TECHNOLOGY

TIME

AND

THE

CONVERSATIONS

OF MODERNITY

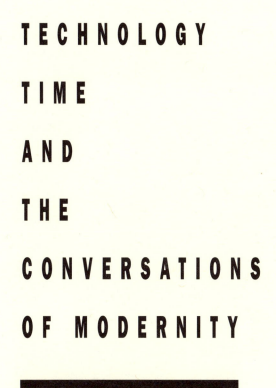

TECHNOLOGY

TIME

AND

THE

CONVERSATIONS

OF MODERNITY

Lorenzo C. Simpson

ROUTLEDGE • New York • London

Published in 1995 by

Routledge
29 West 35 Street
New York, NY 10001

Published in Great Britain by

Routledge
11 New Fetter Lane
London EC4P 4EE

Library of Congress Cataloging in Publication Data

Simpson, Lorenzo Charles.
    Technology, time, and the conversations of modernity / by Lorenzo C. Simpson.
      p. cm.
    Includes bibliographical references and index.
    ISBN 0-415-90771-3 (hb) — ISBN 0-415-90772-1 (pb)
    1. Technology—Philosophy. I. Title.
T14.S553   1994
601—dc20
                                            94-19289
                                              CIP

British Library Cataloguing-in-Publication Data also available

To those who have made possible, and who will doubtless sustain, productive repetitions:

To Lorenzo, Sr. and Bessie, for past enablements; to Marsha, for present sustenance; to Gail, for modeling resolve; and to Sean, with hope for the future.

Contents

Preface   ix

Acknowledgments   xi

I. INTRODUCTION

Chapter 1. The Question of Technology   3

Chapter 2. The Idea of Technological Rationality   13

II. SCIENCE, LANGUAGE AND EXPERIENCE

Chapter 3. Science, Language and Experience:
            Reflections on the Nature of Self-Understanding   27

III. TECHNOLOGY, MEANING AND TIME

Chapter 4. Meaning and Time: An Essay on Technology   43

IV. ON THE USE AND ABUSE OF REPETITION FOR CRITIQUE

Chapter 5. The Use of Repetition for Critique   63

Chapter 6. The Abuse of Repetition for Critique (With Special
            Reference to the Critical Theory of Habermas)   75

Chapter 7. Notes Towards the Trivialization of a Distinction:
            An Interlude on the Conversations of Modernity   95

V. CONCLUSION

Chapter 8. Technology and the Conversations of Modernity:
            Postmodernism, Technology, Ethics and Time   135

Notes   177

Index   223

Preface

This work emerges from my long-standing attempt to understand and assess modernity. It bears the mark of two intersecting sets of concerns: on the one hand, that of discerning the price exacted by modernity in its scientific and technological guises; and, on the other, that of responding critically to particularly important efforts to take the measure of our modern or, arguably, postmodern condition. Accordingly, this book poses the question of technology in the context of a range of issues and themes of current concern; for example, hermeneutics, Critical Theory, rationality and relativism, narrative theory and postmodernism.

The impetus for this book was the idea that technology is an embodiment of our uneasiness with our finitude, of our uneasiness with time. Technology's success in granting our wish to *domesticate* time has encouraged an attitude towards time that is increasingly pervasive in our culture. This book addresses the consequences of this attitude for our self-understanding.

By confronting issues raised in the various theoretical discourses concerning modernity with those engendered by a critical assessment of technology, I hope to elaborate a systematic critique of technology that does justice to our contemporary cultural and intellectual situation. I hope that this essay will prove helpful to those trying to understand some of the recent debates about technology and modernity, many of them inscribed in some of the most important intellectual issues facing us as this century of technological progress draws to an end.

Acknowledgments

My earliest work in planning this book was supported by a year-long Postdoctoral Fellowship from the Southern Fellowships Fund, sponsored by the Mellon Foundation. During the course of its writing, I enjoyed the support of a National Endowment for the Humanities Summer Stipend and another year-long grant, this time a Ford Foundation Postdoctoral Fellowship awarded by the National Research Council. I would like to express my appreciation to those granting institutions. In addition, the research support and collegial stimulation afforded by my appointment as a Guest Scholar at the Woodrow Wilson International Center for Scholars during part of the year of the Ford Foundation grant was invaluable. I am also thankful to Jude Dougherty for the hospitality shown me by the Catholic University of America's School of Philosophy during that year, and to Karsten Harries, who served as my host during stays at Yale University. I acknowledge with gratitude my home institution, the University of Richmond, for granting the two years of leave that allowed me to take advantage of the national awards, for occasional released time, and for a number of its Summer Research Grants.

I have read portions of this book in a number of places. Various versions of Chapter Three were presented to the Department of Philosophy at the University of Virginia; at the invitation of Richard Bernstein, at what was (it saddens me to have to use the past tense here) the Inter-University Centre of Postgraduate Studies in Dubrovnik, Yugoslavia; and at the Stevens Institute of Technology. Versions of Chapter Four were presented at a session of the Society for Philosophy and Technology, where I benefited from a perceptive commentary by Albert Borgmann; at the Woodrow Wilson International Center for Scholars; and to the Department of Philosophy of James Madison University during my enjoyable stay there as Commonwealth Visiting Professor of Philosophy in 1988–1989. Portions of Chapter Seven were presented to the Department of Philosophy of the State University of New York at Stony Brook; to the Department of Philosophy of Howard University as the ninth annual Locke Lecture; to the Ford Fellows Conference at the National Academy of Sciences; and at various sessions of the

American Philosophical Association's Eastern Division Meetings. I extend my thanks to all of these organizations for their invitations to present my work and to the respective audiences for helpful discussion.

A number of individuals graciously and generously offered sage advice at various stages of this project. Thomas McCarthy made helpful suggestions early on. I have greatly benefited from comments, suggestions and criticisms made on earlier drafts of various chapters by Seyla Benhabib, Vlodek Gabara, Robert Gooding-Williams, Karsten Harries, and my colleagues Neale Mucklow, Gary Shapiro and Hugh West. Sabina Lovibond provided a very generous response to my discussion of her work, and Richard Rorty was especially gracious in his detailed response to my criticisms of him. My wife, Marsha, in addition to providing serendipitous inspiration, read the entire manuscript, helping to espy stylistic infelicities. I also found useful the comments of Routledge's anonymous reviewers. I am truly indebted to all of these individuals. Needless to say, I bear full responsibility for the final content.

In addition, I need to acknowledge my remarkably patient, supportive and canny editor, Maureen MacGrogan. My secretary, Beverly Griffin, deserves thanks for the word processing, copying, typing and so forth necessary to get the manuscript into final form. I would also like to thank Professor Randy Pausch of the Department of Computer Science at the University of Virginia for providing the opportunity to experience Virtual Reality technology.

Finally, I must acknowledge with deep gratitude the unearthly patience and support of Marsha, Adelaide and the rest of my family.

An earlier version of Chapter Three was published in *Man and World* 16 (1983), pp. 25–41.

I

Introduction

1

The Question of Technology

It is a commonplace that ours is a technologically saturated culture. For how many of us has not the microwaved dinner or the "fast-food" meal substituted for the time, care and commitment required by the family dinner? Or the brief, purely functional message left on an answering machine for a conversation? And how many of us have not waited impatiently as our word processors whirred away, no matter how powerful their microprocessors?

These are all examples of our being concerned to achieve an end, and to do so quickly and efficiently, but at what price? There are in the literature discussions of such end-oriented or what I shall call value-oriented thinking,[1] but the theme of the involvement of the temporal in technology has received insufficient attention. And when it is addressed, technology's ability to shrink space and time is often viewed only instrumentally, that is, as being merely the ability to decrease by degrees the "distance" separating the desiring subject and the object of desire, and to do so without in any significant way altering the subject or the object.[2]

I claim in this essay that this time-contraction is not only instrumental for, but is also constitutive of, our subjectivity. It is the contention of this book that technology's resources for time-contraction have profound implications for how we experience our subjectivity, for our understanding of who we are as subjects. But technology is not, of course, an independent force, alien to our humanity. As Jürgen Habermas noted some time ago, the concern to control the material conditions of our existence is one of humanity's basic interests. The question becomes one of *measure*, of what place this interest is allowed to assume in the constitution of our experience. The general questions that orient my thinking are: What is the relationship between our allegiance to technological rationality and our options regarding the ways in which we can talk about ourselves, the kinds of stories that we can tell about ourselves, in short, the shape of the human conversation? and Given the technological nature of our culture, how is it possible to reclaim for the concept of who we are sufficient content for us to see the legitimacy of technology and, at the same time, put it in its proper place?

I make my case by focusing on how technology informs our understanding of the meaning of action. I argue that technology, through its emphasis upon efficiency and control, effects a "domestication" of time, a reduction of time to manipulable, dispensable units geared toward future goals. As technology's functional paradigm assumes increasing authority for us, our understanding of the meaning of action is thereby distorted.

My discussion of value is inspired by Heidegger's understanding of the concept developed in his Nietzsche interpretation:

> Value means that upon which the eye is fixed. Value means that which is in view for a seeing that aims at something. . . . The aim in view is value. [Further,] value is posited at any given time by a seeing and for a seeing [and] it is only through this positing . . . that the point that is necessary for directing the gaze toward something, and that in this way guides the path of sight, becomes the aim in view.[3] . . . Values are the conditions of itself posited by the will to power.[4]

From this, I take the idea that, in our age, what matters most is "distortedly" understood as a value, itself understood within an ocular metaphorics as an end, target or goal. Further, there is packed into this account the voluntaristic view that such goals are products of or are rooted in our freedom. By 'value,' then, I mean an end in view that is understood as an arbitrary product of the will. One can find such an understanding of the concept not only in the tradition of Heidegger's interpretation of Nietzsche, but also in the work of Max Weber, insofar as he also understood values in the modern world as subjective posits.

In keeping with this orientation, and despite their somewhat different connotations, I use 'nihilist' and 'relativist' to refer to the standpoint that professes the arbitrariness of structures of meaning and of canons of rationality. I call this standpoint the values-perspective, the perspective from which structures of meaning and canons of rationality are, in an invidious sense, understood to be arbitrary products of the will. I take technological rationality or the technological world picture to be consonant with this. Insofar as from within the technological attitude the world and worldly relationships come to be undersood exclusively as resources, I tend to agree with Heidegger that nihilism and the technological attitude towards the world are aspects of the same phenomenon.

I oppose to the values-perspective a notion of the meaningful. By the "meaningful" I refer to contexts of significance that are not mere items of choice, but that, despite having no transcendental validity, are orders with which we must come to terms. Accordingly, the distinction between meaning and value is central to the argument of this book.

The point of this book is to offer a critique of technology by way of a sustained critique of the values-perspective and its associated temporality. In so doing, I pursue three interrelated projects: (1) to give a phenomenological account of the technological and scientific life-worlds in modernity; (2) to argue that the technological worldview is incompatible with other sources of action, which are also part of our life-world (communication, friendship, love, parenting and so on), and which have a meaning and significance transcending the values-perspective, a meaning and significance that provide us with the conceptual and moral resources from which to criticize technology; and (3) to develop the rational basis of the kind of cultural and social critique of technology which I deploy.

In pursuing the first project, I point out that the technological world picture sanctions certain ways of being-in-the-world and that, by reducing all relations of meaning and significance to the means-ends scheme, such a picture produces the perspective that I call the "values-perspective" and an approach to time that I call the "domestication of time." The second project concerns itself with how moral life and moral reasons can and do arise from *praxis*, and how morality is possible in the wake of what have come to be known as the death of God and the demise of Western metaphysics. I ask: How can a nonsubjective ordering of value emerge from practices and from practical commitments in which we find ourselves already engaged; that is, How can ethical norms be generated from experience or practice? In particular, I seek to show that embedded within my critique is a kind of normative ethics or perspective that enables one to distinguish a good and a bad attitude toward and use of technology, and so to make a distinction between a meaningful and an empty life. In the process I try to reconstruct the notion of *praxis* in a way that is sufficiently rich to highlight the thinness and inadequacy of the modern reception of *techne* and to demonstrate how values emerge from and have their place in meaningful practices. The third project consists in justifying my critical perspective on technological rationality, in establishing the philosophical possibility of critique.

In pursuing these projects, I am led to bring various contemporary discourses into conversation. By drawing a distinction between meaning and value (and their attendant temporalities), I bring a critical discourse about technological rationality into conversation with what Habermas has called the "philosophical discourses of modernity." The latter include, for me, hermeneutics, Critical Theory, the so-called rationality debates and what gets called postmodernism. The discourses of modernity can all be characterized as postmetaphysical discourses in that not only postmodernism, but also both Critical Theory and hermeneutics, as well as the highly influential Anglo-American blend of late Wittgenstein and pragmatism represented by Richard Rorty, mount penetrating critiques of the metaphysical tradition. In Chapters Three to Five, I develop a phenomenological and hermeneutical approach to the critique of technology; in Chapter Six, I give an account of an important Critical Theoretical approach; in Chapter Seven, I examine the philosophical legitimacy of these two approaches, given the post-structuralist or postmodern challenge; and in Chapter Eight, I look at how technology and the postmodern are co-implicated. In the end, I hope to have shown that the philosophical critique of technological rationality (or, for that matter, of rationality in general) need not land us in postmodernist despair.

I should now like to characterize briefly some of the discourses of modernity and their relationship to the question of technology. The rationality debates have primarily to do with the question, Is rationality singular or irremediably plural? Are there structures of rationality that are binding on all of humanity, or are there only structures of merely local validity? The connection between the technological worldview as I have described it and nihilism, relativism and perspectivism invites a response to this worldview that does justice to this rationality discussion, a conversation in which the Habermas-Gadamer debate is also inscribed. The actual dispute between Habermas, the leading exponent of Critical Theory, and H. G. Gadamer, the principal proponent of philosophical hermeneutics, has been over for a while now, though its echoes are still very much with us in current discussions of rationality taking place within both Anglo-American and Continental philosophical settings. It principally concerns the status of epistemic and normative claims in the social and human disciplines. To what extent, if any, can such claims be accorded an objective and universal character, or must some or all of them be viewed as relativistic, that is, as relative to contexts of historical and cultural meaning? Are there critical criteria or mechanisms for resolving disputes within these areas of inquiry that are not "compromised" by context?

Gadamer emphasizes that there is an ineliminable boundary from which any understanding must proceed and which is not itself a product of reflection, but which is rather the effective working of our historical context, a working that is a precondition of knowledge and meaningful experience. He refers to this ineliminable boundary by the term 'authority.' Further, he argues that modern technology and its underlying rationality conspire to deny to human practical life and to human self-understanding that basis of legitimation that is drawn from interpretations of norms and principles yielded by tradition.

Habermas, suspicious of such appeals to authority and to context, is primarily concerned with insuring the possibility of maintaining and justifying critical perspectives on tradition and authority. If Gadamer criticizes technology because it *undermines* authority and traditional contexts of meaning, then Habermas criticizes it because it has *become* authority. Habermas argues that, in our time, science and technology have become self-legitimizing in such a way that practical questions, those concerning the nature of the "good life," are being subordinated to and, indeed, even replaced by, technical questions, questions concerning the most efficient means for the realization of ends, where those ends appear to him to be increasingly beyond our *reflective* control. For him, our challenge is to find ways to preserve, and protect from the encroachment of instrumental imperatives, a space for an autonomous, rational and communicatively achieved consensus about issues of practical life.

Much has already been written about the Habermas-Gadamer debate itself, and I do not intend to address myself to the debate *per se*, so much as to speak to its implications for the critique of technological rationality by viewing it within the context of the rationality discussion. I attempt to do so while doing justice to the tensions between, on the one hand, the two positions in the debate and, on the other, both those positions and what might be called the poststructuralist or postmodernist stance, the latter bearing important affinities to what I have called perspectivism or the values-perspective.

I have spoken of the postmodern challenge. Postmodern sensibilities in many ways sanction an acquiescence to modern technology, and on two levels: (1) those sensibilities and the possibilities ushered in by high technology exhibit elective affinities (the editors of one collection of essays speak of "postmodernist celebrations of the technological sublime"),[5] and (2) technological rationality and postmodernism share a suspicion of critique that, in the case of postmodernism, can be connected with an "end-of-history thesis."[6] The implications of this thesis are that radical critique is dismissed as just another perspective, that the metanarrative of *social* progress has lost credibility, that the idea of alienation, an important cornerstone upon which such critique was to be based, has been discredited as an outmoded modernist notion, and that the only distance on existing social configurations that is sanctioned is the indeterminate negation of irony, not genuinely critical distance.

Our postmodern spiritual situation has been forged in the wake of the "death of God" and of the demise of Platonism and the so-called "metaphysics of presence." It is a context expressive of a world of pervasive and unregulated perspectivism; it thereby threatens to undermine any *critical* understanding of technology by derisively charging that such a critique is just another perspective. Such a perspectivist view I have called "the values-perspective." I emphasize that technological rationality, in its tie to limitless making and its commitment to a homogeneous vocabulary limited to the notions of effectiveness, efficiency and their cognates, reinforces this suspicion of any attempt to privilege values as constraints that would fetter an understanding bent upon control.

There is embedded within this essay an important subtheme, the idea of what I call "humanity as a negotiated, unfinished project," an idea motivated by my response to Richard Rorty in Chapter Seven's rationality discussion. This notion will be seen to provide a critical touchstone for the human conversation, an "outside" measure that would prevent such a conversation from degenerating into a sequence of question-begging monologues. The idea here is to highlight standards that can prevent such a conversation from becoming objectionably provincial and ethnocentric, criteria that would enable a truly rational commitment to an admittedly contingent form of life. My discussion of humanity as an unfinished project is, therefore, the adumbration of an account of a *critical* relationship to our practices that is responsive to historicism, one where contestable, revisable, criterial properties of the "good life" serve as the "outside" measure. This discussion has clear implications for the so-called multiculturalism debates, but the pursuit of such implications is, of course, beyond the scope of this essay.

There are a number of other things that I do *not* seek to do in this book. My primary interest is in the implications of technology for our experience of time and its threat to our continuing ability to find our practices meaningful, not in other aspects or implications of technology except insofar as they relate to my central concerns. I have sought to abstract a general feature of technology in its Western cultural setting (time domestication) and to highlight some of its consequences with an eye to developing (and justifying) a normative standpoint in terms of which our engagement with technology can be assessed. As a consequence, until Chapter Eight I address myself more to technological rationality and to what I have called the technological world picture than to what might be called the technological differentials within our larger technological culture, that is, the differing ways in which that rationality and picture are and have been embodied in material technologies. While the latter would doubtlessly be an extremely important inquiry to pursue, I must content myself here with noting that *insofar as* differing material technologies and technological processes function in instrumental means-ends settings of temporal domestication, my analysis applies to them. And I would claim, further, that such settings are quite pervasive indeed. Lastly, while I devote some attention to the social and political aspects of our relationship to technology, especially in Chapters Two and Six, my concern with hermeneutic questions of meaning places in the foreground what might be called the existential dimension of that relationship.

This introduction has thus far offered a general overview of the book and a delimitation of its scope. A more detailed chapter-by-chapter summary of the book's argument follows.

Chapter Two, a general account of technology and of technological rationality, provides a context for the book's discussion. By 'technological rationality,' I refer to that view of reason which focuses its attention exclusively upon the adequacy of means for the realization of ends, where those ends are not themselves subject to nonstrategic rational adjudication, and to the notion of progress that is consistent with this view.

I briefly take up the conflict between instrumentalist and substantivist views of technology, and consider the relationship between technology and society, politics and the economy. I seek to do so in a way that is responsive to the emerging social constructivist account of technology. The inquiry here also takes up the relationship between science and technology. Though the institutions of science and technology have in common the tendency to neutralize the cultural and historical contexts in which they are inserted, I point out that important differences between them are marked by technology's *practical* concern with altering the world and science's *cognitive* concern with knowing it. This distinction is reflected in the differences between science's and technology's attitudes towards space and, of particular importance for my argument, time.

Chapter Three, in offering a general account of the conditions necessary for the possibility of meaningful experience and self-understanding, concerns itself with the nature of human experience and with how that experience becomes meaningful. It provides an analysis of experience and proposes a way of understanding modern science—a way that is critically responsive to the postempiricist consensus forged by Thomas Kuhn, Mary Hesse, Norwood Hanson et al.—that allows us to see that scientific rationality is unable to do justice to the meaningfulness of experience. In showing the inadequacy of scientific rationality in this regard, the chapter highlights the centrality of the meaning-enabling cultural and historical networks in which we are embedded. In thus connecting meaning with our finitude, the chapter points out that only in light of our concerns does the world and our experience in it become meaningful and make a claim on us.

The hermeneutic of experience developed in Chapter Three—which elaborates the way in which we put prereflectively acquired cultural meanings into play in action and experience—prefigures Chapter Four's discussion of the human experience of time, wherein the "always already" of our cultural and historical insertion gets carried and repeated forward as it informs action and experience. And, through its discussion of the idea of hermeneutic horizons being risked in action, Chapter Three also has implications for the idea of "humanity as an unfinished project" to be proposed in Chapter Seven.

Chapter Four begins with a discussion of the striking and pervasive tendency of our instrumentally saturated culture to fail to distinguish the notion of meaning from that of end or goal, that is, its inclination to collapse talk about structures of meaning into talk about means and ends, into instrumentally rational discourse. I go on to argue against the hypostatization of values or ends-in-view, an hypostatization effected by according values an autonomy or self-subsistence *vis-à-vis* structures of meaning. It is suggested that values understood in this way are worldless, and that a proper understanding of the relation of value to meaning in the context of a life reveals there to be an internal relation between the two.

Chapter Four, by deploying a temporal articulation of the analysis of experience offered in Chapter Three, goes on to motivate the central thesis of the book: technology, in its attempt to subdue time's characteristic flux by harnessing the future predictably and reliably to the present, tends to "domesticate" our experience of time. I argue that technology's means-end rationality projects a self-effacing temporality.

Contrasted with technology's means-ends structure, where significance lies in the end to be achieved, is symbolically meaningful activity or *praxis* which can be understood as an actualization of sociocultural norms, as a more or less creative continuation or repetition of possibilities shaped by our historical past. It is argued that repetition, by rendering explicit the prereflectively acquired interpretations discussed in Chapter Three, reveals itself to be an embodiment of an attitude towards time where time is fully acknowledged as the field of action, not as its alien other, and where the time of repetition is recognized to be productive of meaningful effects.

Chapter Five develops further the consequences of allowing the attitude towards time characteristic of technology to inform our understanding of ourselves. I argue there that that attitude stands as a threat to the continued presence of meaningful differences in our lives and to there being meaning in a life as a whole. Technology's will to contract time, I argue, threatens to marginalize those practices that make a meaningful difference, practices that we engage in for what they are, for what they tell us about ourselves and for what they make of us, rather than for what they achieve. Recent studies of narrative are deployed in this context to explore the issue of "the meaning of life." Departing from such studies, I argue that technological rationality's commitments with regard to time and value stand in tension with the requisites of a meaningful, connected life. The temporality of repetition, through gathering up and giving a meaningful order to our dispersed aims, value orientations and so on, and through restoring the time of action, is claimed to restore connectedness and coherence, thus enabling meaningfulness and a unified sense of self. I close the chapter by briefly raising epistemological and ontological questions regarding the current tendency to identify life and narrative.

Chapters Four and Five present a case for the hermeneutics of repetition. Chapter Six presents an alternative critical approach to the question of technology and meaning, the approach of Critical Theory. It departs from the recognition that attention to coherence and meaningfulness cannot be sufficient, that they cannot have the last word. For the call of the meaningful can be the call of the good or the tempting solicitation of evil. We are thereby challenged to discriminate rationally between the meaningful that is good and that which is not. This chapter and the next purport, then, to examine the possibility and justification of critical perspectives upon meaning and coherence while remaining mindful of the aporetic status of the "values-perspective." In Chapter Six, this concern directly motivates a consideration of Habermas's project and the implications for it of some of the themes sounded in the Habermas-Gadamer debate. Habermas receives focus because his is the most important post-Heideggerian project that critically addresses both the technological and nihilistic problematics. An account is provided of his work, with its hermeneutic weak spots highlighted. Through a discussion of the systems theory of Niklas Luhmann, the parallels between technological or functional rationality and the perspectivism of poststructuralism are pointed out. This allows us to see how Habermas's critique of technological rationality is at the same time a response to nihilism and postmodernism. I argue that, though Habermas's attempts to furnish his notion of communicative ethics—the basis for his response—with rational foundations is beset by hermeneutic or interpretive moments, inviting accusations of unfounded universalistic pretensions from a number of thinkers, there remains considerable critical force in his position, even after its necessary "hermeneutic" emendation. More generally, I argue in this chapter, and more fully in Chapter Seven, that critique need not be construed as invidiously arbitrary, even though our conviction in metaphysical guarantees, in an unproblematic access to an absolute good, or in the very plausibility of such a notion, has been perhaps unalterably shaken.

Chapter Seven, a philosophical interlude, comprises an *excursus* in which I step back from the question of a critical theory of technology in order to interrogate the philosophical status of the approaches presented thus far, namely, my appeal to structures of meaning and Habermas's project of communicative rationality. The point of this chapter is to justify: (1) my appeal to structures of meaning in Chapters Four and Five as a critical counterpoint to technological rationality; and (2) our continuing to take projects of critical rationality seriously in spite of the postmodern consensus over the aporetic status of objectivity.

I begin with an explicit critique of the values-perspective's nihilistic stance by offering a counterargument to philosophical nihilism. I show that the standpoint of the meaningful is not an arbitrary one; our lives are "always already" meaningful, despite technological rationality's tendency to de-emphasize, disregard, disparage and bracket what thus claims us.

In this chapter I argue, moreover, that poststructuralism's insistence that there are no transcendental guarantees does not render incoherent the idea of a nonarbitrary *critical* response to tradition. My argument here includes critical discussions of some of the recent work of Richard Rorty, Sabina Lovibond and Alasdair MacIntyre.

In Chapter Eight, the concluding chapter, I seek to think technology and the postmodern in terms of each other. I am concerned with the relationship of the postmodern sensibility (way of taking up with the world, the real, the other) to the technological attitude toward the world. It is acknowledged that technology must inevitably be understood against the background of its social context. In such contexts, socialized desire influences the rate and direction of technological development. Today that social context is said to be postmodern (at least in the West). In this chapter, I draw together threads of my treatment of technology with those of my allusions to postmodernism in order to make explicit some of the implications of my discussion for ethical life and for the role of technology in it.

This chapter ties the postmodern attitude to ironic detachment, a detachment that characterizes our relationship to the world, to structures of meaning and to canons of rationality. I explore the implications of postmodernism's ironic stance for our relationship with time. It is argued that postmodernism is *risk-aversive* and that technology is complicit in this aversion. Also made explicit in this chapter is the connection between the postmodern temper and the technological attitude insofar as both are expressions of the "will to power." In this context, I discuss the postmodernist phenomenon of the simulacrum—the copy for which no original ever existed, the mere image. The simulacrum is asserted to be the form that value takes in postmodernism and that therefore this book's critique of the values-perspective is at the same time a critique of postmodern desire. The important role of technological media in enabling postmodernist processes of reproduction, and the production of simulacra more particularly, is explored. In so doing, I point out how Virtual Reality technology—computer-based, three-dimensional simulation of concrete objects and environments, capable of completely immersing the viewer in the electronically generated world—is particularly emblematic of a "natural" affinity between technology and postmodernism.

In the second section of Chapter Eight, I examine some of the possibilities for a postmetaphysical ethic. I spell out some of the constraints on such an ethic, and consider several possible responses to our being left to face, without guarantees, time in its uncertainty and unruliness. Part of our task, it is maintained, is to reclaim the ends that we have alienated to technology and to technological modes of action, and to place them in an internal connection to meaningful practices. The notion of the "integrity of a practice" is introduced in this context as a critical touchstone. I invoke health care practices to furnish examples of end-oriented thinking where ends or goals are separated from the dimension of meaning, and to illustrate how meaningful practices, while neither transcendental nor necessary, can provide us with the conceptual and moral resources from which to criticize technology. In this way, I respond to the questions: How can a nonsubjective ordering of value emerge from practices and from practical commitments in which we find ourselves already engaged? or How can ethical norms be generated from experience or practice?

Finally, having acknowledged in Chapters Six and Seven that repetition *per se*, repetition without critically oriented innovation, will not suffice for taking the measure of our present situation, I indicate the importance of interrogating two extreme positions on the idea of technological progress, the extremes of, on the one hand, a backward-looking, antimodernist intervention such as one encounters in the recent work of Christopher Lasch, and, on the other, an uncritical acceptance of technological progress. Accordingly, and in keeping with Chapter Eight's central focus upon the issue of technology, ethics and time, I propose a notion of critical repetition that is informed by the following question: What level of instrumentalization and of technical rationalization is necessary or consistent—under existing, though contestable, conditions of natural or quasi-natural adversity or scarcity—with a socially emancipated life, meaningfully lived?

In order to keep interruptions of my narrative to a minimum, I have in a number of cases reserved qualifications, fuller elaborations, and responses to possible objections for the Notes.

2

The Idea of Technological Rationality

I

This chapter offers the account of technology, consolidated from a range of sources and supplemented by my own perspective, that forms the basis for discussion in this book. Such an account will not only have to make reference to the distinctive characteristics of technology; it will also be incumbent upon me to address, however briefly, questions having to do with the status of technology *vis-à-vis* human values. By the latter sort of questions, I refer to what is a central issue in the philosophy of technology, namely, Does 'technology' refer to an autonomous phenomenon with its own dynamic, or does it refer rather to a value-neutral ensemble of instruments wholly subservient to human needs?[1] While this issue is not an item of explicit concern in this book, it does lie in the background of my discussion. Further, I broach this question at the outset because I think that the dichotomous way in which it tends to get posed—autonomy *or* mere instrumentality—leads to unnecessary philosophical impasses.

A brief sketch of an alternative way to understand the relation of technology to human values will serve to indicate the general orientation taken in this book and to adumbrate a way to avoid those impasses. All technological ends, be they proximate or remote, have their origin in some object of human desire. Our capacities and desires, for instance, for communication, health, transportation, nourishment, security, entertainment, shelter, comfort and so on, will ultimately constitute the hermeneutic grid in terms of which we can understand the point of any technology. In this sense, though technology may generate possibilities that we have not envisioned, its significance derives ultimately from our nature and values. When those values become ends of technology, they migrate into, or are handed over to, the realm of technics, and various branches of technology coalesce around them, for instance, mechanical engineering, electronics, civil engineering, agriculture and so on. And when those ends become the guiding criteria for the various sectors of technology, the ends and the technologies associated with them become autonomous in that the complex of technology (means) and ends, in ways that I explore in the chapters to come, becomes divorced from the context of the human life-world. I shall speak of this in terms of the worldlessness of technology and of the detachment of values from contexts of meaning.

This way of understanding the relation of technology to values allows us to see the truth in, and the dangers associated with, the two positions on this issue mentioned above, and hence, while each has something important to tell us, why we should adopt neither to the exclusion of the other. The danger of focusing exclusively upon the autonomy of technology is the hypostatization of technology as an independent force.[2] The danger of the purely instrumentalist view is that it overlooks what we might call the "internal logic" or structure of technology and the accommodations we are required to make to it. The alternative view sketched above would allow for a response to both the truth and the one-sidedness of each of these two positions when taken singly by suggesting, though by no means offering a full account of, how characteristics of technical autonomy arise from our availing ourselves of technology's potential to address our needs and desires. Technology's autonomy is granted to it by *our* will to power.

To avoid a problematic hypostatization of technology, it might be better to avoid the substantive 'technology' in favor of the adjectival form 'technological.' 'Technological' would then refer to those *aspects* or *dimensions* of a practice that can be characterized in certain specific ways. This would draw our attention to features of practices, including styles of cognition, that we can isolate as being characteristically technological. (Though in the pages to come I will often ignore this distinction and speak simply of technology, this caveat ought to be kept in mind.) The critique to follow in later chapters pursues the implications of the situation wherein what is a feature or an aspect of a practice comes to characterize the practice as a whole. When 'technological' characterizes a practice or an ensemble of practices as a whole, we are then quite likely to be faced with something very much like "runaway" or autonomous technology.

So how should we characterize "technological"? We might start by noting that important features of technology come into view when we understand it to be a response to our finitude, to the realization that we are vulnerable and mortal and that our time is limited. Technology has been a response to our finitude from the beginning. The earliest instances of tool-using in foraging societies were to "increase the reliability and productivity of . . . subsistence strateg[ies] by using time-saving devices."[3] This suggests a theme that will be of central importance in this book, namely, the conception of technology as timesaving.[4]

Technology is end-oriented, implying that its underlying rationality is that which governs those actions Max Weber called purposive-rational (*zweckrational*). Technological rationality is thereby contrasted with a rationality that is oriented by a concern with the way in which an action is done or with the values embodied in it or by the norms governing it. *Qua* technological, action proceeds in indifference to traditional norms and values. Of course, socially sanctioned limits can be imposed from the outside to circumscribe the normative arena within which technology is allowed to operate. However, there is often a "struggle" between the "imperative" of technology to seek more effective and/or more efficient ways to secure an end, or indeed to secure new ends, on the one hand, and the constraints that would fetter it, on the other. Gene-splicing, *in vitro* fertilization and other examples of modern biotechnology are salient here. I speak of this imperative not as an independent force but as part of the logic to which social agents accede as they accept technology's promise. (Insofar as we have acceded, we may speak of "the tendency of technology.") So, to look at the world technologically is to see it either as resources to be used or as constraints to be overcome. Such a technological gaze is guided by an end that has been articulated, and hence understood, in terms commensurate, and indeed consonant, with the particular technology in question. For instance, in medicine one typically speaks in terms of halting the progress of a specific medically defined disease rather than, say, in terms of invoking the concept of health, where health is understood to involve social and cultural as well as medical dimensions.

We can think of technology *per se* as embracing at once a distinctive cognitive style or orientation, a distinctive mode of action, and a distinctive way of taking up with the world. Accordingly, a useful core characterization of technology as such, as opposed to one of technological society or of technology as a form of life, is to think of it as a problem-solving process whereby we make use of the environment to satisfy our wants and desires.[5] Or, thought of as an achievement rather than as a process, one might think of it as the set of knowledge, skills and instruments that are the most efficient and effective at problem-solving.[6] We can characterize the way technology addresses its problems, or the technological approach, in the following way: a need is made explicit, or an opportunity, made available by scientific or perhaps other technological developments, is articulated; within the context of the need or opportunity, a clear and determinate goal is specified; the major steps to be taken and the major pieces of work to be done are identified; the plan is constantly made responsive to "feedback" from the results of the work; and, typically, the work is organized so that each major segment is apportioned within a division of labor.[7] This way of putting it highlights the important point that the end that technology seeks to realize as efficiently and effectively as possible is one that is specifiable and determinate beforehand. It further highlights the importance of planning, or of the rational orchestration of procedure, to the technological enterprise.

If, as is quite fashionable today, we understand 'technology' to designate a social practice, rather than a natural kind or an essence, we can see that some of its features may be historically contingent. This allows us, for example, to think in terms of its transformation, in terms of alternative technological practices. And this is undeniably an important pursuit. However, without essentializing technology, we can also locate features that are, at least relatively, historically invariant, features that survive the transformations, features that enable us to identify and reidentify a practice or some aspect of it as technological. Among these are: (1) the separation of means and ends; and (2) the rationalization of the means for the efficient procurement of ends. To anticipate somewhat, we might think of technology, then, as the set of purposively rationalized practices aiming at putting the future at our disposal. The other, historically variable, features would include those assumed by technological practices insofar as they are situated within a particular institutional framework or a particular set of social arrangements. And, of course, they are always so situated. Such features include, for example, what might be called ideological features or features of social domination, features that typically derive from the social organization of techno-logical labor.[8]

Historically variable also is the always contestable social consensus that deter-mines what means we can avail ourselves of and what ends we can legitimately seek. Also varying with time and place are the available social interpretations of means and ends as well as the social decisions about which possibilities for technological development are to be realized in particular social settings. Among the questions for an investigation into these historically contingent features would be, for example: Time savings for whom? Whose interest is served by the socially available repertoire of means and ends? These are important questions. However, an analysis of the possibilities for technology's historical transformation is beyond the scope of this study.[9] My intention is rather to examine the implications of the relatively invariant core of technological rationality for our ability to find our lives meaningful and rationally defensible, implications that need to be addressed despite the possibilities for transformation.

II

Technology can be viewed as that constellation of knowledge, processes, skills and products whose aim is to control and transform. We often think that technology's promise of control is fulfilled by cashing in on the cognitive achievements of science. But what, exactly, is technology's relationship to sci-ence? By now, much has been written on this complex topic, and I cannot claim to offer anything definitive here. I want only briefly to indicate what I find to be the most plausible understanding of that relationship.

Put simply, *modern* technology is largely based upon science but is different from the latter in some important respects. A conspicuous product of scientific inquiry is an understanding of nature that is expressed in terms of functional relationships between variables representing diverse aspects or properties of natural phenomena. Such functional relationships or laws are often, and perhaps ideally, articulated in quantitative, mathematical form. A standard, and plausible, view of how technology is based upon science, insofar as it is, is that modern technology is grounded upon scientific laws which it transforms into maxims or recipes for action.[10]

Mario Bunge, a prominent advocate of this view, goes on to point out that not all technology consists in the application of substantive scientific theories, that is, theories that articulate a natural causal mechanism. There are also so-called operative technological theories which concern themselves with the operations of persons and person-device complexes in nearly real, simulated situations, such as computer-based models of organizations.[11] These theories involve the use of scientific method rather than specific scientific theories. (For present purposes, we can neglect the important differences between scientific theories and laws.) Examples of such operative theories are decision theory, game theory and operations research. Such operative theories would highlight and guide that species of technical action that Jürgen Habermas refers to as strategic action. So 'modern technology' refers to that cumulative body of knowledge, skills, devices and instruments that, using either scientific theory or method, offers us guidance in the selection of courses of action which are adequate for the realization of a given end or for the solution of a given problem and, further, places at our disposal the means to that realization.[12]

How now should we understand what distinguishes science from technology? An adequate account of this distinction will have to acknowledge that there is considerable overlap between what persons identified as scientists do and what those identified as technologists do. It has been remarked that it is often difficult to differentiate research scientists from research engineers based upon observation of them at work.[13] So if our demarcation criteria are to be sensitive to actual practice, we should think perhaps in terms of a spectrum of activities, interests and kinds of knowledge rather than in terms of sharp dichotomies, and acknowledge that the science/technology "border" is quite fluid. This means that a given person, identified as a scientist or technologist, may find herself on different parts of the spectrum at different times or that her activity at a given time may fall under descriptions drawn from different parts of the spectrum, that is, that there will be different aspects of that activity. Thus one might envisage a continuum, with "pure" science at one end, the traditional crafts at the other, and the subspectrum of academic engineering research to industrial research and development somewhere in between. The end points of such a spectrum should be understood then to designate features more akin to those of an ideal type than to those of an actual practice. But they will be useful for talking about scientific or technological *aspects* of a practice or in speaking of a more or less scientific or technological practice.

The most useful and least contested way of characterizing what lies at the end points is to do so in terms of ultimate aims. Scientific practice aims at increasing our knowledge of the natural and social worlds by offering explanations of phenomena. Technological practice aims at solving the material problems of human life by increasing our power to transform those worlds. An adequate attempt to differentiate between the scientific and the technological, then, must take its orientation from an acknowledgment that science's aim is primarily cognitive, while technology's is primarily practical.

But even here we should be careful to distinguish the aim or purpose of the individual agent from that of the particular institution or form of life in which her agency has meaning. For example, a given problem, indeed sometimes one whose solution requires basic "scientific" research, can be of *intrinsic* interest to an engineer.[14] So it may be misleading to refer solely to the psychological state of the individual researcher in attempting to make our distinction, though no harm is done in referring to an attitude as being scientific or technological or some admixture of the two. But it may be more helpful to ask, What gives the individual's activity meaning within the overall institutional context with which the researcher identifies? So we may speak of scientific and technological settings, defined not so much in terms of the nature of the activity occuring within them as in terms of the primary aim of the enterprises to which those settings contribute. For example, if the results of research issuing from a given setting are communicated and circulated primarily in journals and at fora dedicated to the solution of practical problems or to the application or exploitation of knowledge, as opposed to the expansion of knowledge *per se* without regard for its practical application, then we could call that setting technological even if sited at a university. And even if the basic research of academic engineering constitutes a genuine borderline case, such a fact would not undermine the applicability of the distinction between cognitive and practical aims.[15] My suggestion is thus that we can distinguish between science and technology as enterprises, as social projects or institutions, even though they overlap with respect to the activities, interests and kinds of knowledge exhibited by the individuals engaged in them.

III

Leaving epistemological considerations of theoretical versus practical knowledge aside for now, we might inquire further after the practical aims of technology and their wider consequences. An obvious way to frame this inquiry is to ask, In what does technological progress consist? As we have suggested, the primary measure of technological progress is the imperative to maximize effectiveness (reliability, durability, strength, ease of use and so on) and efficiency in the securing of a given end. (Increased efficiency can be achieved either through the discovery of more productive ways, yielding more for a given "cost" or input, or more "economical" means, providing the same yield for less input, of securing an end.) A further and highly salient mark of technological progress is a shortening of the time necessary for such a securing.[16] Understood in this way, we shall see that technological practices manifest certain tendencies which are sociologically relevant. Perhaps no one has given as influential an account of the social and cultural implications of modern technology as Jacques Ellul's. Among the dispositions that he identifies are a tendency to be autonomous with respect to traditional values, to be self-determining, and to be "totalitarian."[17] In the brief discussion of these characteristics which follows we move beyond the consideration of technology in isolation from its social milieu, in order to gain an angle of vision from which technology in its relationship to more inclusive aspects of our existence can be brought into focus.

Many argue that as technology progresses, techniques are perfected which, in a manner approaching mathematical precision, yield decision procedures for selecting the most efficient means in a given context. As a result, the choice of means becomes subject more and more to the outcome of rational calculation; that is, it increasingly becomes quantitatively determined. This leads Ellul to make the rather strong claim that technological progress is now conditioned by nothing other than its own calculus of efficiency.[18] For him, technology's autonomy and self-determination follow quite directly. Technology is autonomous with respect to traditional values because, assuming we continue to refuse to interfere in any way with efficiency, it is answerable only to technical criteria, which are logically independent of all other estimates of worth.

In particular, technological rationality can be argued to be independent of economic rationality. Even though decisions about which technologies are to be adopted are often, if not typically, made on economic grounds, technical criteria cannot in general be identified with economic criteria. For example, Marx pointed out that technical criteria, or criteria of technological progress, are independent of measures of capitalist economic development. For he noted that technological progress is restrained through the superordination of capitalistic economic imperatives over technical criteria.[19] In fact, for Marx the dynamic of technological development threatened to undermine capitalism, the economic formation whose essential feature is the production of surplus value.[20] Granted, capitalism has clearly been of world-historical significance in its encouragement of technological progress. It will no doubt continue to do so. Nevertheless, to convince oneself that the axes of technological development are orthogonal to those of capitalism, one need only consider that the more efficient method or the more rapidly acting device is not always adopted; for it may be too costly, or its use may lead to overproduction, or its adoption may prevent the amortization of an incumbent device.[21] For example, the basic concept for air bag technology was available long before the automobile industry was willing to invest in it. So technology's conspicuous features cannot all simply be features of capitalism refracted into another sphere.

Indeed, the claimed superiority of communist societies was supposed to consist in part in the contrast that they provided to capitalistic societies' putatively cramped base for technological development. In the former, technical development was to be given free rein. In a recent, far-ranging, critical analysis of socialist societies, *Dictatorship Over Needs*, Ferenc Feher, Agnes Heller and Gyorgy Markus suggest that tendencies inherent in industrialization, tendencies which could become only partially manifest in liberal capitalism, could manifest themselves in an unrestrained form in the new socialist societies.[22] And, to be sure, certain technologies, in particular those of politics and of athletics as well as other so-called human techniques, have been carried further in the erstwhile Soviet Bloc countries than in the West. The notion of centralized economic planning in the "command economies," however inefficient in actual practice, is further indication of the resort to technique.

A claim for the autonomy of the technological might go beyond the assertion that the criteria of technological progress are logically independent of measures of socioeconomic progress. A case might also be made for the proposition that technology has "built-in imperatives" that function and hold sway irrespective of socioeconomic setting. Though recent geopolitical events make this somewhat of a moot point, the features that give shape to the sense of 'technology' under consideration in this book are as much a part of technology in socialist regimes as in capitalist orders. Capitalism has been the primary impetus for the development of administrative, organizational and economic technique, and, along with the military, has spurred the development of material technology. However, as the discussion above suggests, socialist societies have, in the interest of efficiency, adopted Western technology (and, of course, so have the Japanese).

In Russia, where Western thought on technological progress had already been adopted, an intensive process of industrialization began with the rise of Soviet power after the First World War.[23] Given its promised power to liberate, Stalin pointed to industrialization as the sole condition for the realization of Communism, and Lenin spoke fervently of the "indispensability" to Russia of electrification.[24] In claiming that all technical rules and institutions are "identically reproduced" in the socialist state, Ellul claims that technology has, little by little, emptied socialism of any distinctive content, so that radical distinctions between socialism and capitalism have been eroded; technology replaces politics as the master force.[25] Ellul's analysis is confirmed in the view of the authors of *Dictatorship Over Needs*, who hold that trends inherent in industrialization are operative in producing their social effects (often far-reaching and potentially quite oppressive) irrespective of whether industrialization unfolds in a capitalist or noncapitalist social order.[26] Among such effects are the increasing specialization and division of labor, educational and career patterns determined by the division of labor and, in general, a similarity in the kinds of goods that such a society produces, the way they are produced and the configurations that everyday life assumes as those goods are consumed.[27] Technology's autonomy is a reflection of its universal and world-historical significance. Its promise of efficiency, time savings, productivity and reduction of bodily effort secures for it a receptive audience in every corner of the globe. Who among us does not want to "cheat" time in some way?

The mention of "trends inherent in industrialization" strongly evokes the notion of an inner logic that can be ascribed to technology. While the notion of an inner logic of scientific development has taken quite a beating of late at the hands of so-called externalist historians and philosophers of science, such talk is not completely without point in a discussion of technology, particularly insofar as we give ourselves over to the quest for effectiveness and efficiency. Ellul has argued that, to the extent that the choice of methods and of sequences of methods of operation depends upon the results of mathematized decision procedures, technology is self-directing.[28] In this sense, technology itself decides upon the best means, and, to the extent that we increasingly abdicate our power to make legitimate choices—through an almost worshipful attitude towards technology— it becomes self-determinative without any decisive human intervention. While, again, Ellul's statement of the case no doubt exaggerates technology's substantive independence of social forces, it is nevertheless the case that our commitment to the most effective and efficient means forces choices that are taken out of our hands. If one makes effectiveness one's primary aim, then certain other decisions follow as a matter of course, decisions that an algorithm-guided computer can make, and in many cases does.

Our commitment to effectiveness and efficiency allows us to understand how, in recent times, there has been a tendency to rule certain other concerns out of court. For example, the death knell already tolls for Volvo's innovative attempt to make industrial work more meaningful by implementing a "humanistic" assembly process. This process—wherein employees work in small teams each of which builds an entire automobile, giving each worker the opportunity to contribute to the finished product on a much broader scale than in the traditional assembly line process—is destined to be phased out, for it takes three to four times as long to assemble a car in this way as do the best Japanese plants.[29] Witness also the recent controversy surrounding the choice of the drug TPA over the much cheaper streptokinase for use in the treatment of heart attack victims.[30] Even though the evidence in favor of TPA's supposed greater effectiveness is far from conclusive, and assuming that at least some physicians who prescribe it are not doing so because they stand to benefit financially, it seems that at least in some quarters it is taken for granted that its at best marginally greater effectiveness is sufficient reason to discount cost as a factor.

The last claim that I wish to highlight from Ellul's account is the assertion that technology tends to be totalitarian. This characteristic will assume prominence in my subsequent discussions of the systems perspective. In order for a given technical complex to be maximally efficient, all factors which could possibly affect it must be transformed in accordance with the necessities of that complex. With technological development goes an interdependence whereby resources from a variety of sectors must be mobilized in order to pursue a given technology.[31] Advances in automotive technology, for example, both depend upon and occasion developments within petroleum technology, road building, materials technology and so on. Further, anything which might possibly preclude the realization of the most efficient plan must either accommodate itself to the plan or be rendered inoperative. For instance, if worker dissatisfaction threatens to lower productivity, industrial psychology is likely to be pressed into service in order to facilitate adjustment to the technical milieu.

IV

The discussion in this chapter thus far has shown that we can distinguish conceptually a technological advance not only from a scientific one, but from social, economic and political ones as well. This result is not inconsistent with the social constructivist's claim that social, economic and political factors influence, if not determine, which technological advances are encouraged and adopted at a given time and in a given place. But, counter to some trends within the social constructivist orientation, this conclusion authorizes a discussion of features of technology that are (at least relatively) invariant across such contexts.

One of the global features of technology that will assume pride of place in the essay that is to follow—a feature in which many of the characteristics discussed above are implicit—is what I have called its worldlessness. I refer here to the way in which technology takes up with reality or, perhaps better, to the technological approach to reality. By "worldlessness" I mean that the viewpoint of technology is one wherein, first, worldly things are reduced to means, to raw materials, to the potentially exploitable which Heidegger called the "standing reserve" (*Bestand*); secondly, traditional values lose their legitimacy as constraints upon action; and, lastly, ends or values are shorn from contexts of meaning. From this vantage point, the goal of technology is to liberate the idea of pure means and to separate technological procedures from the context of nontechnological forms of life, thus explicitly removing those procedures from the dimension of significance or meaning. The historical process whereby this would come to pass, to the extent that it has not already, can be described as the liberation of *techne* from world. Such a process, one within which technology would burst its bonds, allows us to grasp the purchase of expressions such as "the technological society" and "technology as ideology."[32]

The other global feature of technology that I wish to emphasize here concerns its relation to time. This feature can be introduced via a brief discussion of what Lewis Mumford has called a particularly emblematic piece of technology, the clock.[33] If not *the* key to technology, the clock certainly grants us privileged access to it. The time determination and measurement that clocks procure underlie and are necessary to modern technology. The clock, because it makes possible coordination, comparison and so on, increases our control by enabling us to orchestrate practices and processes and to improve them along the lines of efficiency. F. W. Taylor's classic time-and-motion studies, undertaken at the turn of the century in the interest of heightening industrial efficiency and productivity, would have been impossible without Taylor's dreaded stopwatch.[34] And Ellul concedes that the autonomy of technology is circumscribed by technology's obedience to the clock.[35]

The invention of the mechanical clock in the thirteenth century inaugurated a new *representation* of time. It, like Heidegger's idea of "the world-as-picture" that I shall discuss in subsequent chapters, embodies a homogenizing representation of time, offering a grid within which all events everywhere are commensurable because locatable within the same system of coordinates. Such a device made possible the "hour of equal length," granting us independence from the changing seasons and allowing us to be indifferent to the distinction between night and day.[36] The representation afforded by the clock allows for the coordination of disparate activities on a global scale. Like "the world-as-picture," the temporal representation effected by the clock is rooted in an interest. The clock is a piece of technology that is a means of disposing over, of mastering, time.[37]

The *inevitable, unstoppable* progress of the clock mirrors representationally the inexorable passage of time. If, as has been suggested, the clock issues in a "new time sense [that] finds one expression in [a] heightened awareness of mortality,"[38] then there is good reason to think that we would avail ourselves of technology in order to "stop the clock." The clock, so necessary to the technological project, stands as an ever-present reminder to us of time's relentless march, and is thus at the same time a spur to technological development.[39] So we might say that technology both depends upon and is fundamentally challenged by the clock. In this way, we can begin to see how the clock as a representation of time as linear, as irreversible, as the bearer of the irretrievable, is a key to the technological phenomenon.

A central goal of technology is to "stop the clock," to de-realize time. In the course of this book, we shall see this claim elaborated in a number of ways. Technology seeks to minimize the time necessary to realize a given goal, thus liberating us from "the burden of having to wait."[40] It seeks to give us more time, rendering us in effect closer and closer to being immortal, by reducing the time necessary for a given task or complex of tasks and by rendering us less vulnerable to what occurs in time, to the vicissitudes of time. (Of course, modern medical technology takes the goal of giving us more time as a literal definition of its project.) Finally, as we shall see in chapters to come, the totalized, and perhaps totalitarian, technical project as conceptualized by systems theory places a premium upon the maintenance of an achieved state of equilibrium. Accordingly, the charge to technology is to maintain the equilibrium state and, in the event of a disturbance, to minimize the time necessary to restore that state.

I have suggested that the clock may well be the key to understanding technology. How, more specifically, might this be? The nature of clocks is, of course, overdetermined. Clocks can be understood in many ways. For example, in science, clocks function to provide accurate measures of an abstract, mathematized, elapsed duration that is wholly indifferent to human actions and events. Clocks indifferently mark the passage of abstractly equivalent "nows." In technology, the clock has not only the function of marking time in this way, but it is also a means of synchronization and of the determination of the "time to do something," a means of orienting actions and processes in time. In order to choose among the possible ways of understanding clocks, we need a selection principle. That principle is provided by the nature of technology (which is what is at issue). Hence our inquiry, at this point circular, into the nature of technology is guided by the following hermeneutical question, What is technology such that the clock can be the key to it?

In keeping with what has been suggested thus far, I shall here hazard the following, quite general, characterization of technology: 'technology' refers to that set of practices whose purpose is, through ever more radical interventions into nature (physical, biological and human), systematically to place the future at our disposal. And technology does so, by and large, through the three modes indicated above: through hastening the achievement of a goal located in the future; through control over what occurs in the future ("taking account" of it, in Heidegger's terms); and through maintaining a given state while containing and reducing the period of deviations from it. So the clock suggests itself as an exemplary window onto technology because at least part of what is peculiar about technology is its relation to time, and because of the peculiar nature of its relation to time. Technology demands the temporal metering afforded by the clock, while it is simultaneously a response to the terror of time with which the inexorable movement of the clock puts us in touch.[41]

II

Science, Language and Experience

3

Science, Language and Experience: Reflections on the Nature of Self-Understanding

In order to clarify more fully what I have been referring to by such expressions as 'structure of meaning' and 'context of significance,' this chapter concerns itself with the nature of human experience and with how that experience becomes meaningful. It provides an analysis of experience, and proposes a way of understanding the worldlessness of modern science that allows us to see that the scientific attitude, its own hermeneutic status notwithstanding, is unable to do justice to the meaningfulness of experience. By showing the inadequacy of scientific rationality in this regard, this chapter draws out more explicitly what is distinctive about human experience and its meaning than do current tendencies to point to analogies between the interpretive nature of scientific practice and the interpretive practices of the everyday life-world. In so doing, it highlights the centrality of the meaning-enabling cultural and historical networks in which we are embedded. The hermeneutic of experience developed here—which elaborates the way in which we put prereflectively acquired cultural meanings into play in action and experience—prefigures the discussion in the next chapter of the human experience of time, wherein the "always already" of our cultural and historical insertion gets carried and repeated forward as it informs action and experience.

Much is made today of the interpretive nature of natural science. In her well-known essay, "In Defense of Objectivity," Mary Hesse claims that recent inquiries into the nature of the scientific enterprise suggest that, methodologically, there are no essential differences between the sciences of nature and the human sciences.[1] Other distinguished humanists, practicing both within and without philosophy—Richard Rorty and Hans Küng come to mind—make much of a new rapprochement between science and the humanities.[2] We have learned from the so-called "new" philosophy of science that the data of even the hardest of the natural sciences are theory-laden, and are therefore ineliminably the result of interpretation. Hesse herself has argued persuasively that natural scientific theories have the properties of metaphor. There seem to be no significant differences between the self-consciously hermeneutic practices that inform, say, the humanities, and the activities that constitute the sciences of nature. This would lead us to believe that there is similarly nothing unique about our everyday acts of self-interpretation and attempts at self-understanding, for they stand in an essential continuity with the interpretive practices of the humanities.

Were this true, it would have the effect of defeating many of the arguments against scientism, that is, the extension of the methodology of the natural sciences to the human sphere, from the start. This chapter, cast in the form of a critique of scientism that is responsive to the new understanding of science, constitutes an argument against the view represented by Hesse and others. I argue that there is an important, even a fundamental, difference between the causal-explanatory sciences (the natural sciences) and the interpretive activities implicated in endeavors of self-understanding and in attempts to discern the meaning of our lives. It is this difference that makes a difference for us insofar as we seek an understanding of ourselves—an understanding of our individual situations, of the cultural matrices of which we are parts, and ultimately of the situation which we share with other potential partners in conversation. The first two sections of this chapter offer an account of the nature of experience and of how it comes to be meaningful for us. The third section—while attempting to hold on to the undeniable importance which science *does* have for us, an attempt which many critiques of science fail to make[3]—points out the limits of science as a model of reflection to which we can appeal in our quest for self-understanding.

I

I accept the Socratic maxim that the unexamined life is not worth living. I wish to outline a conception of experience that is able to assign to science its proper place, but is also rich enough to do justice to this Socratic claim. Accordingly, my critique is aimed not so much at science *per se* as at features of science's inadequate self-understanding and, most importantly, at the totalization or hegemony of scientific understanding. I refer to the latter phenomenon by the term 'scientism.'

The demand for critical self-examination thematizes two requirements. First, as I shall show, there is the presupposition of freedom or negativity. Secondly, such an examination requires criteria. Such criteria can be provided, though I do not elaborate upon them here, by situation-bound interpretations of "the good life," interpretations which might be held to be vulnerable to the demand for redemption in something like what Jürgen Habermas refers to as a discourse free from domination.[4] The two requirements can be further related, for a critically examined life requires not an abstract negativity, but an engaged freedom—a freedom oriented to conceptions of the good life. (We would otherwise have the indeterminate negation of nihilism.) In Kantian terms, freedom requires practical reason as a measure. I believe that science's inability to reckon adequately with the themes of freedom and value[5] makes our worry about its hegemony legitimate.

One of our distinguishing features is our ability to extract meaning from our experience as we come to perceive the pattern into which our lives fit. We, unlike the rest of nature, stand as a problem to ourselves. How are we to make sense of our lives? How are we to comport ourselves? What stories are we enacting and ought we to enact? The ongoing response to the question posed by our very existence is the self-understanding attempted and achieved through reflection upon our experience. As self-understanding increases, what it is possible to say appropriately about oneself, both descriptively and evaluatively, is given greater scope as well. That is, our self-descriptions can become more subtle and finely drawn.

What then must be the structure of experience such that we can make sense of this feature of human life? Our reflection here gets its initial bearings from Kierkegaard's *Either/Or*, where we see instructively portrayed two paradigms of experience: the aesthetic and the ethical. In the former case we see depicted the inability or refusal—depending upon the stage of reflection reached by the aesthete—to acknowledge the continuity of the self through time; in the latter, a determination to acknowledge that continuity. The freedom of the aesthete, like that celebrated by Sartre, has no measure; the meaning which is established by that freedom is therefore arbitrary. Moreover, the reflective attitude adopted by the fully developed aesthete is one of detachment. The reflective aesthete becomes a disengaged spectator, a *theoros*-like onlooker who is a mere observer, even of her own life. (More will follow about this tie to the Greek notion of *theoria*.) Kierkegaard's discussion of the ethical stage reveals the impotence of the disinterested attitude when faced with the task of discerning an intelligible shape to one's life. The infinite freedom of aesthetic reflection must be oriented towards a standard if there is to be anything like a determinate meaning to our lives as a whole. While both styles of life, in some measure, are possibilities for us, only that of the ethical—its ultimate inadequacy for Kierkegaard notwithstanding—allows us to understand how we can find our lives meaningful or coherent in such a way that that meaning contributes to our self-understanding, thereby investing meaning with a cognitive dimension. I wish now to build upon this insight by elaborating a conception of experience which allows us to make sense of the achievement of self-understanding and the discernment of meaning.

II

Typically, to use the term 'interest' in a sense made current by Habermas, conceptions of experience reflect interests. The scientific notion of experience, for example, has been argued to betray an interest in an objectivity which facilitates the control of natural processes.[6] We might then say that science embodies a view of experience which is teleologically related to manipulation, while ordinary language, through which the experience that concerns us here comes to be expressed, is tied to a view of experience which is teleologically related to orientation. This is not to deny that ordinary language *can* be used in the interest of manipulation, for instance, through a Freudian rebuff, and thereby can objectify others, but its ability to be so used presupposes its primary orientational aim. In this latter case, language is used to turn against us the world of meanings through which we gain our bearings.

I have suggested that ordinary language is teleologically related to orientation. What does this mean? Understanding the language of a people furnishes us with a map for understanding their world. Through language, we are in the world in such a way that we enjoy a certain freedom from, and an ability to dispose over, what we encounter there; for through language we are able to relate the world to our needs and interests. The similarities and differences which ordinary language expresses are grounded in the relationship of things to our needs and interests. Accordingly, there may be several words for a given thing, depending upon the relationships in which it stands to the interests of a given community and/or upon the importance to those interests of making finer and finer distinctions. For example, there is an African language with two hundred different words for camel and, as is alleged by some, an Eskimo dialect with several terms for snow. Conversely, there may be a single term for a number of otherwise quite different things as long as they all possess the same significance for a given linguistic community. This pragmatic grounding roots language to a culturally and historically defined form of life. The way in which language organizes the world is then dependent upon the projects in which a culture is engaged. Practice determines what are relevant similarities and differences, and language stabilizes them, makes them stand. Ordinary language provides for historical situatedness; we gain our bearings through the language games in which we participate.

To be sure, experience is never for us a concatenation of uninterpreted particulars. Sense making occurs even at a prereflective (but not necessarily prelinguistic) level. Meanings exist prior to reflection. But if we are to learn from experience, it must "speak" to us. Prior to being brought to expression through language, experience is relatively dumb, inchoate and undifferentiated. It must be torn from its mute opacity.

The appropriation of experience in the interest of self-enlightenment involves both an analytic and a synthetic activity.[7] Experience, in its moment of undifferentiation, must first be refracted as are the elements of white light through a prism. This analytic activity is required because we must be made aware of just what the claims are that experience makes on or about us. Undifferentiated experience cannot speak. Experience, once analyzed or differentiated, must be resynthesized and then integrated into the continuum of our life histories. It is through this resynthesis and reintegration that the sense of the claims, the meaning of the totality, emerges. The twofold activity just described is in many ways analogous to the project of interpreting a text written in a foreign language: analysis corresponds to translation, sentence by sentence, and the interpretation of the overall meaning corresponds to synthesis. Only as meaningful or as a contribution to meaning can experience be integrated into the continuum of our self-understanding. The result of this analytic-synthetic process is an articulated totality, as is a text which we have come to understand as a whole and in detail. What results is like a piece of woven cloth whose strands and their connections stand out in relief. The meaning yielded by this process forms part of a subsequent, more inclusive experience, an experience which is now a constellation of interactions and relationships, all of which must be "worked" on in the analytic-synthetic fashion described above, in an ongoing process.[8]

Now, in an important sense, as I have suggested, meanings exist prior to reflection, prior to analysis-synthesis. This is to say that meanings exist, or that sense-making goes on, "behind our backs." These meanings are brought with us to our experiencing; interpretations of this unreflective sort are going on all of the time. For example, within certain cultures, ours included, persons standing very close to one another while talking are perceived as intimates. Or, as another example, one might consider how the Bantu language game, of which the word for person, 'muntu,' is a feature, commits a member of that culture to certain interpretations of individual behavior to which a participant in a Western language game of which 'person' is a feature is not committed. For instance, within the Bantu culture, conceptualizing one's welfare apart from that of one's group is perceived as wrong. The form of life or language game in which we participate always operates, at least partially, "behind our backs." Language is like an infinite roll of tape, in that no matter how much of it we uncover there will always be part of it which lies hidden; there are always unthematized meanings that frame our experience. We participate in a language game unreflectively to the extent that we are unaware of what that game commits us to, what it conceals from us (language game as ideology or as an unavoidable element in a dialectic of blindness and insight), or what lies implicit in it.

Accordingly, our prereflectively acquired meanings typically become clear or explicit, that is, *speak* to us, only after they have been put to "work" in an interpretation of experience. These deep-seated commitments or prereflective meanings are interpretive predispositions that are brought before our eyes only through being put into play in such a way that they are risked. It is the risk of being falsified or relativised "in action" that allows us to become focally aware of them. We, at first, "dwell" in our prereflective meanings and are called out of them—gaining a *provisional* distance on them—only when they fail to do justice to the object of interpretation, where the otherness or alienness of the object throws them into relief, making us aware of their merely hypothetical status. To return to an earlier example, we might not know explicitly just what our notion of personhood commits us to, and what its limits may be prior to encountering a cultural context like that of the Bantu. Or again, in the case of a man of traditional background, the assumption "a woman's place is in the home" would very likely not become an item of his *focal* awareness prior to an experience of a claim to the contrary. In sum, we do not view our prereflective meanings from an extraexperiential standpoint, and consequently our self-enlightenment, enabled by the analytic-synthetic activity described above in a more or less synchronic fashion, requires the *process* of experience.

Not only must experience speak, but it must speak to *us*; it must claim us. Experience claims us in a particular way, in our particularity. In order to be claimed by our experience, we must be placed, situated. It is here that the significance of the prereflective meanings and orientations alluded to above comes into even clearer focus. There is an essential contribution to the process of self-enlightenment made by our original placement, by our insertion into a taken-for-granted form of life with its concerns and commitments. H.-G. Gadamer, following Heidegger, makes sense of this notion of placement through the idea of culturally induced and historically derived "prejudices" or prejudgments. It is only through placing these prejudices or prereflectively acquired meanings at risk in a more or less self-conscious interpretation of experience that self-understanding is achieved. Our interpretive prejudices come to be criticized and corrected as a result of being risked in the act of interpretation. The rehabilitative shaping of the system of our prejudices through this process of confirmation and falsification is what I mean by the augmentation of our self-understanding. The idea of a text as the model for experience again strongly suggests itself, as does textual interpretation as a model for critical self-reflection. For in textual interpretations, anticipations of meaning (what I have been referring to as first-order, prereflective meanings) are both risked and progressively articulated. We live out our prereflective interpretations, writing the texts of our lives as we live, and become reflectively aware of our anticipations of meaning only after an episode of experience, when an anticipation founders, "lighting" itself up.

The prereflectively acquired meanings are claims which are, at least implicitly, held to be adequate to their objects. But through them we are unavoidably tied to a perspective. Experience involves a growing awareness of the perspective-boundedness of those claims. It is the contradiction between the implicit claim to adequacy and the perspective-boundedness of these meanings that is the motor that drives the process of experience. But this means that experience is essentially negative; the meanings that situate us, that, at least in part, define us, are constantly being problematized. Our ordinary language games come to be questioned. Here, in the notion of negativity, we have the idea of freedom thematized. Instead, then, of proceeding with a complacent satisfaction, we are constantly thrown back upon ourselves, upon those prior meanings. Such a reflective return to those presuppositions is what I mean by 'self-reflection.' The process of experience, then, leads to self-reflection. This reflection on my own situation furthers my self-knowledge, expanding my self-understanding.

We now have before us a conception of experience that allows us to make sense of self-understanding as a feature of human life. To summarize, a general account of the conditions necessary for the possibility of meaningful experience and self-understanding reveals the following: (1) that there must be in place prereflective orientations; (2) that the source of these orientations is in historical and cultural tradition; and (3) that these orientations are put to work, put in play, in interpretations of experience. The first condition is especially important, because without it there would be no framework into which to assimilate experience, to make sense of it, no language game in terms of which it would be intelligible, no set of concerns that would reveal its significance. What emerges here as well are two salient characteristics of the language game requisite to such a critical and meaningful appropriation of experience. Such a language must first be capable of giving voice to our prereflectively acquired commitments and orientations. Moreover, such a language, like ordinary language, must be its own metalanguage, must be capable of throwing its own assumptions and presuppositions into question.

III

This section addresses the worldlessness of science and of the standpoint that it encourages. I have said that experience is acquired through negativity, and have intimated that the disinterested standpoint said to be characteristic of science somehow cannot do justice to our experience. But does not contemporary philosophy of science, particularly as it is informed by Karl Popper's doctrine of falsifiability, echo and preserve this insight that we learn from experience through refuting our anticipations? Despite Popper's and Gadamer's shared references to Plato's *Gorgias*—Popper includes science in the field of Socratic dialogues, wherein the loser of a debate is the true winner—the experience relevant to scientific falsifiability is a radically reduced one in comparison to ordinary experience. Also, as we shall see, scientific experience is sought in an ahistorical, unsituated frame of reference.

To be sure, the "new" philosophy of science, as articulated by Hanson, Kuhn, Hesse and others, stresses the interpretive nature of scientific experience and the metaphorical nature of scientific theory.[9] How, then, can I claim an important difference between experience scientifically conceived and elaborated and experience that is conceived and elaborated in accordance with the more or less hermeneutic analysis that I provided in the last section?[10] I shall suggest that the denial of an important difference here rests upon a view of the scientific enterprise which, while it represents a significant advance upon the logical-empiricist view, is nevertheless incomplete.

We have been led to question the nature of both the so-called objects and subjects of knowledge. That questioning led us to suspect that the object does not exist self-enclosed and in itself, independently of our commerce with it, something self-identical, always remaining the same as we attempt to represent it more adequately, something which is preexistent and wholly outside our attempts to represent it. Similarly, the subject is not a disembodied constellation of once-and-for-all conceptual categories; nor can it be adequately conceived of as an attempt to find the *correct* (again, once-and-for-all) categories. Insofar as the self-understanding of science does not reflect an awareness of these themes, science is an essentially dogmatic enterprise, a perspective which is not aware of itself as a perspective. It is this scientistic self-understanding of science, arising from science's lack of self-reflection, that thinkers like Kuhn so admirably expose and criticize. But I believe that such thinkers do not fully expose science's lack of self-reflection, for, as I shall indicate, science operates within a framework which is secured and taken for granted at a level that falls outside of their analyses.

We are always in the midst of what Heidegger calls world (*Welt*), that context, structured by interests, concerns and fundamental commitments, which gives meaning to our practices. The world is the surrounding background of preunderstanding that frames our dealings with persons and things. The notion of world also embraces the conceptual distinctions which are rooted in our cultural practices, distinctions that get marked in the language games we play. Though we have a certain freedom with respect to the objects encountered in the world, we cannot remove ourselves from the world, that is, achieve an aperspectival, extralinguistic point of view. The scientific point of view, however, idealizes such an "escape," and presupposes a distance on the world. The scientific view rests upon a transformation of world into *objectum*.

Given what has been claimed, what is the nature of the distance which science presupposes? How is it to be understood? It consists in part in a willful displacement, a bracketing of the prereflective meanings of which I spoke in the last section. This bracketing or neutralization amounts to the achievement of the value freedom celebrated by Max Weber. This would ideally amount to the achievement of the attitude of Greek *theoria* (except that, of course, *theoria* took values, in what we would now call a normative sense, as its object as appropriately as it did anything else). The contribution of the inquiring subject in terms of its value orientations, aims and perspectives is severely reduced (of course, the immanent concerns of science remain) in the interest of an impersonal objectivity. The scientific conception of experience demands that the individual subject make a vanishingly small contribution, that (ideally) it become a passive receptor. To this end, there is yet another reduction presupposed by modern science, that of secondary to primary qualities, which makes the subject's spatial and temporal location a matter of indifference. I refer here to the so-called quantification of nature. These reductions render the scientific notion of experience ahistorical. They leave us with a value-free, colorless, odorless, tasteless and silent world, a "worldless" world. The scientific conception of experience, in reducing experience to experiment, requires the fungibility of experiencing subjects. The subject, then, becomes a mere marker, is denied a characteristic (*eigen*) contribution, so that experience can be essentially repeatable and controllable.

The idea of the modern subject as a residue or a limit—an idea alluded to by, among others, Marcuse, Lukács, Husserl and Foucault—can indeed be linked to the development of modern science. However, it must also be emphasized that there is a limit to the diminution of the role of the subject, a limit which modern science, perhaps ironically, requires and enforces. The idea of objectivity enshrined in modern science is characteristically tied to the notion of permanence, a permanence which is opposed to the instability and ephemeral nature of subjective experience. Our immediate experience of nature "suffers" from just those qualities to which permanence is opposed. Permanence is achieved only through postulating a mediated realm of scientific constructs and causal mechanisms, a realm which is essentially a subjective contribution. This is, if you will, the other side of the second reduction. The reductions then demand the transformation of the subject that is always located in a particular place into something analogous to a transcendental subject, that is, a "displaced" ideal consciousness.

It is these reductions that allow Heidegger to see the modern age, characterized as it is by science, as "the age of the world picture." The world, the object domain of modern science, is transformed into a picture, a representation, over against which we, the subjects of inquiry, stand.[11] We, the subjects for whom the world is a picture, are out of the picture. That is, we lose our place in the world. This metaphor entails a distance between "man" and world. When the world comes to be grasped as picture, it loses its claim on us (and nihilistic consequences follow). Only that which is susceptible of standing over and against us as a realm of facts can find a place in the picture. The values, commitments, and prereflective interpretations which root us are left out of this scheme. Values find a place here only insofar as they are transformed into facts, for example, into statements about subjective preferences. Such values would then have no more claim on us than would any other fact. I discuss this in terms of a transformation or reduction of meaning to value.

Recall now my claim, in the last section, that *it is only through our being situated, through our being determined in part by prereflectively acquired meanings, that experience can meaningfully engage us.* If, then, we are spoken to only if we are placed, any tendency to displace us in principle, as opposed to provisionally (self-enlightenment always involves a *provisional* displacement in that our prereflectively acquired interpretations are constantly risked), threatens our capacity to encounter our experience in an edifying and meaningful manner. The scientific notion of experience would have us experience in such a way that our contribution is minimized (down to the Kantian constitution of scientific constructs). Self-understanding is won only through placing at risk those prejudices which in part define our situation.

The inadequacy of science to the project of critical self-appropriation and to the retrieval of the meaning of experience can be further illuminated by deeper reflection upon what can loosely be called the conceptual structure of science. The scientific view of experience entails a loss of concreteness which impoverishes experience. Given the reductions alluded to above, a reduced "space" is established within which any theory or model must move if it is to retain scientific status. These reductions then furnish what I shall call an *a priori* of scientific concept formation.[12] This *a priori* of which I speak has the effect of closing off experience. That which is expressed cannot be recognized in its genuine novelty, in its alienness. Only the shell of a radically reduced experience remains. To be sure, such a shell retains sufficient determinateness to make possible the falsification of theories and nomological statements through anomalous and therefore quasinovel experiences, but the space within which falsification takes place remains untouched.

Wittgenstein's notion of logical space might help us here. The scientific anticipation is a predetermination of the most general characteristics of the categories into which the data of inquiry will be fit. This anticipation then predetermines characteristics of dimensions of experience or of logical spaces. It typically functions in an exclusionary fashion. For example, a given physical hypothesis would exclude color, a secondary quality, as a relevant dimension of experience, but might determine, say, electrical current as quantitatively measured to be a relevant logical space. Such an hypothesis would clearly be falsifiable, for it is not fixed *a priori* just what ammeter reading will result; rather, what is fixed *a priori* is that a datum with the general characteristics of an ammeter reading, and only such a datum, is a relevant fact. So, though factual prognostications are vulnerable to experience, the *a priori* commitments to the space in which such claims reside—a space which excludes secondary qualities, for instance— are not. This has the effect of "saying beforehand" what experience can mean. This "saying beforehand" is to be sharply distinguished from hermeneutical prejudgments, for learning from experience requires us to put *those* preconceptions at risk, to test them in the court of the genuinely novel, where nothing has been ultimately decided, where nothing has been ruled out of court. In science, then, the process from which self-reflection issues is short-circuited. Science (and technology too, through its defining concepts of efficiency, functionality and usefulness) "freezes" meanings, making them rigid and atemporal.

What I am proposing here is a three-tiered analysis of science. At the first, lowest level are hypothetical predictions, which are highly and relatively directly vulnerable to experience. They typically take the form of test implications of hypotheses, with the hypotheses themselves often drawn from explanatory theories. In our example, this would be the level at which the ammeter reading prediction would be situated. This level has been amply surveyed by the logical empiricists. At the next level are what Kuhn calls paradigms and paradigm-dependent descriptive categories. At this level of generality, the conceptual frameworks and exemplars which guide and inform a given community of inquirers are elaborated. In physics, for example, it is at this level that the shift took place, as a consequence of the transition from classical to quantum mechanics, from specifying position and momentum in a state description to specifying a wave function instead. In our earlier example, it is at this level that the decision is made concerning the relevance of electrical current as a dimension of experience. Assumptions made at this level, while not directly vulnerable to experience, are subject to change if, over a period of time, they prove consistently unable to accommodate recalcitrant aspects of reality.[13] Kuhn speaks here of "scientific revolutions." It is at this level that his distinction between normal and abnormal or revolutionary science is made. It is to this level also that claims concerning the theory-ladenness of data refer. The third level—most important for my purposes and consistently overlooked by philosophers of science, both empiricist and postempiricist in orientation—is the level at which the most general features of the scientific project emerge, the level at which the scientific view of the world is framed. Here decisions are made with regard to what, in the most general sense, is to count as an object of science or, in other words, what scientific objectivity is to mean. It is at this level that a notion of objectivity is operative which requires that prereflective meanings be taken out of play.[14] It is here that what we might call the scientific "prejudice" comes into focus.[15] The two reductions of experience are situated here. In our earlier example concerning the relevance of electrical current, it is at this level that values and secondary qualities are excluded. I referred earlier to a scientific *a priori*, because decisions made at this level inform the scientific attitude prior to any inquiry and are hardly, if at all, vulnerable to experience. Indeed, what is to *count* as scientific experience is determined here. Assumptions made at this level must be seen as conditioning and framing assumptions made at the two lower levels: conditions on what is to count as a scientific language are determined on this third level; the choice of a particular language is made at the second level; and testable statements drawn from that language are at issue at the first level. In a Quineian sense, claims and assumptions made at each higher level of analysis have relatively greater stability with respect to experience than those made at the level below them; the levels are arranged in the order of decreasing volatility.

Heidegger has perhaps done the most to draw our attention to what lies at this third level of my scheme. He speaks of a category of objectness which is prepared in advance as a defining condition of modern science, as a defining characteristic equally of Galilean, Newtonian, and Einsteinian dynamics.[16] At this level, objects of experience are refined to the point at which they fit into a formal frame wherein nature is represented as a "spatio-temporal coherence of motion calculable [either strictly or, in the case of quantum mechanics, statistically] in some way or other in advance."[17] A detailed analysis of this level need not concern us here, but it is important to note that science, through the reductions and the attempts at the at least quasicausal articulations which inform it, seeks to make nature, to use Heidegger's suggestive term, surveyable.[18] As surveyable, reality would be secured, in that, ideally, experience would be predictable and retrodictable from the vantage point of some comprehensive theory (the goal of the unified science program); reality would, in a sense, be available all at once. As surveyable, all of reality would be placed on the same footing, so that all of it could be dealt with in the same way; the ideal of surveyability, accordingly, suggests the idea of a deep commensurability. The notion of objectness, which is forged here in the interest of surveyability, remains invariant as particular quasicausal frameworks (paradigms, theories and models) change.

I propose a three-tiered explication of the scientific project in order to encourage us to focus on decisions and choices which might escape our notice if we employed a single- or double-layered view. In particular, if we adopted a one- or two-level view, the decision to exclude the prereflective meanings in which our cultural self-interpretations are embedded would not be thematized. The world that is permeated by those meanings, the world in which we ordinarily dwell, is bracketed, and in its place is set the world-as-picture. This amounts to a decontextualization, through which the things that enter the scientific object domain are removed from their manifold relations to human interests. For example, the cloud of the meteorologist is appropriated in a manner which is importantly different from the cloud of the farmer who is concerned for the nourishment of her crops, or the cloud of the couple who desire a pleasant day for a picnic. In the latter two cases, the cloud is wed to a structure of practical interests. The decision to bracket prereflectively acquired meanings is a decision about what can be put into question and what has been secured. The bracketing of these meanings is a refusal to make them objects of reflection, a commitment to keeping them "off to the side," a resolve, therefore, to take them out of play. In short, the realm of prereflective meanings, including the scientific anticipation itself (that is, the incorporation of the two reductions that render science an enterprise of bracketing and quantification), is not problematized by science. (The scientific anticipation is not problematized because it is constitutive of science; our prereflective meanings are not problematized because they are bracketed by science.) As we have seen, this realm must be problematized in a critical hermeneutic experience oriented towards self-enlightenment and the discernment of meaning. Accordingly, the level of analysis at which there comes into view the bracketing of meaning that is characteristic of the sciences corresponds to that at which the problematization of meaning was shown to be necessary for a critical appropriation of experience. This allows for an appreciation of the difference between the degree of self-reflection that is a feature of the work of even metascientists like Kuhn and the *critical* self-reflection requisite to the project of self-knowledge.

I am now in a position to explicate more fully my claim that science presupposes a distance from the world. Scientists do not, of course, and cannot view the world as pure spectators, as pure practitioners of *theoria*, as the ideal of objectivity would demand. They are ineluctably participants, though participants of a very special sort. Just as our attempts to describe the world are made from within some language game or other (none of which imprisons us, however), the scientist's attempts at description are made from within some paradigm or other. Some choice of vocabulary and conceptual categories must be made. Some commitment or other must be made at the second level of my analysis. The scientist is inevitably constrained (and enabled) by the necessity of approaching reality only mediately and, hence, perspectivally through her models and constructs.[19] The search for a language which effaces itself as language must end in failure. This suggests that the ideal of objectivity cannot function as a constitutive idea, but operates rather as a regulative ideal, in that it is presupposed and anticipated in scientific inquiry, and exerts a regulative power over inquirers. Even though, as the "new" philosophies of science tell us, disinterestedness, in the sense of a perspective-free view of reality, cannot be achieved in science, it nevertheless does function as an ideal with specific methodological consequences, for example, the demand for value freedom, for the mathematization of nature, for the related reduction of secondary to primary qualities and so on. These methodological consequences are expressed in the decisions made at the third level of my scheme, decisions which function in the interest of securing objectivity. These decisions are constitutive of scientific practice, in that they inform the scientific attitude, and in that they have substantive consequences for the execution of research programs. What, at least in part, unites the various modern paradigms about which Kuhn writes, and allows us to see them as modern *scientific* paradigms (what Kuhn failed to make clear in *The Structure of Scientific Revolutions*), are these features—the presence of objectivity as a regulative ideal and the constitutive bracketing of prereflective meanings.

It may be objected that the appropriation of the ideal of *theoria* is paradigm-dependent. Does this not sunder the scientific anticipation into a multiplicity of scientific anticipations, making it impossible to talk about *the* scientific attitude as distinct from, say, that of the humanities? I do not believe so, for the decisive point remains that the scientific project is informed by the demand to bracket prereflective meanings and, further, that the *phronesis*-like activity of the application of the ideal of objectivity to paradigmatically structured conceptual frameworks takes place within, and establishes and secures, a very specially prepared formal space, a space structured by the two reductions.[20]

Given the nature of the discussion to this point, it is apposite to ask, What *can* science do for us in our quest for self-understanding? We cannot gainsay the value of science, insofar as science is a project of displacement, as a touchstone for the task which concerns us here, namely, the critical appropriation of meaning. The project of edifying self-appropriation, if it is to embody critical self-reflection, requires displacement as well. As in science, there is a connection here between dislocation and truth. Analogous to objectivity in science, the "good life" stands as a regulative ideal for critical self-understanding. It is true that the "good life" must always be a good life for us in communion with others in concrete cultural and historical situations. But the fact that there is no unproblematic access to an absolute good, or that such a notion may be untenable, does not mean that all conceptions of the good are on a par. Our earnest seeking after "the good life" requires the problematization of prereflective interpretations, a virtualization of the claims they make on us, in that they must be cast into a space of possible alternatives.[21] This is the form that displacement takes in critical self-enlightenment. Such a dislocation is a manifestation of our freedom from the grip of unreflected prejudices, a freedom and displacement which are necessary if we are to continue to distinguish meaningfully between the "good life" and the way we just happen to see things, and to seek the former. (Of course, the vital difference remains between the provisional displacement required by critical self-interpretation and the principled displacement required by science, between problematizing prereflective meanings and bracketing them.)

Science has, of course, further, more immediate value in our cultural life. Not a great deal of reflection is required to see that science can perhaps explain and predict our experiences, making possible a *stabilization* of experience both in a cognitive and, through technology, in a practical sense.[22] Cognitively, this implies the ability to explain and predict; practically, it means the assurance of the effectiveness of our actions and of our ability to secure ourselves against want and the unexpected. This is the clearly desirable fruit of science's impoverishment of experience. And of course it goes without saying that both science and technology are utterly remarkable achievements of the intellect and imagination. What then has been closed off to scientific understanding as possibility? It cannot articulate the meaning of experience. As Rorty puts it: "even if we could predict the sounds made by the community of scientific inquirers of the year 4000, we should not yet be in a position to join in their conversation,"[23] that is, be in a position to know what those sounds were about, what they meant.

Why cannot, then, a scientific self-understanding on our part enable us to articulate the meaning of our experience? I have argued that we must risk who we *think* we are, what we *take* the meaning of our experience to be, in order to be in possession of who we are. Science, I have argued, requires us not to risk who we take ourselves to be, but rather to set ourselves aside. The imperative to set aside, to bracket, is a demand to view our experience from a distance. Accession to such a demand would have the effect of removing us from our experience, of making of it an objectified process. A scientistic self-understanding, one which transforms our experience into an object for us in the sense of an objectified process, would remove us from our experience in such a way that *we* would be no longer present in it to be addressed. Our experience would no longer pose questions to us about our way of being, about how we live our lives. That is, we would lose that experience's claim on us, a claiming which is necessary for our edifying self-understanding. We can start with meaningful involvement in the world and impoverish that involvement to get a simulacrum of "objective" experience, but we cannot start with "disinterested" subjectivity and generate an account of the human experience of the world.[24]

III

Technology, Meaning
and Time

4

Meaning and Time: An Essay on Technology

The last chapter argues that, by effecting a reduction of experience, science is unable to do justice to the meaning of our experience. In drawing upon that discussion, this chapter takes as its charge to demonstrate that technology too, especially through its means-end rationality, effects a reduction of experience. In particular, there is a tendency, pervasive in our instrumentally saturated culture, to reduce questions of meaning to questions of value, to translate talk about structures of meaning into talk about ends or goals. The most profound consequences of this reduction are to be found in the dimension of temporality, within our experience of time. I shall argue that technology, in its attempt to subdue time's characteristic flux, aims to "domesticate" time by harnessing the future predictably and reliably to the present. As a result, being in time comes to be viewed as an alienating rather than as a productive condition. I suggest further that, in predisposing us to experience time as the "other" to be subdued or annihilated, technological civilization threatens to marginalize projects of meaningful doing, the stuff of which stories are made.

On Meaning and Value

Announced by the clarion calls of Bacon and Descartes in the sixteenth and seventeenth centuries, and strengthened by its increasingly scientific foundations since the nineteenth century, the technological project has sought to place at our disposal limitless power. To be sure, our security in the face of an at best indifferent and at worst seemingly hostile natural environment has, from its beginnings, served as the legitimating end for this "will to power." However, what seems to characterize our era, as Heidegger has pointed out, is an emphasis upon "making available for use," virtually for its own sake.[1] We might well speak of this as the technological anticipation, just as we spoke earlier of the scientific anticipation. Such a technological anticipation entails an interest in increasing the arsenal of means. Such a preoccupation naturally leads to our experiencing and interrogating things and action in terms of their manifest utility or potential for use, to our experiencing them within the framework of means and ends.

The elevation of the means-ends paradigm to the status of *the* structuring categories of our technological civilization is a fact of crucial moment to us as meaning-oriented creatures. The means-ends paradigm, I shall argue, makes it impossible for us to give an adequate account of, and consequently must be decisively distinguished from, structures of meaning. As Hannah Arendt suggests in her still-pertinent essay, *The Human Condition*, "meaning," in a milieu exclusively informed by the means-ends paradigm, can be interpreted only in terms of an end.[2] But within a universe fully determined by and consistent with the means-ends principle, there are no *inherent* ends. Any end or goal can be assessed as a means to yet a further one. Utility cannot be an *ultimate* principle, for it will lead to an infinite regress which makes it impossible to assess the value of any given thing or action.[3] As a consequence, the status of ends as meaning-endowers would evaporate into that infinite regress. This suggests that the idea of meaning cannot be given its due within the sphere of utility.

As Heidegger points out, the infinite regress is brought to a nonarbitrary halt only through an appropriate understanding of the phenomenon of significance or of what I shall call 'meaning.'[4] This section seeks to make explicit, more so than do Heidegger and Arendt, the distinction between meaning, on the one hand, and ends, values or goals, on the other. It is important to do so because much contemporary thinking about technology and its relationship to the valuational aspects of our lives has focused upon the idea of the "system" with its attendant notions of goal- or end-directedness.[5] As a consequence, there is a striking tendency to conflate goals or ends and meaning.

Associated with the notion of meaning is the concept of world. Actions and things take on meaning within a world—the context of practices, beliefs, interests, concerns and fundamental commitments that give a point to action and provide a place for things. It is thus common to speak of the world of the Bantu, for example, though, interestingly, much less common to speak of the world of the British or of the French. The Heideggerian metaphor of the world-as-picture can be instructively opposed to the notion of world. As suggested in the last chapter, this metaphor entails a distance between us and the world, a transformation of participation and dwelling into observation and representation. The world becomes a picture, a representation, over against which we stand, leaving us out of the picture, without a place in the world. Such a world, a product of our representing activity, loses its claim on us. The commitments, concerns and interests which root us can find no place on this canvas, even though they may be constitutive in its production.

Without wishing here to pass judgment upon the adequacy of Heidegger's characterization of the modern age as "the age of the world picture," I find the contrast between the idea of world, with its attendant notion of dwelling, and of world-as-picture, with its attendant notion of representability, helpful in illuminating the distinction between meaning and value. Meaning has its natural locus in the phenomenon of world or form of life, and when meaning is made explicit, it emerges from the cognizance of a world. The meaning of an action derives in part from background assumptions and beliefs that inform the tradition in which the action is inserted. For example, one might think of helping one's neighbor paint her house as an action whose meaning derives from actualizing a background cultural commitment to communalism, or of not helping as a way of "living out" such a commitment to individualism.[6] The meaning of a tool derives from its context of use. The end of any process of fabrication or making, the product, derives its meaning from the practices sustained and the projects undertaken in the world in which it figures. If we do not thematize "world" or "form of life," then we cannot thematize meaningful action and meaning, but only behavior and goals.

We are now in a position to think the worldlessness of the scheme of means and ends. That is, both means and ends can be decontextualized. My earlier remarks about an infinite regress refer to the consequences of decontextualizing ends. When ends become worldless they can collapse into means. That is, we can always inquire into their utility or disutility for something else. For example, in a culture in which the family meal (and all that it involves, enacts and effects)— an occasion which, from one point of view, could be understood as significant in itself—is replaced by the "fast-food" meal to fulfill the "nutritive function," it should not be surprising for the question to be raised, Why bother to take the time to sit down together face to face at all in, say, McDonald's? Why not exploit the convenience of the "drive-through," or of microwaved food consumed at different times by the various members of a family? Further, because the means-ends paradigm separates means and ends and grants hegemony to the end, the specific character of the means becomes a matter of irrelevance; it only matters whether the means "work," that is, achieve their respective ends.[7] The means-ends paradigm then invites a decontextualization of means, rendering means worldless as well, "emancipating" them from the contexts of life which alone could grant to any of them its own characteristic and hence specific or peculiar meaning. Moreover, from the perspective of the means-ends schema, means can be made worldless without loss, owing to the possibility of functional equivalence, that is, to the possibility that a variety of quite different means can achieve the same end. Indeed, such an emancipation is a condition of technological progress; it is the basis of technology's rightful claim to universality.

Heidegger suggests that end-oriented talk, value talk, is nihilistic, that it projects values as objects or as properties of subjects, neither of which can have a claim on us. Insofar as values are understood as properties of subjects, the former are rooted in our freedom. What is freely produced can be just as freely retracted. Whereas meaning is worldly, value is worldless. Moreover, insofar as values can be understood as subjective preferences, that is, as facts about individuals, they can be incorporated into the scheme of the world-as-picture, finding there as adequate a representation as do the phenomena of microphysics. This susceptibility to representation suggests the ocular metaphor of "end-in-view" as an appropriate expression for value. The world-as-picture is "out there in front of us" to be surveyed all at once.

Indeed, in both its Platonic-objectivist and its Nietzschean-aestheticist guises, value talk betrays what we might call a spectatorial conception of value. Despite their obvious differences, both approaches are at home in the "world-as-picture" picture, insofar as both suggest values to be somehow out "before" us and not effectively around and "behind" us; they exist either as an object domain "distant" from mind or as the willful product of the will-to-power, respectively. Further, it makes sense to speak of a given goal, value or end as something that one can be closer to or farther away from, something that one can approach or recede from. In short, values and goals lend themselves to spatial geometrical *representation* as end *points*.

Meaning, on the other hand, resists such a reifying representation. I spoke earlier of the world-as-picture as a product of our representing activity. Such a picture is not an autonomous, "free-floating" scheme, but is, rather, rooted in prereflective commitments, in concerns we have as embodied beings. What I referred to earlier as the scientific anticipation, an attitude that is constitutive of the world-as-picture, can arguably be understood as arising out of an interest in an objectivity which facilitates our control. The relation between the scientific anticipation, objectivity and meaning is well illustrated in Charles Taylor's analysis of empirical political science. Mainstream empirical political science, he argues, because of its commitment to objectivity, establishes its object domain as consisting of brute data—including values expressed as subjective preferences and overt behavior—in principle observable by anyone.[8] As Taylor points out, meanings can find no place in such a scheme, for their description can only be the result of interpretation, not observation.[9] However, meanings are not dispensable, for they are presupposed in the very identification and reidentification of behavior as behavior of a certain sort, for example, as religious behavior or as political behavior.[10]

Indeed, given the relationship between meaning and values, a relationship that should be understood, I submit, as one of conditioning to conditioned, it is not much more surprising that meaning cannot be represented than it is that the Kantian categories cannot be experienced. Values emerge from and have their point within meaningful practices and the attendant categorial distinctions embodied in those practices, much as propositions emerge from and have their point within particular language games. (I shall refer to this relationship as the internal relationship between meaning and values.) For example, from the practice of raising a family, the value of security, in its emotional, physical and financial senses, comes to the fore. Values arise from contexts of life as our interpretations of, and as our way of representing to ourselves, what we are about as we participate in those contexts. (Values in this way are partially definitive of practices.) Values can thus be understood as tokens of what has already claimed us, as tokens of meaning. They contribute to the enabling and furtherance of practices by giving us something to aim at, to plan in terms of. They provide the aims that orient the pursuit of practices. They are the signposts representing what we are after; they are the "maps" of our practices.

On the other hand, rather than being a pseudo-object that we can approach or recede from, meaning has the character of the "always already" in which processes of life and action "dwell." Such processes take place in a frame of meaning. If we extend the spatial metaphor, meanings might be understood as the projections of "coordinate systems" in which goals or values have their point. Such a coordinate system would define or delineate space, but would not be "in" space. Meanings can be *transformed* into goals, and *in that way* can be spatialized. But they would then be spatialized *as* goals. They would lose their status as meanings, just as a frame, when *represented* as a frame, ceases to function as a frame, that is, as that which calls attention to the representation, the picture, rather than to itself.[11]

As an example of such a transformation, consider Sartre's claim that our most fundamental aim or value is to be our own foundation, to be God. The impossible aim of "becoming God" is a transformation of the experience of anxiety over the felt foundationlessness of existence, a concern that may or may not pervade human culture. (We need not be misled by the fact that the goal that Sartre has posited, becoming God, is one that we cannot achieve, and that therefore our approach in this case must be infinite. It can still be spatialized as a goal that continually recedes, like the horizon or the point of convergence of railroad tracks, or as a goal that we can get only arbitrarily close to, like the approach of an asymptotic curve.)[12]

What happens in such a transformation of meaning into value? As meaning becomes thematized as value, the manifold connections which operate in part "behind our backs" and which, through informing and shaping our experience, predispose us to experience in a characteristic way, are transformed into premises. The validity of these value-premises, apart from the referential anchoring in the meaning which gave rise to the value, stands or falls with the rational evaluation of those premises. Our inability to provide *purely rational* foundations for such premises, in abstraction from the meaning that gives them point, results in our inability to experience them as binding in a nonarbitrary way. That is, such values *qua* values, that is, in isolation from meaningful practices, cannot claim us. Values, as products of our freedom, have only the status that we, through our choosing, give them. We would have to capitulate to the picture of the absurdity of human existence that Sartre and Camus paint for us if we confined our attention to the level of values only. The only way to avoid such a picture *without* granting a certain priority to meaning would be to maintain a belief, as Habermas sometimes seems to, in the possibility of such purely rational foundations.

Now what is it about technology that demands the transformation of meaning into value, that demands the substitution of the signifier for the signified? Technological activity is result-anticipating activity. Its success is assessed in terms of the efficiency and effectiveness with which it achieves its result. And the result must be determinate and specifiable if we are to distinguish between success and failure and to determine the degree of the one or the other. The "output" then of a technological process, the product, must be operationalized, made measurable. Technology can serve and secure meaning only insofar as meaning is formulated as an end-in-view, goal or aim of which we can render an explicit account, that is, only insofar as meaning is transformed into value.[13] This is what I referred to, in Chapter Two, as the detachment of values from contexts of meaning that is occasioned by technology.

Of course, one might reply to what I have been saying by pointing out that science and technology can themselves be understood as forms of life, as contexts of meaning. The cultures of science and of technology shape the ways in which scientists and technologists make sense of, organize and respond to experience. Scientific activity derives its meaning from the scientific community's concern over an objective representation of what is the case; technological activity derives its meaning from the relevant community's commitment to making things available for use, to efficiency, to functionality and, in general, to solving practical problems by increasing our power to transform the world. The last chapter argues that the scientific attitude toward experience is constituted by a univocal determination of the meaning that experience can have. Central to my thesis there, it may be recalled, is the claim that there are two reductions of experience that are constitutive of the scientific attitude, and that these reductions have the effect of determining beforehand and fixing the meaning that experience can have. I spoke in this regard of a scientific *a priori*. Just as the scientific reductions serve a pure seeing ideally unclouded by subjective orientations and perspectives, technology abstracts from the manifold connections that things, events, processes and actions have to historically shaped and culturally specific forms of life, and views them only under the aspect of their utility. This technological reduction is sustained through paradigm shifts in technology—from, say, mechanical devices to electronic ones— just as the scientific reductions frame paradigm shifts there. The technological reduction reduces experience to resources, tools and products, just as the scientific "world" consists of constructs and pointer readings. We might then well understand science and technology as forms of life, but they are forms of life lacking "depth"; that is, they are essentially worldless. My remarks above concerning the worldlessness of the scheme of means and ends were intended to suggest this in the case of technology.

Let me consider another, though related, objection to what I have been urging.

Cannot notions such as utility and power be viewed indifferently as meanings or values, thus undermining the distinction that I have been at pains to make? Utility is a value *for us* as cultural beings, a value that gives meaning to technology as a social institution. Technology's worldlessness is occasioned by our worldliness. Our desires have occasioned a sector of culture devoted exclusively to the idea of utility. But utility is not only the key to the *meaning* of the technologist's activity; it is also a *value*, or at least a criterion of value, of technology. It is what technology aims to secure. Perhaps the meaning/value distinction does break down within *technology*, a second-order, "nondeep" form of life. Perhaps this is a defining characteristic of such second-order forms. As meanings are institutionalized as values, the meaning/value distinction gets hopelessly blurred within the institutions or second-order forms that serve those values. After all, the inhabitants of scientific and technological communities do self-consciously *choose* to commit themselves to those meanings that characterize their communities. But from *our* point of view, as historicocultural beings who exist, for the most part, outside the laboratory and beyond the test bench, technology's "meaning-values" are to us values, which are tokens of what claims us as finite, insecure, embodied beings in a coldly indifferent universe. In sum, this objection fails to challenge the distinction between world and world-as-picture, the core contrast upon which the meaning/value distinction rests.

Further, utility and power are very peculiar sorts of meanings. For, as I suggested at the beginning of this section, in contexts structured exclusively by them, nothing is valuable or meaningful in itself. Consider again my example about house painting. It was partially used to illustrate the contrast between, on the one hand, action whose meaningfulness or significance derives from the form of life or tradition in which it is situated and, on the other, action whose meaning is derived from the end or goal that it is undertaken to achieve. In the first case I speak of the action's meaning, in the second, of its function. Speaking quite generally, we would consider the first sort of activity to be practical action or what Aristotle called *praxis*, the second sort, technical activity or *techne*. In the first case, the very doing of the action *is* the fulfilling embodiment of a cultural commitment. The activity contains its end, as in acting bravely. In the second case, the end is distinct from and beyond the activity, as a built house is distinct from and external to the building of a house. Now, as I pointed out earlier, helping or not helping one's neighbor paint her house may have symbolic meaning derived from the world in which it is inserted. To this symbolic point of view, or perspective oriented toward structures of meaning, can be opposed the technical point of view. Suppose the neighbor is assisted. It would then also be natural to assess this action in terms of the contribution it makes to achieving the end-in-view, the painted house.

From the point of view of utility, from the technical point of view, all that matters is the result (or, to be precise, the result and the cost of obtaining it). So the action has no significance in itself; its significance lies in its consequences.

It can be replaced without loss of significance by any equally effective means. Such is the fate of anything that falls under the sway of the rule of utility. By contrast, the significance of what I have called symbolically meaningful action, which is one kind of *praxis*, lies in its *doing*, not in its result. As a symbolic gesture it betokens a shape of life, it discloses the subjectivity of the agent, and it confirms and effects a relationship of a certain kind to others.[14] Since under the rule of utility the meaning of anything is exhausted by the end that it potentially serves, and not by what the action itself embodies or is disclosive of, the meaning which lies in the very doing of an action must remain an alien to such a world.

The Time of Meaning and the Time of Ends

Introduction

Reflection upon the distinction between meaning and value, or between meaningful action and functional action, reveals that these opposed notions can be characterized by distinctive attitudes toward time. The distinction between meaning and ends is reflected in the dimension of temporality. Again, Kierkegaard is helpful in providing focus to our reflections here. He contrasts two ways of experiencing ourselves in time: one way is captured by the expression "internal history," the other by "external history." In the case of external history, time is that through which we must move in order to achieve a goal or realize a moment of significance.[15] Time is that which stands "between" us and our goal. In being that which alienates us from the end of our striving, time is at best dispensable, at worst an obstruction. As a consequence, time is not constitutive of goals, and the goals can be conceived of and *represented* purely spatially. The focus in external history is on the *moment* of satisfaction, that is, on the achievement. External history, for Kierkegaard, can be represented artistically, hence spatially and synchronically, because within it time can be contracted without loss. Its time is in principle capable of abbreviation. Indeed, given that time is for external history a source of alienation, we cannot but wish it to be contracted. Through external history time is spatialized as a quantifiable other with which we can only reckon, or at which we can only gnash our teeth in rancor. For significance is concentrated in the end, in the moment of achievement.[16]

Indeed, one is struck here by the similarity between the attitude toward time characteristic of external history and that posture toward time represented by what has been called the "ethics of satisfaction," a position that holds the aim of human life to be fulfillment or completeness, a view that informs the thought of Plato, Schopenhauer and Marcuse, for example.[17] The satisfied individual would want nothing, would be at one with herself. Such an emphasis upon the *state* of satisfaction is inseparably tied to an antagonistic relationship to time, that viscous medium separating us from what "really" counts, and just as surely threatening to sweep us away from any satisfying haven that we might reach.

Given the ideal of satisfaction, existence in time has to be considered a burden. To experience time as alienating in this way is to experience it as the source of constant change, of uncertainty, contingency, loss and irretrievability. The vision of a nonalienated existence would go hand in hand with the project to annihilate time. Time can be contracted without loss; time and value are disjoined.

On the other hand, through the notion of internal history is understood a conception of time that is tied to immanence rather than transcendence. Here, significance lies not beyond, but within; it pervades time.[18] Time is constitutive, and internal history defies spatialization, eschews representation. The passage of time brings us no closer to the thing of significance, for it is, in a sense, already in our possession.

What Kierkegaard refers to as internal history in *Either/Or* is treated by him elsewhere under the rubric of "repetition."[19] "Repetition" captures the experience of time appropriate to what I shall approvingly refer to as resolve. Repetition moves through time, where it is at home, grappling with time and exposing itself to the latter's flux; its task is to persevere in time and to maintain its singleness, identity and continuity within the flux.[20] It seeks, then, not to kill or subdue time, but rather to come to terms with it. In enabling us to come to terms with time, repetition also provides us the wherewithal to cope with loss, be it the loss of a particular object or of objectivity itself.[21] Accordingly, repetition can be understood as a counterpoint to external history's and metaphysics' "ill wills" toward time, to their rancor born out of their yearning for the transcendent.

Now, the notion of external history seems appropriate as a description of our experience of time when the goal-oriented, means-ends paradigm of technology has us in its grip. *Techne* or *poesis*, activity in which the end or product is something other than the activity itself, has, in this sense, external history. Further, just as the time of external history can be contracted without loss, the means can be decontextualized, taken out of time and world, without loss.[22] Action that is inherently meaningful in the sense that its very doing is meaningful, where the means-ends distinction breaks down and the end is not to be distinguished from the activity itself—for example, the Greek notion of *praxis*—such action has internal history.[23]

Technology and Time

Let me state at the outset what I take to be distinctive of the relationship to time that is characteristic of the technological project: on the one hand, technology presupposes an awareness of the openness of the future; on the other, it promises a mastery that would "domesticate" the future through lifting the burden of our existence in linear time, through lifting the burden of our facing an open, uncertain and unmastered future. There is, then, an ambivalence that characterizes technology's relationship to time, a tension between its *presuppositions* with respect to time and its *attitude* toward time.

Technology is an outcome of our attempt to secure ourselves in an indifferent world. The realization of this security would result in granting us immunity from the uncertainty of time: the future would be predictable and controllable. In this way, that experience of time which we might call the "linear experience of time"—where the future is experienced as open, as the locus of possibility and the unexpected—would be "annihilated," in that the future would no longer be open. Through its promise of mastery, technological progress seems to make possible the realization of what I earlier referred to as the "ideal of satisfaction." Such an ideal, one of self-sufficiency, of autonomy, is traditionally tied to the attainment of a standpoint outside time, to the eternal present. Yet technology presupposes an awareness of the openness of the future, of an experience and a conception of time as linear. The remainder of this section will concern itself with the articulation of this tension.

The phenomenon of planning, the activity most characteristic of the technological enterprise as a process, provides a useful starting point. The scope of planning is, of course, broader than that of technology—one plans a vacation, a lesson for school children, a football play—but technology, though itself also more than planning, is always at least and characteristically planning. At the intersection of planning and technology lies the temporality of technology. We must, of course, be careful to distinguish here between the *apparatus* produced by technology, that is, technological artifacts such as devices and bridges, and the *project* of technology, and hence between the time of the apparatus and the time of the project. The time of the apparatus may well be the pointillistic, reversible now-time of science, but the time of the project is not.[24] The time of the project is the time of making, which is a form of the *execution* of a plan.

Planning is a forward-looking activity, where interest is fixed upon the future. In planning we have toward the future an enabling and allowing intentionality, a preparing and making way for intentionality. A plan is a recipe for attaining a future goal-state by means of an ordered sequence of actions. Since the time-scale of a plan can be arbitrarily long, the future envisioned by us as planners must be indeterminately open. The linear or open nature of the time of planning is also underscored by the necessary incorporation into a plan of elements arranged in determinate temporal patterns. Such an arrangement consists in noncommutatively ordered procedures or actions, which must follow upon one another in a determinate temporal sequence and usually within a determinate temporal span. It is clear that the future must be understood as being open enough to accommodate the linearity and successiveness attested to by the "befores" and "afters" constitutive of the plan.

Since planning is an activity of marshalling or orchestrating—collecting and ordering—means in order to achieve an end, it cannot regard time as consisting of a series of wholly indifferent "nows" (as can science or metaphysics). The time of planning is a time of reckoning, where it is always a matter of its being "time for" something, where it makes sense to speak of the "right time."[25] The time of planning is therefore linear in the sense suggested above, though it is not the objective now-time of science that refuses to privilege any given moment.

In that the temporality of technology is the temporality of reckoning or planning, modern technology, or instrumental rationality, also rests on a linear understanding of time. The notion of instrumentality already presupposes the cause-effect relationship, suggesting a temporal ordering with respect to before and after. I introduce the, in some quarters, questionable relationship between causality and temporal order here because, within the sphere of instrumental rationality, we are concerned with the introduction of the element of agency into the causal process, and it is clear that world history, for which agents are in part responsible, does not take place in an instant.[26] That is, there is a temporal spread between causes and, at least, their remote effects.

Further, many would argue that technology has as its objective the *improvement* of means. Such an objective, with its presumption that we have the freedom to create *novel* configurations, has as its most fundamental assumption the modern linear view of time.[27] Quite naturally, then, we are led to the notion of progress. In part, the worldview of modernity owes this idea to technological production, where progress consists in the enhancement of the effectiveness and efficiency of means.[28] The possibility of progress presupposes the possibility of novelty and the reality of becoming. The idea of progress presupposes an understanding of the future as the locus of that which does or can differ in some essential respect from that which now is or which has been. This is clearly incompatible with nonlinear notions of time, assuming that the conception of progress brings with it the idea of a future which extends indefinitely, that is, the idea that there can always be something which has never been. The idea of progress contributes a basic instability to the worldview of modernity, in that it implies that the world is never "settled." This instability or lack of closure is tied to the expectation of change, and both give rise to an experience or existential understanding of time as linear.

The tension to which I alluded in the beginning of this section can, then, be formulated in several ways. Technology, through its incorporation of the temporality of planning and more particularly through its incorporation of the idea of progress, is essentially oriented toward the future, a future which is understood as an open horizon. However, this is an openness about which the technological project is deeply ambivalent. This understanding of the future is compromised by technology's rancor against the uncontrolled past and its concern with predicting and controlling the future. The goal of technology is the "domestication" of time, that is, the prediction and control of that which appears in time. Domestication appears as the will to control. This can be argued to be the will for the closure of history, corresponding to a shift in emphasis from the future to the present. The domestication of time would grant us the assurance that we have the future securely in tow, in a sense, "behind" us. *Technology is fundamen-*

tally an expression of and response to the "terror of history." It represents our quest for security against novelty, through control and order, while presupposing the possibility of novelty. It is the use of created novelty to forestall or defuse contingent novelty. In securing ourselves we want assurances against surprises, against an open and uncertain future. Consider instances of technology's utilization of the novel to "ambush" the novel, instances such as the prediction of the weather through the use of radar, sophisticated instrumentation and computerization; or computer models predicting the vulnerability of various regions to earthquakes; or "high-tech" war games; or the redundancies built into countless technological systems to compensate for subsystemic malfunction. To the extent that its *telos* is security, the "domestication" of time goes hand in hand with the ideal of satisfaction whose project is to annihilate time. For, in lifting the burden of an unmastered, open future, domestication would grant us independence from the flux of time, an independence that is the dream which haunts us hapless wayfarers cast adrift in the stormy sea of external history.

So the tension between understanding time to be open and the will to close it off endows the temporal structure of technology with a certain ambiguity. Technological time, that is, time as it is reckoned for a given instrumental action or complex of actions, is, like scientific time, unambiguously linear. It is the time of the clock. Furthermore, the temporal dimension of the technological worldview, that is, that understanding of time that is consistent with the growth and development of technology, is future-oriented. Speaking very generally, technology structures and quantifies time in the way that science does, but it makes control and prediction paramount. That is to say, that there is a specific technological *interest* that informs its temporality. Explanation, a primary concern of science, is of interest to technology only if it can inform rules regulating possible future control, whereas for science prediction serves explanation. What is significant here is that, although technology is future-oriented, it is so in a way that seeks to annihilate the future *qua* future, that is, as free possibility, so that the future remains open, but open for increased control. In such a preempted future, prediction and control would secure us against eventualities with which we would otherwise be unprepared to cope.

Of course even technology's guarantee of mastery and control turns out to be as much threat as promise. As Horkheimer and Adorno have argued in *Dialectic of Enlightenment*, the project of control over external nature sublates itself in the project to control internal nature. We become as much the objects as we are the subjects of techniques of mastery and control. Technology's domestication of linear time is born out of the practical concern for a type of satisfaction which ultimately technology, because of its own requirements, cannot deliver. It promises to deliver us from the renunciations made necessary by a recalcitrant, unyielding and indifferent natural world. It promises to grant us autonomy, to make of us wholes. Yet it requires that we remain parts, that we subordinate ourselves to larger wholes. As Jacques Ellul and others have amply documented, progress in the control of objectified natural and social processes requires techniques for integrating the "human factor" into the whole in order to fully realize technology's potential, techniques as various as propaganda, amusement and vocational guidance.[29] Thus, while technology promises a satisfaction which is ideally linked to autonomy, where here I mean freedom from determination by blind natural and social forces, it issues in new constraints, in a new set of renunciations.

In our yearning to be liberated from the linear time of external history, we find ourselves in thrall to the time of technology. In technology, time is destined to be reified, to be transformed into a commodity to be quantitatively reckoned, distributed and parceled out. Within the context of instrumental action we are always concerned to "save time" and "make time," and we fear "wasting time" and "losing time." Of course it is we who are subject to the pressure to husband time. Clock time replaces the temporal determinations that evolve from the life rhythms of a people. We, too, become instrumentalized. Our own wants and needs are subordinated to the requirements of the technical complex and, specifically, to time.[30]

The line of argument sketched in the two preceding paragraphs has been developed by others. I rehearse it here to highlight the ambiguity of technology's promise, and to suggest where the talk of wholes and parts and of integrative human technique leads us. The fear of leaving anything to chance gives rise to, and nurtures, the ideal of control. Habermas has validly suggested that the technical interest in security and control finds its natural outcome in the demand for the establishment of self-maintaining systems regulated by cybernetic feedback. He refers to such a cybernetically self-regulated organization of society as a "negative Utopia of *technical control over history*" (emphasis mine).[31] For, as Ellul has emphasized, progressive control requires an integrative coordination of all functionally implicated elements or parts in order to insure that possible perturbations of a trajectory to a given end or disturbances of a given end-state can be rationally anticipated and counterbalanced. We and our techniques are increasingly subjected to an all-embracing technique or a metatechnique arising from the "need to master trends which affect the security and well being of mankind."[32]

The most consistently articulated elaboration of this ideal is provided by general systems theory or the "systems perspective." From its standpoint, the ideal of security is transformed into the ideal or goal of systems maintenance. The idea of self-monitoring and self-correcting systems where the functional integration of parts assures the viability of wholes—both at the level of the device, for instance, "on-board" computers to monitor and coordinate the various functions necessary to the efficient operation of automobile engines, and at the level of society, for example, the practice of organizational management—captures the direction of technological development. Both for the sake of technical progress itself, as Ellul has argued, and in the interest of economic and political management and control, as Habermas has argued, technology's "means-ends" motif is being applied increasingly not only to its "proper" domain of devices themselves, but also to society as a whole. Functional integration for the sake of the stability of the whole assumes priority. (And the achievement of such integration characteristically requires both the application of existing technological knowledge and the development of new technological knowledge in order to address recalcitrant aspects of a system, aspects that Thomas Hughes calls "reverse salients," both of which augment our fund of technological know-how. And in the manner characteristic of cybernetic systems, much of the resultant know-how is destined to become new "input" for refining and enhancing the potential of the system for growth, efficiency and productivity.) It is here that some of the most pressing issues concerning the consequences of technology for our self-understanding arise, when technology's promise of an emancipation from our thralldom to nature is redeemed as a social promise.

The functional or means-end rationality characteristic of systems, and of technology in general, projects a *self-effacing temporality*. The project of the domestication of time finds its fulfillment in the idea of the system, in achronic structures characterized by nonsuccessive relations. This ideal's emphasis on the maintenance of an achieved goal-state confers upon time the derivative status of being merely the measure of deviations or lapses from a synchronically understood stable equilibrium. Consequently, time or the diachronic dimension is understood as a lack, as nonconstitutive, accidental and unreal. Again, we understand technology as participating in metaphysics' "ill will" toward time; technology's time is the time of value and of external history. The tendency of the technological systems framework is to reduce action and its novelty to behavior and its programmability.[33] Through the projected realization of an already constituted goal that closes off the future as real possibility, a reductive demand for commensurability is enacted.[34] The negative ideal of the control over history issues in the history of control. Such a history holds the future to be the locus of the elaboration of techniques and metatechniques of adaptation, and signals an end to the notion of an open future. For the future is represented by a *telos* accepted *a priori*— by systems values which are not treated as problematic.

The Time of Praxis

The hermeneutic of experience developed in Chapter Three—where the way in which we put prereflectively acquired meanings into play in action and experience was elaborated—prefigures the temporality of repetition, where the "always already" of our cultural and historical insertion gets repeated forward as it informs action and experience. *Praxis* can be understood as an actualization of sociocultural norms, as an activation or repetition of possibilities shaped by our historical past. We recall that, because the technological project's focus is on securing an end, its attitude toward temporality is that time, in its unruliness, must be domesticated, must be brought under control. Opposed to this "ill will," *praxis* fully recognizes time as its field of action and as an enabling medium—for instance, the meaningful action of *praxis* is an application or repetition of the past understood as an historical legacy—and seeks, ideally, to maintain the singleness of individual identity through the vicissitudes of temporal existence. Indeed, our singleness, identity and integrity are both forged and confirmed by the way we comport ourselves in and through time, for instance, through promise-keeping or by demonstrating patience. For example, a temporal reference is constitutive of a claim to, say, integrity as a character trait, for the conditions for the application of the term require the comparison of at least two temporal moments with respect to whether a person exhibits self-sameness or loyalty to self. *Praxis*, like repetition, does not, therefore, seek to annihilate or even to domesticate time; it seeks, rather, to come to terms with it.

Our understanding, bearing the imprint of historical effects (*wirkungsgeschicht-liches Bewusstsein* in Gadamer's terms), bearing the marks of the past, has toward the present a future orientation (action-oriented self-understanding in Habermas's terms) enabled by hermeneutic anticipations of meaning. Thus, the "moment" of repetition is a present doubly determined: we orient ourselves in terms of predispositions inherited from the past and in accordance with our solicitous concern about our future, that concern itself in part a legatee of our cultural heritage.

Repetition is not a mere "repetition of the same," abandoning itself wholly to the past.[35] It is, rather, a matter of being a *new* application of already existing possibilities, a unique appropriation of tradition.[36] The temporality of *praxis* effects a fusion of the horizons of the past and the future. Repetition in *praxis* is an applicative recollection oriented toward future action. Praxial temporality is thus at once the time of both preservation and invention.[37] Arendt emphasizes the aspect of novelty in action. She understands actions or deeds to be beginnings or inaugurations.[38] Political deeds, for instance, institute ways of living together. She, of course, emphasizes the inaugural quality of action in order to distinguish action in its novelty from behavior in its predictability. But meaningful actions or intelligible deeds are new enactments of the *already possessed*. They must take place in a frame of meaning in order to be understood *as actions*. And that frame of meaning cannot be wholly incommensurable with what has gone before, lest the action be unintelligible. So perhaps it would be better to think of actions as *creative* continuations, as novel appropriations, but as continuations nonetheless.

Remaining with Arendt's categories for the moment, we might say that the temporality of action or *praxis* is a kind of dialectical synthesis of the temporalities of what she calls labor and work.[39] Labor, for her, is pure meaningless repetition, a Sisyphean toil bearing what Hegel calls a "bad" or "spurious infinity." Work or *techne* has the absolute directionality of beginning, middle and end; it has the progressive temporality of external history. Action can be understood as a *repetitive unfolding*; its temporality has the "proper infinity" of a self-relationship, of an internal history. In repetition the self is brought forward; in external history the self is preempted by the moment of future satisfaction. Further, action's tie to novelty and the essential unpredictability of its consequences give it an openness that distinguishes it sharply from both the cyclical understanding of time characteristic of labor and the closed future of technology's temporality.

If repetition does not abandon itself to the past, it is also true that it does not aim at progress, at least not as the latter is usually understood.[40] As the transmission of tradition, of the "always already," repetition does not so much advance beyond as dig deeper, rendering more and more explicit what I have called our "prereflective meanings."

I have implied that, in contrast to the time of *techne*, the time of *praxis* is productive, is in fact constitutive of the self. What time holds and what gets repeated forward is a history which bears the conditions of the intelligibility of action. Repetition is therefore meaning-enabling. The repetition which is an explicitation is also productive of self-knowledge, and in a double fashion. First, as our prereflective orientations are projected forward into action in the way described in Chapter Three, they can be brought from "behind our backs" and made objects of focal awareness, thereby enabling and furthering self-understanding and self-critique. As I argued in that chapter, the thematization or explicitation of our prereflective meanings occurs in action guided by, or in experience shaped by, those meanings. So critical experience as I outlined it is at the same time recollective experience. I have suggested, therefore, that repetition can be understood as a mediated self-relation. The implicit or latent self is brought forward in action and experience which render it explicit or manifest. The explicit "presentation" allows self-recognition which, when appropriated, effects a "return to self," but a self that has been transformed by its newly appropriated self-understanding. Repetition is productive of this growth, of this self-transformation. Thus, secondly, the productive temporality of repetition grants us new and "deeper" ways of looking at the world and ourselves in it. Further, given that what gets recollected (and can thereby be criticized, relativized or *consciously* adopted) is action-orienting, the retensive intentionality of repetition also functions protensively as it enables forward-looking action.[41] The conscious interception of such a repetition can generate interventions leading to renegotiated futures.

The foregoing discussion treats repetition more or less as an ontological phenomenon, as a general feature of the human way of being. But the role assigned to repetition, *Wiederholung* and *Geschichtlichkeit* in the work of Kierkegaard and Heidegger suggests also a decidedly "ethical" dimension, that is, a dimension having to do with the determination of the will, as is suggested by the pivotal use of such terms as 'authentic,' 'choice' and 'resolve.' In this sense, 'repetition' connotes a steadiness, even a steadfastness.[42] To choose repetition is to resolve to accept in earnest the challenge thrown down by time. The time of internal history is a testing time, a time through which who we are is forged and revealed.

Repetition is an act of *constitutive discovery*. "Existentialists" like Sartre and Camus, and other value-oriented thinkers, emphasize only the aspect of constitution. It is to the credit of hermeneutic thinkers like Kierkegaard, Heidegger and Gadamer that they also give the ontological dimension of discovery its due. But these latter too, especially Kierkegaard, stress the significance of choice. Heidegger speaks of resoluteness as the repetition of a possibility of existence that has come down to us via tradition.[43] Authenticity lies here in making the possible, as it has been forged by our tradition, our own through repetition.[44] Understanding the self to be resolutely brought forward in repetition suggests two starkly contrasting ways of making the future present: on the one hand, through technological security; and on the other, through the moral bindingness of, for example, promise-making. In moving from the former to the latter, the locus of domestication shifts, from time to the self. Domestication thereby shifts from being a technical intention to being an ethical intention.

I shall bring this section to a close by briefly amplifying my beginning remarks about repetition and identity. Alasdair MacIntyre has put forward the idea of a self whose unity resides in the unity of a narrative that links birth to life to death as narrative beginning to middle to end.[45] The unity of the self, he argues, can best be understood through the notion of a story and of the kind of unity of character that a story requires.[46] This is a very suggestive tack, and I pursue further such a narrative account of the self in the next chapter. But I introduce MacIntyre's account here in order to further articulate, by indicating some reservations I have about his account, what I intend by the idea of repetition. Of the three difficulties that I shall mention, only one will be pursued at any length here. First of all, it is not clear how his account solves the difficulties that beset traditional attempts to understand personal identity. What entitles us to claim, for instance, that the episodes that are linked narratively are episodes in *my*, as opposed to some other's, single life story, other than an appeal to criteria such as bodily identity or memory, the very criteria upon which the narrative account of the self supposedly represents an advance? Secondly, MacIntyre's discussion suffers in general from his failure to give the underdetermination thesis its due. This thesis, though originally at home in the philosophy of science, is now a virtual commonplace also in literary theory and historiography. It asserts that accounts of facts, be they theoretical accounts or narrative accounts, are not uniquely implied by those facts. Contrary to this thesis, MacIntyre often seems to write as if there is for each of us a unique narrative account, or at least a unique *sort* of narrative account, spanning our lives from birth to death.

As a consequence of understanding the unity of the self as the unity of a narrative, MacIntyre holds that to ask about the "good life" is to ask about the kinds of stories we want told and to be able to tell about ourselves and the communities in which we participate. Though, again, this is a suggestive way of putting the matter, we need to be especially careful in our selection of the narrative models that we choose to privilege for these purposes.[47] MacIntyre claims that the unity of our lives is the unity of a narrative *quest*.[48] Care is necessary here, because central to the notion of a quest are the notions of an end or *telos*, and the linear structure of beginning-middle-end. If the concern of the narrative is largely with the achievement of the end, then time tends to get experienced as a limiting concept, as a coefficient of resistance or adversity to be nullified. On this model, our narrative representations, our biographies and autobiographies, would all read like histories of science and technology, in that they would be mere chronicles of more or less successful or failed attempts at achieving an end, that is, chronicles of making, as opposed to doing. History would become the history of control rather than the story of action. This, what I will call a technological model of narrative, does not do justice to the productive character of time, and consequently restricts the sort of narrative understanding that we can achieve about ourselves, the kinds of stories that we can tell about ourselves and, hence, the shape of the human conversation.

Of course, in life we never begin at the beginning. Since it is always already begun, we are in the midst, in the middle, from the outset. Here we discern the face of repetition, suggesting that in our repertoire of narrative models should also be those wherein the linearity of beginning, middle and end is replaced by a circularity in which ends are returns to beginnings, and a repetition in which ends are already contained in beginnings—narrative models realized in texts such as Proust's *Remembrance of Things Past*.[49] Repetition endows with themes lives understood in terms of these narrative models. The theme of such an enacted narrative gets carried forward in the episodes of a life through what Heidegger calls a "steadiness which has been stretched along," a steadiness that binds birth, death and their in between together. So an authentic life, at least, is a unified or connected life in virtue of its repetition. Now, only if MacIntyre's quest is interpreted broadly enough to accommodate the quest for who we already are can it be an adequate model for understanding life as an embodied narrative. For the movement of repetition is a movement toward a deeper understanding of who we are, and hence a movement to become more deeply who we are. It is in this inward voyage toward ourselves that we narratively disclose the "who" of our *praxis*.

IV

On the Use and Abuse of Repetition for Critique

5

The Use of Repetition for Critique

In painting ideal-typical portraits of symbolically meaningful action, on the one hand, and technical action, on the other, my discussion has set the stage for a critique of technological rationality: the growing hegemony of the temporality of making (*techne*), at the expense of temporalities of doing (*praxis*), stands as a threat to the continued presence of meaningful differences in our lives and to there being meaning in a life as a whole. If our self-understanding is a narrative understanding, as MacIntyre and others suggest, then in order to understand how technology affects our self-understanding we must attend to how the temporality of technology predisposes us to choose certain narrative models for emplotting our lives over others. This chapter pursues the discussion of the narrative qualities of a life with the aim of highlighting this threat posed by technology's orientation to time.

As I suggested in the last chapter, the romantic quest seems peculiarly well-suited as the counterpart to technology's external history. In viewing our lives as such quests, we want to "hurry the plot along." Think, for example, of Mozart's Don Giovanni, who "exists" only at the moment of conquest, who exists only pointillistically or paratactically. What gives actions their value in such a setting is their ability to telescope the time between the present and the attainment of the object of desire. This criterion of telescoping ability confers upon actions the kind of commensurability that does not allow for meaningful differences, only for quantitative distinctions, because the specific qualities of action cease to matter—any functionally equivalent action will do.

Through its wish to derealize time, technology denigrates the field in which meaningful differences are deployed. Does not the technological consciousness wish to repress the memory of the history of even its own achievements? An influential student of technology, Langdon Winner, has spoken of technology as a "license to forget":

> Is not the point of all invention, technique, apparatus, and organization to
> have something and *have it over with*? One does not want to bother any more

with building, developing, or learning it again. . . . Technology, then, allows us to ignore our own works. It is *license to forget.*[1]

Winner is speaking here of us, the consumers of technology, taking our species' achievement in the technical realm as license to forget. However, it seems that the technological consciousness or the institution of technology itself, as distinct from society at large, is also characterized by a kind of forgetfulness. Before elaborating upon this, it might be well to remind ourselves explicitly, here, of a distinction between two perspectives upon technology, that of society and that of the technologist. From the point of view of society, ends are understood in terms of what a device, technique or organization is used for, what its function is, while the device, technique or organization itself, along with the process of its construction or development, is viewed as a means to that end. For the technologist, on the other hand, the device, technique or organization is understood as the end, while the process of its construction or development is taken as the means. For the technologist, use or function serves as the pretext or provides the context for her activity. That is, what serves as the end for us enframes or gives meaning to the technologist's activity and product, but, strictly speaking, does not constitute her end. The end for the technologist, along with what counts as means for her, is for us merely a means.

This distinction between perspectives suggests a principled demarcation of the institution(s) of technology from those of the rest of society. However, we should not, of course, regard such a demarcation as being indicative of an hermetic seal. As the history of technology amply demonstrates, there is in general no device-invariance, given a specific function. That is, technology, in general, not only perfects a given kind of device, but also serves up different kinds of devices for fulfilling a given function. Witness computational devices ranging from the relatively primitive, if ingenious, abacus, to mechanical calculating machines, to high-speed electronic computers. Or, in the area of transportation, devices include everything from Greyhound buses to supersonic transports, space shuttles and the contemplated superconductor-based magnetic trains. This suggests that the gaze of the technological community, too, must pass beyond a given paradigmatic device, since for a given function devices vary, and fasten upon the function to be served. So the principled distinction between the ends of technology and the ends of society should be viewed not as establishing a watertight boundary between the two but, rather, as drawing attention to a semipermeable membrane that allows use or function to serve as the technologist's (remote) end as well as society's.

Now, to return to technology's own forgetfulness. The state of the art in a given domain of technological endeavor is taken to be the determinate measure of that which is to be surpassed. We remember, in keeping with the distinction between means and ends, that it is not the activity that counts, but the result. The activity, the enabling process, is cast into the accidental, derealized time of the means. But further, the result, the achievement itself, stands as a point of departure for yet another surpassing.[2] An achievement, once secured, can be safely forgotten and put behind one. It is the archival or commemorative consciousness, not the technological consciousness, that is fixated on past or even present technological accomplishments. The technological mind, when satisfied in an achievement, becomes potentiated for yet another quest.

These reflections suggest important differences between technological achievements, that is, achievements having to do with the intervention into nature and quasinatural processes, on the one hand, and historical-human achievements, that is, achievements having to do with the intervention into intersubjectivity, on the other. I mean here roughly to distinguish achievements in the domain of making from those of acting or doing, though I mean to set aside here the complex domain of art as a form of making and to distinguish strategic action from other forms of doing.[3] I want to focus on the domains of, on the one hand, what Habermas calls purposive-rational action (which, broadly construed, includes strategic action) and, on the other, what he calls communicative interaction. The salient difference between our responses to a technological achievement and to a human doing is that we want to use and surpass the technological but *appropriate* the human. Though we might admire and marvel at a technical breakthrough, we could not, even arguably, *privilege* such an achievement as we might in the human arena. Even exemplary or paradigmatic technological achievements are made to be surpassed. Think about the current and continuing flurry of activity directed at finding or constructing materials that exhibit superconductivity at higher and higher temperatures, or the quest for faster and faster microprocessors for computers.

As Hannah Arendt has observed, action produces meaningful stories.[4] Action is disclosive of an agent and of a set of possibilities for us. Somewhat like poetic discourse, exemplary action stands, among other things, as an invitation to expand, to reconfigure, or at least to reconsider the maps of our social and moral situations and, through reconsidering what matters, to entertain new possibilities of speech and action. Exemplary actions, in ways that command our attention, publicly disclose novel, though not incommensurable, hermeneutic situations. Like good literature, they extend the range of scenarios in which our social, moral and psychological concepts are at home, as they lead us to refine and rework the networks in which our concepts figure. If we accept the invitation that such actions proffer, then our own predispositions to interpret, or what I earlier called our own "prereflective meanings," will be reinformed. By the ability of exemplary actions to reconfigure and extend the range of the paradigm scenarios where our concepts find application, the (proto)scripts for the embodied narratives that are our lives get rewritten. New story lines emerge as our prereflective meanings undergo revision. These are the practical effects of what Gadamer calls the "fusion of horizons." The thought of surpassing such human achievements is the thought of not stopping to accept the challenge that they throw down to us to win through to a new space of possibilities for the course of our lives. Such a thought of surpassing misses what matters about these interventions, that they matter because they prompt us to rethink what matters.

Exemplary actions inform and become elements of the traditions that historically affect our consciousness; they are repetitions, extraordinary to be sure, that inform our repetitions. They seize and reveal the creative possibilities of the hermeneutic situations from which they arise. Every such action is an appearance of situated freedom in the world. We can continue to avail ourselves of what appears thereby only insofar as the stories that such actions produce are remembered, are kept alive. The forgetfulness associated with the technological enterprise would militate against our maintaining these appearances in a manner that keeps them continually operative.

This is an appropriate place to state explicitly a theme that undergirds much of what I have been saying—technological rationality is reflective of a distinctive response to our finitude. To time, the contingency that it bears, the loss that it brings, and the irreversibility that it insures, technology responds with a feverish will to surpass, ever haunted by the spectre of insecurity, of undomesticated time. Constant progress (constantly shedding the skin of time past) stands in contrast to the *situated* temporality of repetition. Technology attempts to come to terms with our finitude by denying it. Symbols of this denial, and of the nihilism that follows in its wake, abound. One might think, perhaps surprisingly, of word processors. With their ability to reverse quickly and painlessly any conceivable mistake, to revise easily, and consequently to enable an aesthetic, distanced and playful attitude towards our written acts of establishment, they can be seen to be symbols of immortality and to provide us, within a very limited domain to be sure, with a species of functional immortality. The ease with which writing can be revised tends to undermine the investment in the original act of writing, in the original act of establishment; any given act of this sort loses its "weight." Lowering the threshold for "getting something on the paper" goes hand in hand with a relative indifference towards what gets put on the paper (it can always be "fixed up"). We can hardly avoid seeing the similarity between this indifference towards the content of an act of establishment and the *Gleichgültigkeit* or absence of meaningful differences that characterizes alternative courses of action in a nihilistic world; or the similarity between the ease of reversibility that these devices afford and our ability to undo, and hence render meaningless, any missteps that we might make in the fullness of time, were we granted the "gift" of immortality. I may be accused of a rather disingenuous, and even perverse, construal of these wonderful devices, and perhaps with some justification (after all, these lines were typed on one at some point in their history). But sometimes extreme construals are helpful in bringing to the foreground quietly persisting features of our world that warrant our concernful attention.

I have suggested that technology denigrates the field in which meaningful differences are deployed. Meaningful differences lie in what an action *of itself*, *by its very nature*, does to or for us through our engaging in it, while that action secures an end, an end which other, different, actions are also capable of securing. The meaningful difference is determined by what it, as opposed to another action, does to or for us as it secures its end. Indeed a mark of an action that makes a (positive) meaningful difference is that its end often serves only as a pretext or excuse for engaging in it. Among the things that actions do to us or for us is to shape our experience of time, and whatever else they do for us, it is clear that technology's idealized elimination of the time of action is the idealized elimination of their meaningful effects, for the production of those effects is inseparable from an action itself *as it unfolds in time*. It is a matter of the quality given to time. Consider walking as a way of engaging with the environment (and with our bodies) versus its being merely a means of locomotion.[5] So the ideal of the elimination of time is at the same time the ideal of the elimination of the field in which meaningful effects are deployed.

The specific meaning of an action has to do, at least in part, with the character that action gives to time, with how we experience time during it. Meaning lies in part in the shape and texture that we give to the time in and through which we live, and not only in the end that is beyond the time of action (or even only in the cultural world of which action is expressive, though I have placed great emphasis upon this aspect). Different experiences shape or focus our experience of time in different ways. Music is an obvious case in point here. But think also of how time gets sculpted, say, in playing a game or in lovemaking. One could maintain that there is an end or, if you will, a goal, in both sorts of activity— winning the game and sexual climax, respectively. Yet the meaning does not of course lie exclusively in the end or in the moment of its realization. The time of such activities is a time of delight in the activity itself, a time of expressiveness (for example, how the game is played), a time of expression (for example, of affection for one's partner), a time, to be sure, that is punctuated by moments of condensation (for example, a particularly good move and those other unpredictable occurrences of tension, release and thrill characteristic of games and sex), but which nevertheless is just as real for us between the punctuations. At any given moment in such an activity, the memory of past condensations, the expectation of future ones and the relation between the two gives the experience its stamp and integrity. There is thus the rhythmic yet progressive temporality of bicycling, the more punctuate temporality of a ball game, the irregular yet progressively intense temporality of lovemaking and so on. Moreover, the time of these activities is one of sensual, bodily and, especially in the case of lovemaking, emotional engagement.

A recent study offers a phenomenological analysis of the way actions, events and experiences configure time. It discusses the shape of time first of all in terms of the beginning, middle and end structure characteristics of a given experience, event or action. But then, within the framework provided by this closure, the configuration of time is further delineated in terms of characteristic relationships between beginnings and ends, relationships such as those between departure and arrival, departure and return, means and end, suspension and resolution, and problem and solution.[6] Meaningful differences will in part have to do, then, with differing relationships among beginnings, middles and ends. Further, meaningful differences, within the temporal dimension, are also made through the characteristic ways in which *middles* of actions, not only beginnings and ends, have significance.

When we return to take up specifically the symbolic or referential dimension of action, where we again emphasize its world-disclosive nature, here, too, we can speak of differences that make a difference. Meaningful differences can arise in ways that they cannot when action is viewed under its technical aspect. We have spoken of action as an expression of a cultural repertoire by an agent. It is thus revelatory of the cultural insertion of the subject of action and of the subject herself. Different sorts of action, occasioned by similar goals or ends, can, though of course they need not, be revelatory of different aspects of culture and self or of variations on a common aspect. So, though both helping a neighbor paint her house and voluntarily watching her children are expressive of a communal orientation, and are both gestures of solidarity, they ring changes on that theme. The latter action could well be expressive of a subjectively felt responsibility not only to a particular existing community but also to a wider future community. When viewed exclusively under its technical aspect, such a difference in action *cannot* effect a meaningful or qualitative difference, for here meaning is exhausted in the end, in this case, of placing some discretionary time at the neighbor's disposal. Technical action, like a *sign* that merely serves to point beyond itself, is ideally functionally degenerate. Like merely conventional signs, there are often many ways to get the job done; technological progress consists in the proliferation of functional equivalents, the more efficient and the less "time-consuming" the better. On the other hand, *praxis*, like expressive discourse, can be more readily likened to a *symbol*, and especially so the closer such action approximates the status of a social practice. Such action has characteristic meaning. It does not thereby merely indicate, point or refer to; like symbols, it represents. We might say then that, though technical action can be meaningful, practical action *embodies* meaning; the latter bears the trace of a certain range of conceptual-linguistic distinctions and of a complex of cultural concerns and commitments subjectively refracted. And again, needless to say, all of the sources of a meaningful difference that I have so far mentioned—the shape that action gives to our experience of time itself, the nature of bodily engagement during action,[7] and what action discloses and intersubjectively effects—differences that cannot be separated from or exist apart from the *doing* of certain actions, all such sources require for their very being the *time* of action.

If technology is a license to forget, to get time behind us and thus to undermine a condition for the possibility of meaningful differences, repetition is a matter of living as if time is always before us. Repetition does not regard with alarm the perpetual "restarting of the clock"; it even commends it. Heidegger suggests that the authentic person always has time. Repetition is living each moment as if the clock were restarted without its being an occasion for frustration or despair. But did not this Sisyphean picture capture for Camus the very essence of meaninglessness? The problem in the Sisyphean picture lay in expecting a standing achievement that is separable from the activity itself. Given that repetition or internal history takes seriously time and its proper unfolding, without a wish to telescope it, this way of life enables the history of productive effects to take place. Repetition is the struggle against technology to keep open the field in which meaningful differences appear, and thus to combat the marginalization of those practices that we engage in not for their utility, but for what they are, for what they tell us about ourselves and for what they make of us. Consider the practice of letter-writing versus the phone call or the consumption of information via electronic "mail," or the making of music versus the use of preprogrammed electronic synthesizers, or the preparation and eating of a meal as a social event versus the staggered consumption of microwaved products.[8] In the latter case, time-contraction can assume a graphically tangible form in the collapsing of a sequence of courses into one product.

Much has been made of late of the similarities between life and narrative, some authors going so far as essentially to identify the two.[9] While there are, as I shall suggest later, both epistemological and ontological reasons for questioning too ready an identification of the two, using the notion of narrative as a metaphorical frame for our picture of life is, as was suggested in the last chapter, a useful way of going at things. In particular, it provides a helpful way of approaching the issue of "the meaning of life."

As we move from talk about action to talk about "life," we will be interested in how the actions, events and experiences that make up our lives are strung together. The story of our lives has as its basic components the circumstances in which we find ourselves (events and situations) and the activity that we undertake, activity of basically three sorts or with three aspects: *techne* (fabrication or making); *praxis* (action proper or doing); and play (subjective expressiveness). The story of our lives is woven from these threads. As I have suggested at some length, these kinds of activity are informed by different and, particularly when found in a single life, competing temporalities. What I have been urging is that we take care to prevent the temporality of domestication, fully legitimate in its place, from arrogating to itself the entire temporal domain and thus marginalizing the important practices that make a meaningful difference. As we turn from a focus upon actions to life, we shift our concern from the temporality of action to the incorporative temporality of life. For instance, life as a repetition can be a repetition of a certain admixture of the three temporalities, of technology's domestication, action's repetition and the characteristic temporality of play. It is to this incorporative temporality that we now turn.

An occurrence, in the sense of an action or a set of circumstances, gains significance through being placed, and from its place, in a story. Of course, as my discussion suggests, we can also speak of actions having meaning that is not derived exclusively from narrative contexts.[10] Meaning can originate as well from the cultural milieux of which actions are symbolic. But the meaning of a life has to do with how actions relate to other actions and circumstances, with how actions cohere. Hence the focus here primarily on narrative contexts. In any case, the narrative meaning of actions will ultimately be derived from the cultural settings in which the relevant stories are circulated. For the stories that we can recognize or acknowledge, the stories in which the actions figure, will be drawn from the repertoire of (proto)scripts that are culturally available, from the template of plots that, in a reciprocal manner, inform those predispositions to interpret that I earlier called our prereflective meanings. So the distinction here between actions having narrative versus symbolic significance is not sharp. It will turn out, moreover, that a meaningful life, in placing a requirement upon the relationship among actions, also places a requirement on the meaningfulness (in the symbolic sense) of the actions so related.

Our ability to construe our lives as meaningful depends on our ability to place the actions and events which constitute our lives into a story, and to articulate the thread that allows us to grasp the unity wherein what we have done and has happened to us, what we are doing, and where we are headed, are held together. That thread is the theme or meaning of our lives. According to Paul Ricoeur, this unity is the unity of the Aristotelian *mythos*, the plot.[11] How are we to understand the "hero" of such a story? How is the nature of the "who" who lives that story related to our experience of time? How is our self-understanding, our apprehension of our subjectivity, shaped by the apprehension of time that technology fosters?

The being of a "who" and the existence of meaningful differences are co-implicated issues. When ends or goals are understood as states of a subject to be achieved, and this view is encouraged by technology's will to contract time and by the means-ends distinction that informs technology, then technical means of achieving such states can in principle replace without loss those activities in which we would otherwise engage that tend to be productive of those states. I think here of some of José Delgado's science-fiction-like, but all too real, devices, one of which consists of an electrode stimulating the brain of a patient to produce a euphoric state upon demand. Another such device that comes to mind is Woody Allen's fanciful "orgasmatron." Or contrast a "high" achieved by drugs with "runner's high." These examples indicate yet another dimension of the reduction of meaning to value,[12] a dimension where value attaches to subjective states. A view of the subject is encouraged wherein the latter is no longer understood to be rooted in and informed by meaningful practices, but rather where the subject is understood as a seat of preferences related to it as accidents are to substance.

This aesthetic-technological self would exist both pointillistically or paratactically *and* multifariously in terms of the ends it sets for itself. A life lived and understood in terms of the imperative to contract the time between the present and a desired subjective state is a life in which only disconnected moments of satisfaction are highlighted, is a life consisting only of a concatenation of moments of satiation or of failure to achieve satisfaction. The character living such a life "flashes" rather than develops. One is reminded here of the intermittent flashing on the screen of a video game, itself a reflection of the intermittently existing self before the screen, a self which lives for the excitement induced by the play. The pointillistically existing self lacks connectedness, lacks a thread to hold itself together, and is therefore bereft of what is requisite to its living and understanding life as a continuous, developing story.[13] The forgetful self of technology lacks the means to weld an enduring identity. The life of such a self would thus lack coherence along what we might call the time axis or the diachronic dimension.

But further, the *multifariously* existing self, also underwritten by the temporality of value, lives incoherently as well, for it lacks focus; it lives in dispersal or in "spread-outness." The aesthete, having adopted the value position and cast herself in the image of the disengaged observer, is a relativizer not claimed by meaning. The standpoint from which no one goal has any more title to a legitimate claim on us than any other, the standpoint from which all validity claims are relativized, is one from which any meaning must seem arbitrary. The "values-perspective," emphasizing our freedom with regard to values, allows for a virtual omnidirectionality of aims. From this perspective, the ends or values that orient our aims, because they are purely products of our freedom, in and of themselves form no coherent pattern or picture. An internal relationship to meaning, such as the one described in Chapter Four, would provide values with a grounding from which such a pattern might emerge, and would be therapeutic for this self's "schizophrenia," but this would clearly require a move beyond the values-perspective.

So we can understand how the dispersal associated with the values-perspective can be overcome through again attending to the level of meaning.[14] A repetition which carries forward a "field" of meaning would connect and gather together the otherwise disconnected and dispersed aims of aesthetic-technological existence. The temporality of repetition, by allowing the dispersed value orientations to find a place in a meaningful order and by restoring the time of action, would enable a less scattered and more unified sense of self.

Before proceeding further, it is fitting here to raise again the issue of the status of repetition. Is it an inescapable ontological fact about us that holds no matter how diverse our aims, and how ill-fitting the pieces of our lives, appear to be? If so, then it would be difficult to see how "repetition" functions as a standard of *critique*. If our lives are, willy-nilly, already a repetition, then what critical force can this standard have? Would it not then be superfluous, unless we invoke something like an essence-appearance distinction and the point is to get us to *see* ourselves as we *really* are? On the other hand, if it is not constitutive of our being, what recommends it to us? What are its credentials? Could it not become the object of an arbitrary choice, a choice that could with equal justification embrace or reject it? After all, the life of Kierkegaard's aesthete or of an Oscar Wilde has its appeal for many thoughtful observers, Richard Rorty and Harold Bloom among them. Are these partisans of an aesthetic-poetic existence, with its multifarious and polythemic character, simply choosing one "life-style" from among other, no more intrinsically worthy, ways of life, or are they somehow deluded or mistaken? In no simple way is either the case. Their position is, I believe, symptomatic of a pervasive malaise afflicting postmodern culture. The perceived loss of stable patterns of meaning has occasioned a variety of responses, from an ironic aestheticism that would claim to be at home with such a loss, to, say, so-called New Age practices that would stave off the emptiness that such loss would entail. And even practices such as the latter, which acknowledge the significance of patterns of meaning, are often nevertheless unwittingly complicit in the very values-perspective that they would combat. They attempt what I would call an aesthetic retrieval of lost meaning, an attempt, as I shall show in Chapter Eight, that undermines itself. Much in our culture seems stuck in the techno-logic of the values-perspective.

I suggested earlier that a life of repetition digs deeper, that it is a life that is progressively revelatory of the self. Michel Foucault, a central thinker in the postmodern canon, would reject this surface-depth distinction and the essence-appearance distinction on which it appears to rest. A defense of repetition against the postmodern or deconstructive challenge would in part involve showing how the postmodern critique presupposes, in many cases, the distinctions it wants to deconstruct. (Chapter Seven takes up the task of justifying the "standpoint of meaning" *vis-à-vis* postmodernist gestures.) Such a demonstration can be provided, but for now I shall provisionally adopt a position to the side of this controversy and claim a hypothetical justification for the notion of repetition. I will allow that repetition is not so much a description of life, even of life at its deepest level—if by "deep" we mean something like "essential"—but of a certain kind of life, of a life lived with the concern for being *a* self. What is at stake is coherence as a self, the unity and integrity of personal identity.[15] So the interest in coherence is, as I indicated near the end of the last chapter, a moral concern. Taking our lives seriously as our own requires the constitutive discovery of the characteristic (*eigentliche*) tie that binds. The demand for narrative coherence is, then, the demand made in the behalf of a self who wishes to be authentic (*eigentliche*).[16]

Obviously, my earlier remarks about Heidegger and the role of repetition in an authentic life, a self-owning life of loyalty to one's self, are apposite here. The "connectedness of life," for Heidegger, is enacted through the temporal stretching along that is achieved in virtue of our historicality (*Geschichtlichkeit*).[17] Our self-constancy is a temporal achievement which we are. The "anchor" for this achievement and the root of our finitude are the possibilities housed in our tradition, possibilities that inform what I earlier called our prereflective meanings. Repetition is the mode of making explicit and owning these culturally sedimented dispositions to act or experience.[18] Repetition underwrites the connectedness of life.[19] So the authentic life is lived in pursuit of the self that we in an implicit sense already are. Nevertheless, it bears reemphasizing that authentic repetition cannot be mere repetition of the same. To own our history is *to take responsibility for it* and to do so in such a way that responsibility for and (critical) *response to* are co-implicative. As Carr suggests, "inauthentic" is as appropriate a label for a life of too much coherence as it is of one with too little.[20] There is a dialectic here between the individual and the cultural heritage, wherein the individual takes up collective categories and does something characteristic or distinctive with them. So the protagonist of our life story should not be understood as a self-enclosed, degenerately self-identical character, but rather as one who develops through time while improvising on a theme.

Having taken advantage of the notion of narrative coherence for the light that it sheds on the idea of life's bearing meaning, we should remain mindful of the differences between life and other sorts of narrative. The last two chapters implied that because of its constantly deferred ending, life lacks the closure of a text, even that of a text whose ending is, as in the case of the so-called "new novel," inconclusive. Closure is important, for it is the standpoint from which the significance of elements comprising a totality emerges. From its vantage point, and often only from its vantage point, are patterns confirmed and the role of the parts in the whole decided. Barbara Herrnstein Smith points out that any temporally organized work of art is structured in terms of introduction-complication-climax-resolution, where the sense of stability or closure is deferred until the end.[21] Closure provides "ultimate unity and coherence to . . . experience by providing a point from which all preceding elements may be viewed comprehensively and their relations grasped as part of a significant design."[22] No matter how recondite it may be, literary texts have closure. As Ricoeur points out, an inconclusive ending can well be a fitting ending, and hence contribute to closure, when it delimits a text that self-consciously raises a problem the author considers unsolvable.[23]

Life is obviously unlike a text in a number of important ways. Objects of art are designed; our perception of their structure is, no matter how complexly and problematically, somehow dependent upon what has been constructed or structured in prior to our experience. It would indeed strain the notion of "life as a work of art" to understand a life as so fully contrived. The successful work of art is one where all the elements contribute to a desired effect, where nothing necessary is left out and nothing that exceeds the sufficient is put in. Life, clearly not a product of such control, has meaning that is, if anything, even more underdetermined than is that of a text.

The condition that we do not in life have the totality as a designed whole before us leads to the other salient difference between texts and lives. The standpoint from which we survey life's meaning is part of the temporal process of life itself, and thus (except perhaps, as Aristotle observed, when we reach the end of a life) the end is always before us. Closure is constantly deferred.[24] Moreover, a consideration departing from the notion of repetition further underscores life's (or at least the authentic life's) lack of closure when compared with a literary text. For in repetition we live each moment as if the clock were restarted. We never, therefore, get time behind us, for the end is constantly postponed.

Both the idea of control implied by our seeing our lives as the product without residue of our design, and the idea of occupying the standpoint from which we have in view ultimate or final closure, suggest Godlike ideals of omnipotence and omniscience. The idea of "life as a work of art" bespeaks the control of the aesthetic ideal, the atemporality of having the "text" at hand in advance. But of course, that this condition is not "true to life," that we do not have ultimate closure at our disposal, does not mean that we cannot understand our lives as meaningful or coherent. To live an intelligible life, I have suggested, is to act out interpretations of the social roles or protoscripts that form our sociocultural horizon. Coherence and meaning can be achieved at the level of understanding just what protoscripts and roles one is living out. This gives us coherence but not closure, for, unlike an actor in a play, we do not know how the play will end, what will become of the characters, how roles will intersect, conflict and so on. An awareness of the roles we are enacting will give us some guidance with respect to how to act, but otherwise we are inventing ourselves in a field of contingency as we go along. Life is thus more like improvised acting, with a theme but not much in the way of a script, with coherence but not closure.

Yet, in making sense of our lives to ourselves and to others, we *do* tell stories, with beginnings, middles and ends. This sense-making is enabled by *provisional* points and hypothetical *projections* of closure; thus St. Augustine tells the story of his becoming a Christian, or Proust, of having become a writer. To find meaning is to be able to tell such provisional stories, such *petits récits*, each with its own kind of closure.[25]

6

The Abuse of Repetition for Critique

(With Special Reference to the Critical Theory of Habermas)

Chapters Four and Five present a case for a response to technological rationality in the form of a hermeneutics of repetition. Mindful of some of the putative limits of hermeneutics, in this chapter I present an alternative critical approach to the question of technology and meaning, one that has developed in part through a dialogical response to hermeneutics, namely, Critical Theory. This treatment will focus on Jürgen Habermas's articulation of Critical Theory, for he is arguably the most important post-Heideggerian writer to address critically both the technological and the nihilistic problematics. After briefly recapitulating Heidegger's understanding of the connection between technology and nihilism, I give an account of Habermas's critique, pointing to some of its affinities to Heidegger's and to some of its weak spots *vis-à-vis* hermeneutics. Further, though a concern with temporality *per se* does not figure prominently in this chapter, the discussion here of systems theory offers further confirmation of my thesis of the domestication of time. The next chapter, an excursus, steps back from the question of a critique of technology in order to interrogate the philosophical status of both the hermeneutic and the Critical Theoretical approaches in light of what might be called a postmodern consensus over the aporetic status of objectivity.

The preceding chapters have rather explicitly suggested linkages between the technological project and nihilism, where the latter is understood as the absence of meaning and of meaningful differences. To recapitulate a representative line of argument: to the extent that technological or functional rationality holds sway, actions are assessed only in terms of their functional contribution to the achievement of a given end and to the contraction of the time necessary for such an achievement. To the extent that there exist functionally equivalent actions—and technical progress consists in part in the proliferation of such equivalents and in improvement upon them—there can be no meaningful, that is, nonquantitative, differences among them. Though I have sought to provide a new angle of vision on the connection between technology and the loss of meaning, the assertion of the connection itself is, of course, not new. This theme assumes prominence in Heidegger's writings, especially in those on Nietzsche and on technology.[1] In these writings, Heidegger locates the roots of modern nihilism, and of the pervasiveness of the technological rationality to which it is linked, in what he calls a "subjectivism" that finds expression in Nietzsche's thought of "the will to power."

For Nietzsche, value is what the will to power posits in the service of itself. As Heidegger puts it in a gloss on *The Will to Power*:

> "Values" are in the first place the conditions of enhancement that the will to power has in view. . . . Will to power and value positing are *the same*, insofar as the will to power looks toward the viewpoints of preservation and enhancement.[2]

The importance of this understanding of value is twofold. First, not only does it reflect Nietzsche's explicit intention to undermine metaphysical conceptions of value, conceptions whereby values enjoy a transcendent status *vis-à-vis* human strivings. It also, by grounding valuation so firmly in the will to power of a subject, licenses the abstraction of values from their internal connections to meaningful practices.[3] So, in this respect, it serves to underscore my earlier elaboration of the "values-perspective." And if, as I have suggested, technology incorporates the values-perspective, then Heidegger's charge that Nietzsche's conception of value is nihilistic would be consistent with my earlier discussion of the worldlessness of the schema of means and ends and of technological rationality's implication in the loss of meaning.

This internal connection between value and the will to power would sanction a framing of the world in terms of a mobilization for use, in terms of a standing at the ready in reserve.[4] It would license an instrumentalization of the world of which modern technology is the fullest realization. We recall that the technological refers to the organization of means in the interest of maximizing the efficiency and effectiveness with which an end is secured, that technological rationality is functional rationality. If the relation of the world and, indeed, of values themselves to the will to power is understood in the functional terms that Nietzsche suggests, where worth is conferred on qualities, institutions and practices only insofar as they serve the will to power, then it is not surprising that Heidegger would say that Western metaphysics has, through its development in and by Nietzsche, culminated in technological rationality.[5] Insofar as technology is the means of rendering the world at our disposal, is the means of empowering us to dispose over the world, the technical perspective is the values-perspective *par excellence*. It is a perspective or a point of view wherein our concern is with conditions of the preservation and enhancement of our control, of our power. This perspective therefore marks a way in which things are disclosed for us. Reality is disclosed under the aspect of the serviceable.

Linguistic disclosure is a signally important mode of world disclosure; it is a way of framing the world that is marked by the sets of rule-governed distinctions that constitute language games, which games are themselves situated within forms of life shaped by various interests, concerns and projects. A technological civilization predisposes us to experience and to frame our talk about things in terms of their manifest utility or potential for use—to experience them within the framework of means and ends. Along with utility and the means-ends distinction, other central and privileged items in such discourse are terms such as 'efficiency,' 'effectiveness' and 'control.' These characteristic features of the vocabulary of technological discourse describe the technological reduction of the world, the technological anticipation or presupposition. (Our world is one where we strive, for example, for ever more efficient sound reproduction—through compact discs and so on—despite the often indifferent aesthetic merit of what gets reproduced.) So the end of technology is the mobilization of the world within the framework of this anticipation, a framework wherein rationality can be understood only as functional rationality.

Heidegger's diagnosis of the nihilism of our technical age remains tied to ontological claims and commitments, in particular to his understanding of European nihilism as the stage at which the concealment of Being has reached its completion.[6] In my discussion of technology and meaning I have sought to avoid such commitments by remaining on the level of the phenomenological. Many latter-day admirers of Nietzsche, for instance, Rorty, Foucault and Jean-François Lyotard, convinced of the gratuitousness of a notion of Being that transcends a given language game, power/knowledge regime or local narrative, would not find Heidegger's charge to be a particularly damaging or worrisome indictment. Aside from the hermeneutic tradition departing from Heidegger, only the school of Critical Theory as it is represented by Habermas and K. O. Apel understands itself as a philosophical response to the challenge posed by both the technological and the nihilistic tendencies of our age. It is in the discourse of modernity, whose participants include not only Nietzsche, Derrida and Foucault, but also Max Weber, that Habermas is able to uncover the nihilistic themes that so preoccupy him. Habermas's critique of functional reason is meant at the same time to challenge the assumption that the legacy of modernity must expend itself in a dialectic of Enlightenment that stands impotent before European nihilism. Nihilism, for him, is not so much the condition of being ontologically unmindful of Being, but rather of being bereft of the critical resources that would enable us to recognize ontic conditions of domination.

There are parallels between Heidegger's critique of subjectivism and Habermas's polemic against what the latter calls "subject-centered reason." Their lines of thought converge tellingly in their respective critiques of Nietzsche and functional reason. Heidegger, as has already been indicated, finds in Nietzsche the expression of the full-blown nihilism in which modern global technology is rooted, while Habermas finds it significant that Nietzsche's deconstruction of the distinction between truth and illusion is an important aspect of modern functional rationality.[7] So we shall presently want to consider Habermas's response to nihilism as a response to functional rationality. Habermas understands the critique of functional rationality to be today a critique of systems theory. So it would be useful first to look again at how we get from technology and its means-end rationality to systems theory.

Chapter Four made reference to the importance of systematic means of anticipating contingencies that might undermine our control. I spoke of the importance of an integrated coordination of functionally implicated elements to insure that our planning issues in the desired results, and that those results will be secured. The perspective demanded by such a concern is one wherein the implicated elements are understood as being related in such a way that they comprise a system—a whole articulated into parts whose functional integration assures the stability and viability of that whole—with self-regulating resources that allow it to accommodate and compensate for contingencies. Further, such a coordination of elements in accordance with the systems approach is a means of increasing the efficiency and effectiveness of specifically technological components, that is, machinery, devices and processes, making them more effective than if they functioned independently, and is thus a means of increasing the power of our technology.[8] And is it not natural for us to want to increase the power of that which increases our power? The systems perspective thus serves our will to power by encouraging us to look at the world from the point of view of the maximization of efficiency, effectiveness and control. As the application of knowledge derived from the empirical sciences—both social and natural—in the interest of achieving efficiency, effectiveness and systems stability, systems theory is the technology of organization in general, is the most general expression of functional rationality.

The foregoing suggests that technology operates from a cramped base not only, as Marx suggested, where capitalistic demands for surplus value choke technical innovation, but also where any aspect of reality that might impinge upon its functioning escapes the technological reduction. Insofar as we accede to the "internal dynamic" of technology to place ever-increasing power at our disposal through its "will to surpass," that is, insofar as we will it to reach its full potential, we will increasingly allow the systems perspective to colonize our world. As Niklas Luhmann, one of the most sophisticated of the contemporary systems theorists, suggests, we live in an age where factors that are not relevant to technological functioning have no significance.[9]

The danger that we thereby confront is that, as the meaningful gives way to the functional, we will find it increasingly difficult to understand and experience ourselves as meaning-oriented creatures. Indeed, this development should be a source of concern, not only for the hermeneutic tradition which places great stress on the significance of structures of meaning, but also for the existentialist-cum-emotivist tradition, wherein we are understood as authors of values whose only foundation rests in our having freely willed them. For the authorial subject would also be undermined by its transformation into an objective component of administrative, economic and social systems organized along functionalist lines.[10] This postmodern dialectic of Enlightenment can be succinctly described as follows: we can trace a trajectory spanning the stages from our enlisting technology in the service of our will to power (by its mobilization of the world) to, because of the objective necessity of *total* control, our becoming objects of a system, in order to maximize a power that we have come to regard as important in its own right. When technological progress comes to assume such a self-legitimating status, that is, when, in Habermas's terms, technology becomes an ideology, then we will experience the replacement of "the culturally defined self-understanding of a social life-world . . . by the self-reification of men under categories of purposive-rational action and adaptive behavior."[11]

Now, of course, there is the obvious distinction to be drawn between *understanding* society from the systems point of view, and *organizing* society along lines consistent with that view. We are interested in tendencies of the latter sort, tendencies which are, of course, especially well captured if not actually guided by the analytical perspective of systems theory. Even though we must respect the fact that this distinction between theory and practice can be drawn for the purposes of analysis, it can be argued, and indeed even seems to be acknowledged by Luhmann, that systems theory is itself to be understood as a mode of the *functional* self-understanding of systems.[12] That is, systems theory can itself be seen as a factor relevant to technological functioning; it can be understood to stand in a functional relationship to self-maintaining systems. Nevertheless, since it would not be self-contradictory to conceive of systems theory being exploited to *undermine* systems, I shall respect this distinction for now.

We can view systems theory as articulating the will to power, not of the subject, but of the system. Systems are organized, their elements are mobilized, so as to maintain and enhance their viability. That the attribution of will to power to systems is not merely metaphorical is apparent from systems theory's projection of self-enhancing self-maintenance as the goal of systemic functioning (recall Heidegger's discussion of the viewpoint of Nietzschean will to power). I have already suggested that the system fulfills the ideal of the domestication or annihilation of time. The achievement of a fully coordinated system—immeasurably enabled by modern computer technology and its ability to integrate and respond to information from a bewildering variety of sources—would realize our dream of an independence from the flux of time.[13] The desire for domestication appears as the will to control. The will to power, too, wills to domesticate time. Its abhorrence of time and contingency is evinced by the will's gnashing its teeth at time, at the "it was." Is not Nietzsche's doctrine of the eternal return the means whereby the will to power domesticates time? The technological will's "ill will against time" is thus a refraction of the will to power's rancor.

There remains one more theme to set in place in order to fully appreciate Habermas's critique of functional rationality as a response to modern nihilism. That is the motif of functional rationality as a species of perspectivism.[14] (As we shall see, what is perhaps most telling in this regard is the role played by "meaning" in the functional perspective of systems theory.) In his important early essay, "Science and Technology as 'Ideology'," Habermas questions Weber's analysis of Western rationality, an analysis that portrays means-end rationality or purposive rationality as *the* distinctive and characteristic achievement of modernity.[15] Purposive rationality, Habermas suggests, does not exhaust the legacy of the Enlightenment. Weber's analysis, he holds, is one-sided.

The intellectual lineage connecting Weber and Nietzsche is rather easy to trace. Adopting a Kantian fact/value dichotomy, and understanding values as products of sheerly arbitrary willing, Weber explicates a notion of rationality that is at once functional and perspectival.[16] Sabina Lovibond captures the notion well in holding that the currently dominant notion of rationality is a technical one, whereby rationality as such is identified "with an ability to find the *objectively* right means to a *subjectively* determined end" (emphasis mine).[17] Weber counsels that, in the case of the choice of ends, "[s]cientific pleading is meaningless in principle because the various value spheres of the world stand in irreconcilable conflict with each other," meaning that we are confronted with "the struggle that the gods of the various orders and values are engaged in," a struggle in which "the individual has to decide which is God for him and which is the devil."[18] Here Weber clearly articulates his well-known decisionism. For him, modernity has shaped a form of self-consciousness wherein our points of view and value orientations can no longer be understood as being susceptible to grounding in objective structures, but must, rather, be understood as being the objects of sheer choice. The perspectivism of Weber, where even reason itself becomes a mere item of choice—the value of science itself cannot be scientifically settled—led him to despair, for with the loss of stable structures that command our conviction there goes also a loss of meaning, the loss of a secure sense of "how things hang together in the most general sense." He despaired of our breaking out of the "iron cage" of modernity, for this is where reason has brought us, and there is no turning back.

The thesis of Habermas's *The Philosophical Discourse of Modernity* is that the "dead ends" betokened by metaphors of iron cages and by dialectics of Enlightenment can be avoided, not by despairing of reason—as the postmoderns, their precursors and fellow travelers suggest—but by attending more fully to the legacy of the Enlightenment. Habermas's notion of communicative rationality is an attempt to carry out this project. The nihilism of Weber, the postmoderns and even of Adorno and Horkheimer is a result, Habermas feels, of a one-sided view of rationality as instrumental rationality and "subject-centered reason."[19] The self-destruction of reason is by no means inevitable.

In Chapter Four, I suggested that the transformation of meaning into value deprives values of a referential anchoring in such a way that our only option is to view them as arbitrary products of our will that can have no claim on us, unless there are modes, modes that warrant our respect as moderns, of rationally adjudicating such commitments. Habermas's notion of communicative rationality is offered as just such an antidote to what I have called the values-perspective and its indeterminacy. I will consider later the cogency of communicative rationality as a response to perspectivism, but I want first to make explicit Habermas's critique of functionalist reason.

Already in "Science and Technology as 'Ideology'," Habermas argued that, in our time, science and technology have become self-legitimating in such a way that practical questions, those concerning the nature of the "good life," are being subordinated to and, indeed, even replaced by, technical questions, questions concerning the most efficient means for the realization of ends, where those ends appear to be increasingly beyond our *reflective* control. For him, our challenge is to find ways to preserve, and protect from the encroachment of instrumental imperatives, a space for an autonomous, rational and communicatively achieved consensus about issues of practical life.

Today his critique of functional rationality is deployed in terms of a distinction between system and life-world and between their complementary concepts of purposive-rational and communicative action, respectively. The life-world has cultural, social and psychological dimensions.[20] In its underlying cultural dimension, it corresponds more or less to my description in Chapter Three of "world" as the reservoir of our prereflective meanings, the source of our predispositions to interpret and the context, structured by our fundamental commitments and concerns, that gives meaning to our practices. It is the prereflective, linguistically sedimented and shared realm that gets implicated in all subsequent speech and action. Habermas speaks of it as a culturally transmitted and linguistically organized stock of interpretive patterns, a stock of knowledge that is "always already" familiar.[21] In its social dimension, the life-world refers to normative orientations that facilitate group solidarity or social integration.[22] Psychologically, the concept refers to motivation structures, socialization and the acquisition of various speaking and acting competencies.[23] In general, the life-world provides the backdrop against which, or the coordinate system within which, communicative action unfolds.[24]

By system, Habermas understands society from the point of view of action consequences. From this standpoint, society is conceived as a system of actions that is maintained and stabilized through functional interconnections, where each action has a functional significance in terms of its contribution to the maintenance of the system, thus allowing the system to become independent of the life-world.[25] The economy and public administration form two central subsystems in late capitalist societies. Furthermore, Habermas claims that the systems aspect of society comes into view necessarily as a consequence of adopting an objective observer's point of view, while the life-world can come into focus only by entertaining participative "I-thou" perspectives.[26]

Purposive-rational action indicates that aspect of action that is oriented towards the realization of defined ends or goals under given conditions.[27] It is end-rational action. Communicative action or symbolically mediated action indicates that aspect of action that is governed by shared norms, and requires at least two actors, each of whom acknowledges the other's recognition of the norm.[28] Communicative action is therefore action oriented by mutual understanding.

Making use of the concepts briefly explicated above, Habermas makes much of a distinction between what he calls social integration, on the one hand, and system integration, on the other, two notions that systems theorists, he claims, conflate.[29] Social integration refers to the coordination of action that harmonizes the action *orientations* or *intentions* of participants by means of a normatively secured or communicatively achieved consensus.[30] System integration, on the other hand, denotes the functional integration of action *consequences* in order to stabilize the *unintentional* interconnections of actions, where this integration is achieved by a regulation of individual decisions that is *not* mediated by the recognition of norms on the part of social actors.[31] System integration is equivalent to the process of system maintenance. Habermas maintains that both orientations, towards issues of social integration and towards those of system integration, are requisite to an adequate social theory.[32] I can briefly summarize Habermas's position here by saying that action, including linguistic behavior, has not only meaning but also function.

I can now indicate the tenor of Habermas's critique of functionalist rationality. The danger that modern societies face is that systemic imperatives, and the one-sided rationalization of economic and bureaucratic subsystems in accordance with purposive rationality alone, will have a disintegrative effect upon the essentially communicative rationality of the life-world.[33] The life-world reproduces and maintains itself through processes of cultural reproduction, social integration and socialization. These processes are sustained through communicative action, and it is only through it that the life-world can be reproduced.[34] So the processes whereby life-worlds are sustained—mutual understanding, the coordination of action orientations, and socialization, all achieved through the medium of language—are short-circuited by the essentially monological character of functional rationality.

The life-world can itself provide the setting for communicative practices that repair breakdowns in its requisite consensus. When the background consensus requisite to cultural reproduction, social integration and socialization breaks down, when what has been taken for granted becomes problematic, participants in interaction have recourse to discursive argumentative procedures in order to reestablish agreement. Moreover, in such cases of breakdown, these discursive practices are crucial if communicative action is to continue without resorting to force.[35] The argumentative reestablishment of agreement can take place with reference to any of three categories of intentional objects or "worlds," the objective, the social and the subjective.[36] What follows is a brief account of Habermas's conception of argumentative discourse, with special reference to practical discourse aimed at agreement concerning social norms. In the special case of practical discourse, such agreement is to be secured in a distortion-free dialogue oriented towards what Habermas calls generalizable interests.

In the elaboration of his theory of communicative action, Habermas proposes a version of a consensus theory of truth. What is perhaps most novel about his conception is the suggestion that in the very process of communicating through meaningful utterances, we, with something very much like transcendental necessity, anticipate a dialogue situation which is ideal, and in which the truth claims of our utterances could be consensually redeemed. Such an ideal speech situation is structured by what he refers to as symmetry conditions, conditions which supposedly insure that interlocuters are swayed only by the force of the better argument. Such conditions amount to the requirement that the participants in dialogue be fettered by no restrictions to the symmetrical exercise of the option to employ various speech acts, that is, to make various moves in the dialogical language game such as asserting, contesting, questioning, disclosing, prescribing and so on. In short, these conditions are to guarantee that there be an unlimited interchangeability of dialogue roles.[37] The symmetry conditions further allow the freedom to move from a given level of discourse or a given way of framing a discussion to increasingly abstract levels of discourse and to alternative ways of framing a discussion, that is, to call into question and modify the originally accepted conceptual framework. For example, in a discussion structured by a particular normative ethical framework, participants are free to move to a metaethical discourse that calls that framework into question. The importance of this freedom becomes apparent once we recognize that the cogency of an argument will depend partly upon the conceptual or linguistic frame in which it is formulated. For example, theologically based argumentation increasingly loses its cogency after the seventeenth century in the West. The point, then, of the ideal speech situation is to uncouple *participation* in discourse and *acceptance* of truth claims from *power*.

Analogous to the idea of truth in theoretical discourse, the idea of generalizable interests stands as a regulative ideal for practical discourse.[38] Basically, for Habermas, interests are needs that we become aware of when they are not being met.[39] Furthermore, he denies that all needs or interests are irremediably subjective and ultimately intersubjectively irreconcilable. Those that *are* irreconcilable in this way, he refers to as particular interests. If *all* interests were sheerly particular, then we would have to resign ourselves "to an impenetrable pluralism of apparently ultimate [and incommensurable] value orientations."[40] Opposed to such sheerly particular interests, generalizable interests are those that can be communicatively shared, those that reflect an unforced consensus about what *all* could want. Therefore, the question to keep in mind when assessing the generalizability of an interest is: Would the norm expressing and/or regulating that interest be one such that *every* person affected by the norm can with good reasons accept the consequences and side effects that are expected to result from the *general* observance of that norm?[41] A particular interest would be one that fails to meet the conditions of this test.

Generalizable interests, for Habermas, are not simply preexisting attributes or properties of persons that can be empirically found (through, say, questionnaires), nor can they be simply imputed from the outside (say, by theorists claiming a privileged access). They are, rather, shaped and discovered through the linguistic medium of communication in a practical discourse among all persons concerned.[42] It becomes convenient, therefore, to speak in terms of "need interpretations." Both norms regulating interests or needs and the interpretation of the needs themselves form the subject matter of practical discourse. That need interpretations are themselves discussable in an ideal discourse (where symmetry and the freedom to change levels of discourse are secured) is an important safeguard against deception and self-deception.[43] The freedom to choose levels of discourse means that participants need not accept any need interpretation in which they cannot recognize what they truly want. That is, the deck cannot be stacked against them, either by themselves (self-deception) or by others (deception). For example, think of women whose needs are interpreted within a linguistic or conceptual framework structured by the following dichotomy: either restrict yourself to home and family or consider yourself selfishly ambitious. Could the need for self-respecting self-fulfillment find an appropriate interpretation in such a framework? The interpretation of needs must take place within some linguistic or conceptual frame or other. Needs are interpreted as needs for x in linguistic or conceptual frame y. It is, therefore, important that the chosen framework not be inappropriate, that is, that it not reflect an understanding of social life such that needs are perceived as being met only in certain arbitrarily (that is, unreasonably) limited ways. Think again of the acceptance of a psychological conceptual bind in which one faces the alternatives "be self-sacrificing" or "you are not doing right by your family" so that the need to be responsible gets (falsely) interpreted as a need to relinquish autonomy.

So the discourse situation will, or is likely to, alter one's *conception* of one's needs. But no matter how much it is altered, no need interpretation can be valid in which an individual cannot recognize what she wants. In these terms, the distinction between particular and generalizable interests can be posed in terms of the following question: Does a need permit of an interpretation in which *everyone* can recognize what they can want or not? If so, that need gives rise to a generalizable interest; if not, it remains sheerly particular.[44]

When the life-world permits of greater and greater scope for argumentative procedures oriented towards the validity claims of truth and normative rightness (as reflected in agreement upon norms that express generalizable interests) we speak of the rationalization of the life-world. Habermas's critique of functional rationality thus appeals to a further distinction, that between the rationalization of systems and the rationalization of the life-world.[45] By the former, the rationalization of systems, he understands the movement towards increased complexity, the development of a self-regulating capacity and an increased ability to adapt to crises.[46] He understands the rationalization of the life-world to imply the extension of communicative practices in the dimensions of cultural reproduction, social integration and socialization.

The rationalization of the life-world, while clearly salutary for Habermas, is an ironic and problematic process. It is ironic because the systemic and functional imperatives that threaten the integrity of the life-world ultimately have their roots in the disenchanting delegitimization of tradition, the very process that goes hand in hand with the spirit of cultural modernity as it quickens the critical and argumentative temperament throughout the life-world.[47] It is a problematic process because what was once settled—worldviews, social norms, personal identities—is submitted to argumentative renegotiation. The rationalization of the life-world corresponds, then, to the burdening of competent speakers and actors with the responsibility for the argumentative redemption of the claims of tradition, of social norms and contexts of socialization, a burdening that renders cultural reproduction, social integration and socialization demanding, fragile and risky achievements.

Habermas's critique of instrumental rationality is that systems rationality, in particular, economic and bureaucratic rationality, threatens the communicative processes that sustain the life-world. Orientations to argumentatively redeemable validity claims are displaced by purposive-rational, functional orientations on the part of self-interested subjects strategically pursuing private ends.[48] The penetration of the life-world by functional systems imperatives constitutes what he calls a "colonization of the lifeworld" that issues in a variety of pathologies.

Money and power, the media whose circulation effects the coordination of action in the economic and bureaucratic subsystems, respectively, increasingly function as steering media that replace language with symbolically generated incentives and disincentives as a means to coordinate action. This "technicizing" or "mediatizing" of the life-world allows strategic influence to be exerted upon actors while *bypassing processes of consensus-oriented communication*.[49] Habermas insists that this mediatization of the life-world can come into view neither from the methodological standpoint of hermeneutics nor from that of systems theory; it comes into focus only from the communications theoretic angle of vision.[50] This incursion of the system into the life-world takes the form of a *systematic* deformation or distortion of communication, a condition his theory of communicative competence was formulated to analyze. When systemic mechanisms suppress forms of the symbolic reproduction of the life-world, for instance, forms of social integration, in areas where a linguistic consensus-dependent coordination is *indispensable*, then mediatization assumes the form of colonization, and pathologies are imminent.[51] So this thesis of the so-called "internal colonization of the lifeworld" does not apply to processes of material production and work, processes where, to be sure, systems of rewards and punishments functioning as action-coordinating media will indeed have an impoverishing effect, but where such a means of action coordination will not threaten the integrity of those very processes themselves. It is when processes of cultural reproduction, social integration and socialization themselves are subjected to such an incursion that pathological conditions arise, conditions such as the loss of meaning, anomie, alienation, an array of psychopathologies and so on.[52]

The encroachment of the system into the life-world renders patterns of meaning functional, in that they serve to legitimate the imperatives of the system, patterns of meaning such as the work ethic, material sacrifice and postponed gratification.[53] These performative meaning patterns can be successful in consolidating functional action orientations even if the actors are not cognitively invested in the plausibility of these patterns *per se*.[54] The systems theorist Luhmann speaks approvingly of this "technizing of the lifeworld" and functionalizing of meaning, citing its role in "relieving the interpretation processes of experience and action from having to take up, formulate, and communicatively explicate all meaning relations that are implied [in the lifeworld context of communicative action]."[55] So the transfer of action coordination over to technical steering media represents a relief from the risks of communication.[56]

The colonization of the life-world by systems imperatives pushes moral-practical considerations out of the private and public spheres of life; practical questions are more and more replaced by technical ones.[57] For example, the imperatives of the economy reward purposive-rational orientations among consumers and employees. Competition and performativity become behavior-shaping forces conducing to consumerist and possessive individualist orientations. The imperatives of the administrative system lead to a disempowering of democratic will formation, and demands for substantive justice are met with claims to a merely procedural legitimacy of laws.[58] Questions of justification and of justice tend to be discounted in favor of questions of the functional exigencies of the political economy.

Socially integrated life contexts become redefined around the roles of consumer and client and subjected to the demands of system integration.[59] Even the otherwise progressive social-welfare state bureaucracy, in attempting to reduce life risks at the expense of failing to honor the integrity of contexts of life shaped by communicative interaction, contexts such as the family and the school, contributes to the disintegration of life-relations. It does so through its excessive demand that the relationship of the client to the bureaucracy be mediated by an ever-expanding network of legal prescriptions and remedies, by an ever-increasing net of administrative regulations. As a result, clients become objects of negotiations and proceedings among experts, rather than communicative participants in them.[60] For example, arbitration in divorce cases, rather than legal negotiation, would be an instance of a concrete initiative in the direction of decolonization, of emancipating the life-world and turning it over to its own communicative practices.

We should be generally concerned about such transformations of the practical into the technical because, when a problem is viewed as technical, its interactive dimension drops out of view. The interactive dimension, discussed in Chapters Four and Five, is the dimension of what gets enacted and effected in the very doing of an action, rather than in its result. A solution to a problem viewed technically, a technical solution, suffices only where the point is in producing or maintaining a given *state*, where the state is external to, and can be specified independently of, the means used to achieve it. But many characteristically human problems, problems indigenous to the life-world, are matters of assuring a certain kind of *interaction*, an interaction engendered as a good internal to a practice and/or enabled by and identified with *praxis*. We recall that '*praxis*' refers here to action where the end is described in the progressive tense, where the end is actualized or effected in the doing of the action. The description of the state to be achieved through *praxis* is either just one of the appropriate descriptions of the actions undertaken to achieve it, or what is achieved in the performance of an action itself. Closely related to this, a good that is internal to a practice is one that is specific to a given practice, and is effected by virtue of the very doing of that practice. For mundane examples, note the difference between the consequences for interaction (and for temporal experience) of the use of a dishwasher and, say, a husband and wife doing the dishes together; or preparing a meal in a microwave oven and the communal preparation of a meal.[61]

I have made claims for the confluence of Habermas's critique of functional rationality and his response to the problem of nihilism. He sees and takes aim at both nihilism and instrumental rationality through the sights of a theory of communicative rationality. His critique of nihilism departs not from what I have called the meaning perspective (although, as I shall point out, there are significant affinities between the two positions), but from the perspective of rational critique and of a conception of the aporetics of poststructuralism. In what ways can we understand the postmodern or poststructuralist stance to be implicated in functional rationality? A key to understanding the postmodern temper is the recognition that, for it, the distinction between truth and illusion has lost its purchase. As Nietzsche would put it, truth, as the correspondence between language and reality, is, like all values, an artifact concocted to serve the will to power.

With regard to social meanings, the dissolution of the distinction between truth and illusion takes the form of the dissolution of the internal connection between meaning and validity. This severance of the link between meaning and validity is precisely what is effected by conceiving of meaning in exclusively functionalist terms.[62] When social meaning is understood functionally, that is, when social meaning is transformed into (instrumental) value, we have entered the systems perspective, a perspective which is itself tantamount to perspectivism. The actual validity of a social consensus no longer matters; what counts are the effects of holding it as true.

Further, from the systems perspective it is desirable that social systems become more complex in order more efficiently to reduce complexity in their environments. One obvious avenue for such growth in complexity is the provision of functional equivalents, fail-safe mechanisms structured into the system, to handle environmental contingencies. Functional degeneracy, the state of being endowed with functionally equivalent mechanisms, is a systems equivalent of value pluralism or perspectivism. For, given *functional* equivalency, there would be no *privileged* social practices or social values. There would only be the *Gleichgültigkeit* of whatever works to enable the system to reduce complexity and maintain systemic differentiation. There would be no rational basis for adjudicating competing functionally equivalent practices or values if functionality is the ultimate criterion. In fact, for the systems theorist Luhmann, values such as those of human rights, equality and economic justice are appreciated simply as solutions to systemic problems, problems such as maintaining social pluralism and differentiation, not as being at all justified on extrafunctional rational grounds.[63]

Luhmann elaborates a very sophisticated, subtle and exploratory conceptual scheme to which I cannot do justice here, but certain lines of force are apparent. In particular, we should take note of his cynicism regarding truth and justice. He suggests that because of the radicalization of the sceptical critique initiated in the nineteenth century and continuing through today, a critique that turns back on the criteria of truth and justice themselves, and the complexity of social systems, the critique of existing conditions in light of the standards of truth and justice has become anachronistic.[64] The attempt to employ these criteria to anchor a vision of what should be preferred inevitably turns ideological, he claims. He sees such criteria as empty, underdetermined, if not indeterminate, ideals, in that they do not themselves announce what content they should be given, and when we do try to fill them with content we find that, in spite of ourselves, that content is ideologically skewed. Moreover, given Luhmann's essentially Weberian position of value relativism, for him the appeal to truth and justice as values cannot be rationally privileged in a universally valid way as an expression of what counts most about us.[65]

Instead of such appeals, he proposes "a theory of organized and reflexive decision-making processes that treat values *opportunistically* and view programs as capable of yielding decisions" (emphasis mine).[66] The Nietzschean overtones of this proposal are unmistakable. Criteria such as truth and justice are adjudged functionally deficient with regard to the standard systems problem of guiding decision-making processes in the interest of reducing environmental complexity. Meaning critiques, he claims, are possible now only as immanent critiques of systems.[67] Hence dysfunctionality is the most basic critical category ratified by the theory of systems. To speak of an "ought" independently of a given relevant whole, a whole such as "the all-encompassing system of society itself," and of that whole's ability to master its environment, is to speak nonsense, is to commit a kind of category error. Practical questions, in the sense of those which critically suspend ends as well as means, give way to purely technical ones. We cannot coherently raise the question, as Diotima did for the young Socrates, of the *goodness* of the whole.

Habermas quite explicitly links systems theory to the perspectivism of postmodernism. He thinks Luhmann understands meaning-elaborating social systems in the way that Foucault elaborates his, Foucault's, notion of power/knowledge regimes.[68] As indicated earlier, 'meaning' for Luhmann refers to our experience of processes of selectivity, processes which can be experienced as meaningful because they take place within an horizon of possibilities where some possibilities are excluded by the selection.[69] Patterns of meaning reflect principles or patterns of selectivity or, what is the same thing, patterns of exclusion. In his celebration of the neutralization of history and historical meaning, Luhmann advocates our liberation from the fetters of a historicity that limits our options with regard to selectivity. Social meaning, then, should be rendered independent of the operativeness of history, of Gadamer's *wirkungsgeschichtliches Bewusstsein*. As Luhmann puts it:

> Technology . . . unburdens us from rehearsing the subjectivity and historicity underlying the meanings things bear. We are thereby able to acquire a wider range of possibilities and a greater selectivity.[70]

Technology would relieve us of the burden of having to engage in the essentially contestable interpretive processes that inform our attitudes towards competing social practices, interpretive processes that, from the standpoint of systems theory, are arbitrarily constrained by the historical self-understanding to which they profess allegiance. Technology, in other words, would relieve us of the "burden" of the temporality of repetition. So the "loss of meaning" decried by critics of technology, myself included, is for systems theory a condition for increasing our capacities, for enhancing the ability of social systems to reduce complexity. Hence social meaning is to be understood only through functional spectacles sensitive only to the ability of patterns of meaning to enhance the power of systems.

This is similar, as Habermas points out, to the power-serving and -enhancing status that Foucault attributes to discourse formations. The difference is that an analysis that was for Foucault the occasion of a critical, suspicious posture towards discursive formations, is for Luhmann, who finds the critical intention jejeune and passé, simply the revelation of an unproblematic normative ordering of the way things are.[71] Since Luhmann eschews the notion of a critique of reason, what Foucault denounces in the name of an unfettered subjectivity, Luhmann accepts and merely describes.

There are obvious consequences for moral argumentation of meaning's divorce from validity and its wedding to power. Moral argumentation, as I have already suggested, gets set aside in systems theory, and quite explicitly so in Luhmann's version. It gets replaced by functional arguments whose exclusive point is to demonstrate systemically necessary correlates of the process of differentiation. For example, Habermas points out that systems theory does not have the conceptual resources to represent reification and objectification, the subjection of social life to instrumental control, as negative phenomena, for they enhance, not detract from, the ability of systems to master complexity.[72] So, from the point of view of systems theory, the colonization of the life-world cannot appear as a cost.[73] In replacing "validity" by "functionality," we capitulate to a vocabulary that closes the gap through which the wedge of critique could enter. 'Rationality' is translated 'functional rationality' or 'end rationality,' and ends are disconnected from both argumentation processes and traditional contexts of meaning, that is, from the acknowledgment of subjects.

The totalization of functionalist reason, then, has two salient consequences: one, it renders the encroachment of the system into the life-world immune to rational critique, for the "outside" from which such a critique could be waged is sealed off in the dustbin of quaint, antiquated and impotently implausible value orientations; and two, systems theory itself, when understood in its own terms, can claim to be no more than a useful "fiction." Systems theory itself, at least as Luhmann understands it, stands in a functional relationship to social systems; it assumes a basically affirmative stance *vis-à-vis* such systems. One might view such a theory as a mode of the self-consciousness of social systems. Understanding all cognitive acts, including its own, in terms of their contribution to the system's achievement of the mastery of complexity, systems theory is, in principle, resistant both to the moment of critique and, as well, to any moment of an unconditional warrant of its *own* assertibility.[74]

These considerations suggest that we can pinpoint what Habermas would earlier have called the cognitive interest of systems theory, and that such an insight would highlight systems theory's status as what Nietzsche would call a "necessary illusion," a belief that is instrumental to, if not required for, our getting on with things in a certain fashion, but to whose validity we cannot attest. Systems theory's own reflexive self-understanding would require it to surrender claims for its own validity.[75] It, like its own understanding of social meaning, becomes a "fiction" produced by a highly specialized subsystem of society—the academy—for the enhancement of the social system itself. So, my qualifications earlier in this chapter regarding systems theory's self-implication in the functional *organization* of social systems notwithstanding, Luhmann's cynicism regarding truth makes of him a candidate for the very sort of question that we are so tempted to put to Nietzsche (knowing full well that it violates the spirit of his teaching): "But is the doctrine of the will to power true?"[76] By this I mean, assuming that it has no "objectivist illusions"[77] about its status as an autonomous description of an independently existing reality, and that it understands its validity to be parasitic upon the interest in promoting the self-maintenance of systems, why should such a systems theory warrant *our* assent?

Before turning away from this discussion, it is important to note that, and make explicit how, my central concern with time and temporality is very much implicated here. Habermas speaks of the risks of communicative action, and of how they can be diminished by allowing processes of action coordination to be driven by systems imperatives.[78] The fear of risks and of being vulnerable to chance and contingency is, I have argued, emblematic of an uneasiness with time. What Habermas calls systems theory's technicizing of the life-world is a response to our uneasiness with time. Luhmann's call for the "defuturization of the future" (see Note 13 above) is explicit testimony to the will of systems theory to defuse contingency, to neutralize time.

Indeed, Luhmann makes a concern with temporality central to his social theory. He holds that "*the differentiation of system and environment produces temporality* because . . . [p]reserving the system requires time."[79] Further, he sees system differentiation as "a structural technique for solving the temporal *problems* of complex systems," that is, problems arising from the fact that responses to the environment take time (italics mine).[80] To understand temporality as being produced in this way is to understand our relationship to time as one of impatience with its burdensome character and/or of anxiety over its frightening character. Time makes us anxious because what is not yet present is uncertain. The expanse of time as the spread between the present and the future is the site of uncertainty. As I have argued at length, the point of technology is to transform such an open future into a domesticated future, in Luhmann's terms to transform a "present future" into a "future present." In systems theory, time becomes defined negatively as a coefficient of adversity much like the neo-Kantian definition of the thing-in-itself as the beyond of an ever-receding limit, as an ever-vanishing residue, as that which has yet to be mastered—in short, as an adversary. While time, in the sense of an open future, is viewed with uneasiness, the idea of the future as the locus of a projected *determinate* state assumes central importance for modern social systems. Extensive functional differentiation, the considerable autonomy of subsystems in modern societies, and abstract functional perspectives, all contributing to the complexity of such societies, have made the idea of harmony among the various components of modern societies an idea that can be realized only as a future project.[81] This determinate ideal of harmony or compatibility gives priority to the future. So the shift from the past (history) to the, albeit defuturized, future as the temporal horizon that controls present selections can be understood as a response to the systems problem of absorbing complexity.[82] The goal orientation of what I have called external history is again seen to go hand in hand with the systems perspective. In general, my thesis of the domestication of time is given a striking confirmation by Luhmann's analysis.

To pick up the threads of this chapter's main discussion: if, as systems theory and the postmodernists counsel us, we uncouple meaning from validity, then my consenting to an assertion in no way obliges me to be committed to the notion that any rational agent would or should grant their assent as well.[83] The perspectivism or nihilism at the heart of systems theory allows Habermas to paint his critical picture of both functional rationality and poststructuralism with the same broad brush.[84] That brush is furnished by his theory of communicative rationality. Such a theory of rationality forms the essential basis upon which

Habermas's project of Critical Theory rests.[85] As I suggested above, his theory of communicative rationality is an expression of his fundamental concern to block dialectics of Enlightenment and nihilism.[86] I now turn to a summary appraisal of that theory.

Habermas's notion of communicative rationality—captured by the idea of an orientation towards truth or validity claims that are understood to be redeemable in an ideal speech situation, that is, where consensus is forged through reason alone—"lays claim to a universal validity binding on *all* 'civilized men'."[87] This rather extraordinary claim is buttressed by his belief that the exemplary status of this conception of rationality can be exhibited through a rational reconstruction of learning processes or of the development of structures of rationality. The strategy of rational reconstruction would provide grounding for such a universalist claim through demonstrating communicative rationality to be the *telos* of an evolutionary process.

In his attempt to defend the view that the rational is what emerges from a free and unfettered dialogue among all those concerned, an attempt pursued by demonstrating such a view to be *the* culmination of a cultural learning process of *universal* significance, Habermas has met with stiff resistance.[88] Countering charges that by grounding a normative theory of rationality in an evolutionary result he has committed naturalistic and, perhaps, ethno- and phallocentric fallacies, Habermas responds that in an actual rational reconstruction, normative and empirical claims are inextricably wed in such a way that empirical results can *indirectly* redeem normative claims, thereby providing them with an objective foundation.[89] The idea seems to be that a rational reconstruction not only yields hypotheses about, say, intuitive moral know-how, but that it also embodies hypotheses concerning the *hierarchization* of that know-how (from, say, morally less adequate to morally more adequate levels). That is to say that such a reconstruction must be informed by a moral theory. The presupposed moral theory serves to provide the descriptive categories which inform the concepts of, for example, a developmental psychological theory about moral reasoning, and to provide a developmental *vector*, a direction of development corresponding to putatively higher moral stages. Confirmation of the moral theory, and ultimately of the status of communicative rationality, is won through coherence with the psychological data obtained with the theory's hermeneutic guidance. If, for instance, subjects do not in fact prefer what a given moral theory claims to be a higher stage of moral reasoning, then that theory would be placed in question.[90]

Habermas's intent to provide not only a critique of functional rationality but also the means to pursue a critical assessment of competing norms, values and contexts of meaning is testimony to the ambition of his project. Can he make good his claims for communicative rationality? The attempt to provide objective foundations in the manner described above cannot do for a rational reconstruction what Habermas seems to want it to do. What such a confirmation would secure is not the universal validity of the moral claims, nor the uniqueness of the rational reconstruction, but, rather, only the heuristic power of the moral theory that informs the reconstruction. Like textual interpretations and scientific theories, rational reconstructions are underdetermined, that is, are not uniquely implied, by the relevant data. So, by extension, Habermas's attempts to place the concept of communicative rationality "in the evolutionary perspective of the rise of modern structures of consciousness" ought not be viewed as grounding communicative rationality as *the* unique *telos* of that development, as the only way of giving those processes a coherent structure. Perhaps other postconventional theories of morality would do. Furthermore, as Habermas acknowledges, one *would* commit a naturalistic fallacy if one asserted that a reconstruction, corroborated *on this basis*, demonstrates what morality or rationality *ought* to be.

Consequently, the privileging of Habermas's notion of communicative rationality will require more than rational reconstruction. It will also ultimately require the kind of hermeneutic dialogue that stands in tension with attempts to provide objectivist foundations.[91] Habermas's project, it would seem, cannot escape a hermeneutic moment.

However, this need not worry Habermas as much as it seemed to in his celebrated debate with Gadamer, or as much as it sometimes seems to even now. The critique of the universalist pretensions of communicative rationality need not lead one into the arms of poststructuralism, historicism and decisionism. Critiques of this sort need not leave us bankrupt as we pursue a critique of the values-perspective. Critiques of objectivism could do so only insofar as we found ourselves in the grip of a false dichotomy, only insofar as we found ourselves having to choose between objectivism and relativism, between, on the one hand, the view that there is a notion of rationality that can be *fully* justified, in terms of which competing notions can be critically evaluated and, on the other, the view that all such standards are simply conventional through and through, with the consequence that each is refractory to nonarbitrary critique. Often Habermas writes as if he fears that failure to make good his claim that communicative rationality is necessarily somehow binding on all cultural beings is tantamount to succumbing to historicism and decisionism. His anxiety over providing a convincing demonstration of the exemplary status of his procedural concept of communicative rationality is born of his predisposition to believe that only such a demonstration can disarm relativistic arguments that purport to show that standards of rationality drawn from the plurality of forms of life are thoroughly unadjudicable.

But I spoke of this position as entailing a false dichotomy, because between the extremes of objectivism, where reasons are held to be conclusive, and an extreme form of relativism, where reasons are held to be irrelevant, is the position of what can be called, following Gadamer, judgment, where reasons are held to be relevant but not conclusive. Much of what is important to my project in Habermas's work is, I believe, compatible with this third position. One consequence of this is that, in a sense that will become clearer in what follows, in the debate between Habermas and Gadamer, I would declare Habermas the phenomenological winner, while to Gadamer should go the ontological honors.

An exploration follows of ways of responding to poststructuralism and its values-perspective,[92] modes of response that are sensitive to the critique of Habermas's universalist and foundationalist aspirations. I pursue this exploration by exploiting the resources of the middle ground between objectivism and relativism.

7

Notes Towards the Trivialization of a Distinction: An Interlude on the Conversations of Modernity

What I have alluded to as the "postmodern consensus" refers to an orientation, attitude or sensibility that reflects a suspicious if not cynical posture both towards projects of rational critique and towards hermeneutic projects that grant privilege to structures of meaning. Within such a consensus, the products of both projects tend to be regarded as invidiously arbitrary. Accordingly, given the purchase that such an agreement seems to have on our current intellectual and cultural life, either explicitly or implicitly, it is incumbent upon me to address directly the challenge my project faces from this direction. That is the point of this excursus. My aim in it is to provide a philosophical justification of the basis for the critique of technology that I have developed in these pages.

The general tenor of my justification will be to draw a distinction between two senses of 'arbitrary,' a distinction that relativists, writers who affirm postmodernism and others very often fail to make. While allowing that both structures of meaning and Habermas's standards of critical rationality are arbitrary in one, perfectly innocuous sense, I argue that they need not, and indeed in the case of structures of meaning, in an important sense cannot, be regarded as arbitrary in the other and, for my purposes, quite significant sense. I mean to understand 'arbitrary' in the first sense in opposition to 'necessary,' where the latter is to be taken in the sense of being strictly universally binding, transcendentally guaranteed, or metaphysically underwritten. I mean to oppose 'arbitrary' in the second sense to what members of a given community must take *seriously*, that is, to oppose it to what cannot be regarded as question-begging within that community. I point out that to call a structure of meaning or standard of critique arbitrary in the first sense is not really to disparage it, for it will turn out that the notion that contrastively defines 'arbitrary' in *that* sense has no currency for us, that in the wake of the "death of God," such a notion is empty. I go on to argue, *pace* the postmodern consensus, that structures of meaning and standards of critical rationality need not be arbitrary in the second sense. What *can* be shown to be arbitrary in this latter sense would indeed be invidiously arbitrary and, as we shall see, could thereby become a legitimate object of rational critique.

In the first section of this chapter, by offering an argument against philosophical nihilism, I defend my appeal (in Chapters Four and Five) to structures of meaning in posing a critical counterpoint to technological reason. In the second section, I defend taking the project of the rational critique of tradition seriously, the postmodern consensus over the aporetic status of objectivity notwithstanding.

I

This study has been concerned throughout to expose the threat of instrumental rationality to our ability to experience our lives as meaningful. The last chapter emphasized a particular aspect of what it means to lead a meaningful life, namely, to have good *reasons* for doing one thing as opposed to another. The emphasis in earlier chapters centered upon notions such as connectedness, continuity, coherence and differences that make a difference. The shift in emphasis from earlier chapters to the last does not entail a shift in subject matter, but, rather, enables another sort of approach to the problem of nihilism, an approach from the perspective of critical rationality. The excursus which follows continues such an approach in, first, justifying an appeal to the meaningful by offering a critique of the values-perspective. This critique will, secondly, remove an impediment to our taking seriously the idea of a nonarbitrary critical response to tradition, be that tradition technological or not.

In order to see the connection between these two aspects of the meaningful, that having to do with coherence and so on, and that having to do with having good reasons, it suffices to note how an orientation in terms of a particular structure of meaning is at the same time an implicit claim about the nature of the "good life," which sort of claim is what the goodness of good reasons for acting ultimately depends on. This is in keeping with my assertion in Chapter Three that prereflectively acquired meanings are *claims* that are implicitly held to be adequate to their objects. As Sabina Lovibond suggests, in the language analytic idiom of the later Wittgenstein, in order to *use* sentences, as opposed to just mentioning them, we must draw upon our own conception of how the world is, of what is plausible to us.[1] When we become explicitly aware of such claims, and we can be led to do so in a number of ways, we *may*, with reason, decide to reject such a claim, again for any number of reasons. This consideration foregrounds the possibility of rational critique, rational critique of the meaningful understood in terms of coherence and so on, while remaining within the ambit of the meaningful. Such awareness puts us in a position to acknowledge that the call of the meaningful can be the call of God or, as the "Heidegger affair" has taught us, the tempting solicitation of evil. These considerations suggest that we continue, as I shall do in the second part of this chapter, to press the line of investigation pursued by Habermas, by accommodating questions having to do with critical perspectives upon meaning and technology's implications for such questions, even as we remain sensitive to hermeneutic and postmodernist responses to Habermas's project.

This book's analysis of the implications of technological rationality for our self-understanding has thus far explicitly availed itself of a distinction between what I have called the "values-perspective," on the one hand, and an orientation towards structures of meaning, on the other. Technology counsels the values orientation of the worldless, disengaged, aesthetic-observer. The technological world picture threatens to undermine critical standards by derisively charging that such criteria are merely expressive of an ultimately arbitrary perspective. From the standpoint of technology's functional rationality, there can only be ironic, if not cynical, suspicion of the criteria that would guide the conduct and examination of a life. To experience our standards in this way is surely to flirt with the loss of meaning.

The first task here will be to examine ways of dismantling the values-perspective and its claims *from within*. I shall focus on a central presupposition of the values-perspective's nihilistic stance, and attempt to undermine the cogency of that position by calling into question a key distinction upon which it rests, namely, that between the disillusioned observer and the naive participant. This is *a form* of a distinction that has so far had only an implicit presence in this discussion: that between, on the one hand, those earnest souls who *participate* ingenuously and seriously in a particular form of life, those who are claimed by a structure of meaning, and, on the other, those ironists who merely *observe* from a detached perspective the passing show mounted by the diverse forms of life without being able to muster an allegiance to any of them except through what they would understand as a sheerly *arbitrary* act of the will. This distinction between the inner or participative standpoint and the outer observer's perspective, the latter a standpoint from which the claims on the participants under review are neutralized by something very much like a phenomenological *epoché*, is prominently invoked, if only to be challenged subsequently, in the writings of David Wiggins and Jürgen Habermas.[2] The observer's viewpoint can be directly linked to the aesthetic-theoretical standpoint of disinterested contemplation. Chapter Three argued that to adopt such a standpoint is to suspend the enabling conditions of meaning. As Habermas points out, such an orientation also stands in tension with taking seriously the project of rational critique.[3] Since from the observer's viewpoint each formation in the panoply of structures of meaning is indifferently regarded as if it were the product of an arbitrary "will," none can be claimed to warrant privilege over the others. Thus the observer's standpoint can be linked to what I have called the values-standpoint and to a Nietzschean perspectivism that deflates straightaway any pretension to a rational critique of values, belief systems and social practices. By contrast, from within the inner or participative standpoint, the two aspects of the meaningful, that of coherence and that of having good reasons, can be brought together.

The values-perspective of emotivism, existentialism and much of poststructuralism comes into view when we attend to the theoretical attitude, the standpoint of *theoria*. This disengaged observer's point of view is the site where meaning and validity claims are placed in suspension. From *this* standpoint it is only as a *naive* participant that one can be claimed by meaning and by validity. So the aesthetic observer can acknowledge the believer as well as herself only through invoking a distinction between observation and naive participation, between a standpoint from which life is objectively meaningless and one which is implicated in essentially *illusory* notions of objectivity, importance and significance.[4] The postmodern consensus is informed by *this* distinction. Invoked from the external perspective of the observer, this distinction entails that, whenever matter from the participant's perspective is brought to the attention of the observer, it must appear in quotes. That is to say, it cannot be taken seriously; its validity claims must be suspended. We shall presently want to ask, Is it possible for everything that we as participants take seriously to be presented in this fashion?

From the other point of view, how does the skeptic or systematic ironist appear from the perspective of the participant? Assuming that the skeptical observer is not written off as being simply perverse or of diminished capacity, there are a number of possibilities, none of which require, however, that the participant take seriously the ironist's counsel proclaiming the arbitrariness of all commitments. The observer and the message she bears need not force the participant to make conceptual room for a being whose relationship to structures of meaning and to canons of rationality is different *in kind* from that of the participant. Let us consider the possibilities. Think of the observer as the subject of a Sartrean "look," as the outsider whose gaze threatens to reveal the arbitrariness of our practices. The participant might well view such an outsider as a potential participant who simply has not yet been convinced of the cogency of the participant's practices. Or, even if the believing participant can entertain the possibility that she is wrong, she might yet believe that there are criteria to which both she and the skeptic can appeal that will decide the issue or, in the case of *phronesis*, help to decide the issue, and hence that the skeptic is still a coparticipant. For to believe that reasons are relevant, that they have compelling force, is to be a participant in, is to be implicated in, the forms of life that give those reasons their purchase. And even if the skeptic cannot be seen as a *co*participant, she may well be understood as owing her allegiance to another form of life, and will therefore be seen as a participant nonetheless.

And what if the observer insists upon her nonparticipatory status, upon her difference in kind? Then the participant need not take her or her message *seriously*. Such an ironist can well make us feel uneasy about taking a given set of practices seriously. But to be seduced into "stepping back" from our form of life *as a whole*, not to mention the project of "stepping back" from all forms of life as such, is to throw into question the very condition of our taking *anything* seriously. So we need not follow our observer to this point, for as participants we will be committed to language games in which the contrast between the worthwhile and the frivolous has nonironic currency.

Similarly, if the skeptic insists that the notion of a good argument, as opposed to one that is *merely* successful for a certain audience at a certain time, is a chimera, the participant could respond by asking for a justification of this view, for a good argument for it. The skeptic, under pain of self-refutation or pragmatic self-contradiction, may refuse to offer an argument. In this case, the participant will accordingly see the skeptic as merely willful, as merely *asserting* her view. If, on the other hand, the skeptic, quite consistently, responds not by understanding herself to be giving a good argument (an illusion, in her view) but by advancing reasons that, just as a matter of fact, the participant is likely to accept, then the participant may respond by pointing out to her interlocutor that by 'good argument' the skeptic must not mean what she, the participant, means by the expression. The skeptic means something like 'the kind of argument God would advance,' and this is not a notion that the participant needs or is likely to intend. All the participant will need to distinguish between a good argument and one that is merely successful is a notion of a good argument as one that is fully consistent with and sensitive to the most highly refined canons of rationality and rules of evidence available to her form of life. Hence in neither case would the participant have to take the skeptic seriously. In the first case the skeptic would be seen as refusing to defend her position, while in the second, she could be charged with misusing the participant's language.

Indeed, the observer does seem to assume an artificially alienated posture. The moment of reflection, which occurs on occasion as a rupture in the stream of life, is transformed into an autonomous self-subsistent perspective. When the observer's perspective is absolutized, what is an aspect of a life lived intelligently is hypostasized into a style of life itself. However, such a stylized posture, its own self-understanding notwithstanding, retains its connection to life and action. The observer is also an embodied being-there (*Dasein*) who cannot thematize her whole life at once. Insofar as she continues to speak and act, and must she not do so, the rest of her life must be understood by her as naive participation. One cannot pursue a life from the vantage point of the observer; from such a perspective one can only hover speechlessly above life. Hence the observer will require some notion of participation. The standpoint of participation is unavoidable. However, the participant will not be required to acknowledge a standpoint from which her standards of rationality must all be cast under suspicion. Hence only the theoretical attitude seems to *require* a form of the participant/ observer distinction, and it requires it in the form of a distinction between a knowing or disillusioned observer and a naive or deluded participant. (Plato's myth of the cave represents perhaps the first attempt to give philosophical expression to the distinction in this form.)

In keeping with my suggestion that, for the theory of communicative action, language has not only meaning but also function, Habermas understands the perspectives of the participant and of the observer to be complementary moments or aspects of an irreducible approach to social action.[5] He warns against absolutizing either moment.[6] The moment of theory is required to explicate structures that operate "behind the backs" of social actors, structures that are not mediated through the consciousnesses of such actors. The systems theoretic analysis of *The Theory of Communicative Action* proceeds from this vantage point. However, such an analysis is illegitimately absolutized, Habermas thinks, in the hands of a Luhmann. For Habermas, thinkers like Rorty, along with Luhmann, absolutize the perspective of the observer.[7] Habermas's theorist is a "relative" observer, not the paralyzed aesthetic-observer, but one who takes seriously the integrity of the communicative rationality that sustains the life-world, as well as one who is fully aware that she is a participant in a discursive communication community herself. To absolutize the observer pole is to accept the form of the participant/ observer distinction that we shall presently want to question, that is, the distinction between the illusionless observer and the gullible participant.

Intellectuals, as Habermas reminds us, are burdened with the status of being both participants in, and observers of, culture. As participants, when engaged in theoretical or practical discussion, they cannot help but take seriously the distinction between the valid or legitimate, on the one hand, and the merely socially sanctioned, on the other. As observers, they *might* want to say that theirs and others' notions of validity and legitimacy are merely conventional. As Kant suggested, from the point of view of action, we must consider ourselves as autonomously related to a morally rational law; from the point of view of disinterested theory, we must see ourselves as determined. Perhaps this dual status *is* in some sense irreducible, and conclusive grounds cannot be given for privileging one over the other. From the nature of the case there is probably no neutral, non-question-begging standpoint from which to adjudicate this issue.[8] One way of putting the project in this chapter is that it is a search for ways to reconcile these two seemingly incompatible self-images.

Before turning to an assessment of the participant/observer distinction, it is important to fix in mind the relationship between the two central distinctions invoked in this book thus far: the meaning/value contrast and that between the participant and the observer. By 'meaning perspective' I emphatically do *not* intend to call to mind the state of being *naively* claimed, where such a state is understood to be *opposed* to the state of being aware of the contingency of those claims, as if, were we merely to be aroused from our dogmatic slumbers, we would straightaway have to adopt the standpoint of the ironist. I intend, rather, to call to mind the angle of vision which allows us to recognize that we are always already claimed. The meaning perspective allows for, and even encourages, a full recognition of the fact that consciousness is the issue of historical forces, that it is in Gadamer's terms a *wirkungsgeschichtliches Bewusstsein*. But further, it insists that some such issue is the condition of there being any understanding at all. So the distinction between the observer, sophisticated in the ways of the history of Being, and aware of the demise of the metaphysics of presence, and the naive participant cannot capture the meaning/value contrast as I intend it.

When we take *seriously* what comes into view from the perspective of the participant, even while aware of its historical contingency, then the meaning/ value contrast *is* a projection of the participant/observer distinction. The values-perspective results when values are understood apart from those contexts of meaning that alone give them their point. The perspectivism of the values orientation arises from: one, the demand to see things from an *aperspectival* site; and two, the failure to find anything that is compelling from *that* position. *The aperspectival is thus the measure of perspectivism.* The values-perspective, then, entails the observer's point of view. Hence our challenge of the latter viewpoint will also be a challenge to the values-perspective.

The critique of the values-perspective that follows will proceed by questioning the plausibility of the strict separation of participation from observation that those who purport to philosophize from the observer's position seek to institutionalize. The first point to be made is that the very attempt to give an account of the content of the participant's perspective, of what the participants are saying and doing, will require that the observer, too, be a participant in the sort of structures of meaning that she, *qua* observer, eschews. Now, this claim can be understood in a number of ways, and in at least three. It can be construed to mean that the observer must bring prior participative experience of the very kind of form of life of which she wants to render an account, and that she may do so while either being invested in that form of life or while withholding commitment to it. And in withholding commitment to it, she may be either neutral or judgmental. In addition to these three possibilities, the claim can also be understood to echo the now commonplace assertion that in order to understand human action one must decipher the rules governing the behavior in question, or interpret the structures of meaning that provide the context for that behavior. Such an understanding cannot proceed exclusively from an observer's point of view, for such rules and structures of meaning are not observables. This assertion of the *verstehenden* approach to social inquiry does not of itself require that the observer, in "going native," have the beliefs that she ascribes to the "target population," or that there be any particular prior participative commitments on her part. All that is required is an after-the-fact (of the encounter) participative understanding of what members of the target population say and do when they say and do it. And, typically, for *verstehenden* social inquiry, no further claims are made about the role of prior participative engagements.

I have already alluded sufficiently, in the context of Chapter Four's reference to Charles Taylor's work, to a defense of the now hardly controversial thesis of *verstehenden* sociology.[9] I do want to suggest, in the course of the discussion, however, that, in the hands of many of its proponents, the thesis does not go far enough, that, in rendering an account of a practice or of a form of life, the participative commitments of the inquirer *are* engaged, that her hermeneutic situation is a knowledge-productive factor. One's ability to give an account is limited by the forms of life one participates in, or can imagine oneself to participate in. If I am right about this, then the thesis of interpretive sociology can be folded into one of the three modes of prior participative understanding mentioned above.

If my claim here is contested, I would reply that not only is it true that behavior will appear arbitrary unless one has access to the rules governing it, but, further, that the rules themselves, even if we *could* gain access to them independently of our hermeneutic situation (and I have reason to doubt that we could), will seem arbitrary, merely gamelike, unless we can understand the practice that they govern to be analogous to some practice that *we* could find significant. To refer to it as anything other than a game in such a way as to convey information is to employ descriptive categories that are part of, or that can be intelligibly linked to, *our* repertoire. [10]

Moreover, the need to bring our engagements into play has the heuristic benefit of suggesting potential applications of the vocabulary corresponding to *our* relevant practice to regions of the target population's practice in such a way that new hypotheses for understanding that population would be generated, hypotheses that would not be generated were we to be restricted exclusively to the rules regulating observed behavior. I have in mind here something quite analogous to the situation in *natural* scientific inquiry. In her *Models and Analogies in Science*, Mary Hesse argues for the importance of interpreting the mathematical calculus of scientific theories into models, that is, into antecedently understood structures. [11] Though a purely formal theory, that is, the mathematical calculus, could account for observed physical phenomena, the model, she argues, has the indispensable heuristic value of suggesting new testable applications of a theory to physical systems, and hence new lines of inquiry, that would not be suggested otherwise. The analogy that I wish to highlight can be seen by identifying "antecedently understood structure" with "practice with which we are already familiar." Then, for example, if we understand a given rule-governed practice in terms of *our* notion of a religious practice, we will have hermeneutically guided anticipations of meaning that may "light up" aspects of the incompletely understood practice that would otherwise remain in the dark. For example, we may be led to ask, Is there an aspect of their practice that marks a distinction between the sacred and the profane?

Lastly on this score, even if it is granted that we can gain access to the rules governing a practice without engaging all of our being, it cannot reasonably be claimed that we can achieve this insight without engaging *some* of our being, without some presuppositions. In particular, our notions of rationality and of what it means to follow a rule will be presupposed. In deciphering a code, for instance, we must not only assume that the arrangement of the ciphers is rule-governed, but also that their arrangement is intended to convey information, and so on.

Incommensurability is the limiting case that proves the point. At the level of language analysis, incommensurability amounts to nonintertranslatability, to the inability in principle on the part of speakers of two languages to translate one language into the other. Donald Davidson points out the conceptual pitfalls in attempts to make sense of notions of both radical and partial incommensurability, arguing that the idea of totally incommensurable linguistic or conceptual schemes is incoherent, and that partial incommensurability is undecidable.[12] Any linguistically structured form of life can be translated into my own *if* I can recognize it as being so structured. Such translations are effected through a principle of charity which has transcendental-pragmatic status. A condition of the possibility of the translation of an alien linguistic scheme into my own is that I assume that much of what the speakers are saying in the as yet to be translated language is true, that is, that we inhabit, at least to some extent, a common world. So if I am able to recognize another language as a language, I am pragmatically committed to presupposing that I share at least some of my experience of the world with the user of that language. Some commensurability is a condition of the intelligibility of another tradition.

With regard to moral traditions, incommensurability, in the sense of a radical difference in the criteria for the application of moral concepts, would mean that it would be difficult to see how we could be in a position to know that participants in a tradition so radically different from ours in this respect were indeed engaged in *moral* discourse. So some degree of commensurability is a condition of our recognizing moral discourse *as* discourse of just that sort. In general, if a practice is so utterly unlike our own that our own *participative* understanding cannot be brought to bear upon it, then we cannot *describe* that practice as being of any given sort, for example, as argumentative activity or ethical activity. And without the linguistic resources enabling us to bring it under a description, save that of 'game,' we would be hard-pressed to go on with an account of it. For accounts of phenomena are accounts of them under a description, a description that is in part an artifact of the language game or theoretical scheme from which the account is drawn.

Habermas and Wiggins support my claim that an account of the participant's language game will require that the observer draw upon some participative appreciation of that language. They stress the point with regard to argumentative practices and moral discourse, respectively. As Habermas suggests, we would not know what it means to engage in argumentative conduct, and hence would not be able to identify such conduct, without our already having acquired the experience of what it is like to participate in argumentation.[13] And that experience is one in which we understand our claims to aspire to more than merely local validity.

Argumentative practices are structured by the perception of internal relationships among propositions, by the perception of some propositions as grounds for others. In order to recognize others performing this sort of activity, I must have experienced it myself, must myself have had the experience of taking some propositions as grounds for others and of recognizing the distinction between validity and invalidity in argumentation. To have participated in argumentation is to have engaged in the practice of distinguishing good grounds from bad grounds. A regulative ideal for a participant in argumentative conduct is success in adducing grounds that would command the noncoerced respect of anyone at any time. The proof that such an ideal is operative is that, whenever a participant in argumentation is made aware of the merely provincial basis of her argument, she will seek less provincial grounds, or be called upon to *justify* not doing so. Making claims about the provincial nature of an argument is a way of *criticizing* it. All things being equal, the less provincial an argument is, the better it is. So the ironic observer's denial of the distinction between the valid and the merely local contradicts the very experience that is necessary for the recognition of argumentative activity at all.

Now, nothing in what I have just argued is subverted by the claim that argumentation always takes place in a historical context, or that what counts as a good argument is hermeneutically determined, claims to which Habermas is not always as sensitive as he might be. For within a given hermeneutic horizon we can still distinguish meaningfully between the merely local and the less so; between reasons for a belief and fear, prejudice or habit as a basis for belief; between that horizon's *ideal* of a good reason and what is in fact *accepted* as a good reason; and, further, between challenging or questioning that horizon and passively accepting its limits.

Perhaps this is the place to say more generally that, if Habermas were to relax his strong universalistic claims and to adopt instead what I would call a more modest, hermeneutically self-reflective standpoint, it would have a salutary effect. He could, I believe, preserve his central and important insights while avoiding many of the criticisms of his universalistic pretensions.

One of those central insights is the claim that, if we are to take another seriously, be it another person or another society, then understanding that other inextricably involves evaluation or taking a position with respect to the other's expressions.[14] In making this claim, Habermas takes a step beyond maintaining that the recognition of argumentative conduct requires experience in the *use*, not only the mention, of the valid/contingently acceptable distinction. Such recognition will also ineluctably involve us, he claims, in the evaluation of that conduct. So the "observer" will not only have to call upon participative experience of the sort of which she is rendering an account; she will also be called upon to take a stand *vis-à-vis* the conduct and the claims she has made thematic. She will be called upon, willy-nilly, to be a participant in evaluative practices, a participation that undermines the cogency of the notion of a fully disengaged neutral spectator. That understanding entails evaluation is claimed not only for argumentative interaction. It holds, Habermas would claim, for any practice that can be assessed along the dimensions of truth, normative rightness, truthfulness or sincerity, and/or comprehensibility.

Understanding, then, involves the assessment of validity claims. To understand another and to take that other seriously, that is, from within a nonobjectifying attitude, is to treat her expressions not merely as causal results, but as claims which are criticizable or redeemable in appropriate ways. Habermas argues, further, that we cannot avoid taking the other seriously if we want to understand, and that understanding *tout court* is evaluation:

> But if, in order to understand an expression, the interpreter must *bring to mind the reasons* with which a speaker would if necessary and under suitable conditions defend its validity, he is *himself* drawn into the process of assessing validity claims.[15]

> And [further] he cannot take a position without applying his *own* standards of judgment, at any rate standards that he has made his own.[16]

So it is a presupposition and an enabling condition of a rational interpretation that the participants be taken seriously as responsible subjects, that their claims be withdrawn from the neutralized and indifferent suspension of the phenomenological *epoché*. And if the participants are either explicitly or implicitly engaged in argumentative discourse, then the observer who aims to understand must necessarily be an engaged coparticipant in the practice of assessing reasons.[17] If this line of argumentation is correct, the distinction between the disenchanted observer and the naive participant, a distinction which is, as we have seen, crucial for the values-perspective, will again fail to hold. For the observer who understands cannot distance herself from practices which require taking *seriously* standards of evaluation.

The claim that understanding entails evaluation means that there can be no purely neutral or "value-free" account of systems of belief, of the variety of forms of life.[18] The observer is always already engaged in judgmental practices in such a way that the "anything goes" species of relativism cannot be valid from her point of view. And it was only from her point of view that such a relativism was espoused. Is the argument that understanding entails evaluation a sound one? I think it is, but it needs to be qualified in a way that I shall presently suggest. In understanding an expression or an action, we look for reasons—typically beliefs and desires in the context of socially sanctioned rules—that underlie it. We do not have to evaluate the beliefs and desires *qua* beliefs and desires in doing so, but we must evaluate them as *reasons*, that is, as being *understandably* connected with the utterance or action in question. That is, we implicitly evaluate the internal connection between background beliefs and purposes, on the one hand, and expressions, on the other. Thus, so far, it appears that understanding necessarily entails evaluation, but that it entails evaluation neither of background beliefs and purposes nor of the expression in question itself, but only of their connection.[19] We try to ascertain whether or not an expression is reasonable in context.

Now, both Habermas and, in a recent publication, Thomas McCarthy want to go further than this and claim that an account of a system of belief entails not only an evaluation of the reasons for holding such beliefs, but also an evaluation of the system of beliefs itself. In referring to the case of interpreting mythical narratives and modes of thought, Habermas asserts:

> [w]e understand them only when we can say why the participants had good reasons for their confidence in this *type* of explanation. But in order to achieve this degree of understanding, we have to establish an internal relation between "their" sort of explanation and the kind we accept as correct. We must be able to reconstruct the successful and unsuccessful learning processes which separate "us" from "them"; both modes of explanation have to be located within the same universe of discourse.[20]

Accordingly, we pass judgment not only on the reasons, but also, in this case, on the explanation itself. If we are *correct* in assigning to them the same purposes in elaborating a particular mode of discourse that we have when treating a given subject matter, say, the course of nature, then judging their discourse in terms of its success in fulfilling those purposes is perhaps inevitable. *If* mythical narratives are offered as a species of explanation in our sense, then we would have to find them wanting. And we could presumably establish connections between the special circumstances or context of beliefs that we would appeal to in understanding why they have confidence in this type of explanation and what we now take to be the case about the world. Further, we could do so in such a way that what we now take to be the case about the world and the type of explanation that we offer can be understood as the result of a learning process. But suppose the mythical narrative is *not* intended as an explanation, but rather, say, as a *dramatization* or *expression* of some facet or other of the human condition.[21] Then to understand it as a deficient *explanation* is to make a category mistake. It is to run the risk of, to use the words of McCarthy in another context, construing practices in other cultures "as exhibiting a more or less deficient mastery of our competencies rather than as expressing a mastery of a different set of skills altogether."[22]

The insight that understanding entails evaluation should then be qualified by a nod to hermeneutic modesty, a modesty born of the awareness of a dialectic of blindness and insight. This dialectic, in which understanding is inscribed, keeps practices in the dark whose point falls outside the purview of the informing assumptions of *our* understanding. And this qualification cuts even deeper, to the evaluation of reasons themselves. Our assumptions about the purposes or intent of an expression will guide our selection of what is to count as a good reason for it. The reasons adduced for the production of an expression will be relative to the purposes that such a production is taken to serve. Hence, if our assumptions about the purposes of an expression are "off the mark," then our assessment of good reasons for it will be compromised as well.

Further, for Habermas, the notion of a learning process, be it cognitive or moral, refers to a sequence of stages of development which can be described and ordered in terms of a developmental logic, a sequence of stages of problem solution that can be reconstructed on internal logical grounds.[23] A learning process is thus a *directional* process, structured, for Habermas, in terms of a definitive and invariant hierarchy of stages.[24] Many have challenged the idea of unique patterns and/or *tele* of cognitive and moral development.[25] If we cannot rely upon universal patterns which structure learning processes, then the notion of a nonarbitrary evaluation of an expression is severely at risk. One way to put part of the point is that Habermas is perhaps too quick to assume that there is a nontrivial level of description at which all social actors face the *same* set of problems. Without some such assumption of the continuity of problems across cultural boundaries one cannot *compare* problem solutions in such a way as to rank them hierarchically.

In sum, it may be pragmatically unavoidable that understanding entails evaluation. However, the methodological pitfalls adumbrated here, at the very least, cast suspicion on the cognitive hubris of such evaluations. These important qualifications notwithstanding, I take Habermas to have secured the claim that the observer who understands cannot be construed as a disengaged spectator, but must, rather, be seen as a participant in the same sorts of evaluative practices in which the more reflective among those whom she observes may be engaged.[26]

Let us now examine in greater detail how the participant's standpoint gets described by the observer, as the observer is understood from within the values-perspective. The expressions 'naive,' 'inviduously local,' '*merely* conventional,' and 'rationally ungrounded' (used critically) come readily to mind. Such descriptions rest upon untenable assumptions about the limits of doubt, about objectivity and about rationality. As Lovibond, following Wittgenstein, points out, rationality itself presupposes socialization into a language game; such socialization is a condition for the possibility of rationality in thought and action.[27] It is therefore odd to claim that there is a standpoint from which it makes sense to say that a convention of ingenuous participation *qua* such a convention is *not to be taken seriously* because it is rationally unfounded. For rationality itself is constituted by a shared way of life, by conventions of ingenuous participation. Rationality is in *this* sense conventional. Wittgenstein's private language argument suggests that the transcendental basis for any judgment pertaining to the rationality of a practice or form of life is itself a form of life. To be or to fail to be rational is to follow or to fail to follow rules. All serious, non-ironic talk about rationality, then, presupposes *participation* in a shared mode of life. There are no standards of rationality *outside* some such social context that will enable us even to talk of conventions of ingenuous participation as being irrational or rationally unfounded.

So our intrepid observer may forego serious talk about rationality, regarding such talk to be antithetical to her requirements of intellectual hygiene. She will concede that all standards or criteria regulating or constraining discourse are internal to some form of life or other, and will go on to say that they are all *naively* held. We might first point out to her that the constraints on *her* discourse are then presumably naively held, and, thus, that on her own terms we need not take her claim seriously. Apart from pointing out the self-referential infelicity of her claim, we might also point out that its *meaning*, as well as its truth, is in jeopardy. In order for the expression 'naively held' to mean anything, to convey any information, we must be able to make sense of the sorts of standards with which we want to contrast those that are naively binding. We would have to make sense of a sort of standard that is not naively held, of a sort that, in accordance with the demands of our observer, is not grounded in some nonnecessary form of life. But we cannot. Any sort of reasoned insight that *we* could attain would be enabled by canons of rationality acquired at least in part through socialization processes that are not fully transparent to reason. So the idea that standards that are internal to a form of life are *naively* held *because* they are internal standards loses its point. At most it is an acknowledgement of our finitude.

Both sides, the observer's as well as the participant's, agree that it is only from within the internal or participant's point of view that there are criteria for judging. While the observer is concerned to point out the *merely* local validity of those and hence all standards (thus espousing relativism), the internalist might want to suggest, with Habermas, that some of those standards are privileged and should command universal assent, or, more modestly, might want to point out that disparaging talk about the limit of their validity is pointless because, *ex hypothesi*, we can give no content to the contrasting notion of a standard whose validity is *not* limited. For all standards, by hypothesis, are internal, all of which, on the externalist's view, have only local validity.

The externalist's point of view would imply that all forms of life and the standards derived therefrom are conventional in the sense of being of only local validity, and hence that each as a whole is immune to nonarbitrary critique (since all critique will be in terms of standards drawn from a merely conventional form of life). This position is one horn of what I describe in the last chapter as a false dilemma. The other horn is Habermas's contention that some standards are of universal scope, and that reasoning in terms of them is legislative for all rational discourse. If we think of Gadamer's position as the claim that *all* thinking is done in terms of prejudgments or prejudices, and hence that the idea of a non-*vorurteilenden* thinking is incoherent, making it incoherent to speak of prejudice based thinking *as such* as irrational or of *invidiously* local validity, then we can identify Gadamerian hermeneutics with the second, more modest, internalist response mentioned above. This angle of vision allows us to take issue with the externalist's claim that standards of rationality can have only local validity, if "local" is intended invidiously. For nothing could be nonlocal except from God's vantage point. *Hence it makes sense only from such a vantage point to speak invidiously of local standards of rationality*; the aperspectival is the measure of perspectivism. That is, it is only from that peculiar absence of perspective that is God's "point of view" that the term 'local' would do any work when applied to standards of rationality *qua* standards of rationality (though it may, of course, be usefully employed to refer to particular standards of rationality for particular reasons). Accordingly, to say that all of our standards are local is to say no more and no less than that we are finite.

Why should the view sketched above not be considered a species of relativism? If the "anything goes" form of relativism is untenable because the observer who understands also judges, to what extent can the contextual account of rationality just adumbrated be understood as a kind of relativism? If the account is correct, we can understand the notion of a *subjective* view of reality to have sense. For we can contrast such a view with the view that the best available or potentially available practices of our culture lead us to hold. But we cannot cash in on the contrast term in comparison with which the view commended by our ideally realized actual and potential cultural practices can be labeled nonobjective, especially if, for us, God is dead. The idea of relativism, be it cognitive or moral, would only occur to one still haunted by the spectre of acontextual principles of rationality.

In its search for a language that effaces itself as language, the aesthetic project of the external observer is fraught with internal contradictions. For to make sense of anything requires that it be assimilated to a framework or scheme. This will, at the very least, entail applying a rule for classification; such rule-governed activity will be, in principle, public in nature. Such an activity will, in principle, require an ego and an alter. One person alone cannot objectify the world; one can do so only as a participant. For example, is it not precisely because of shared rules for the application of terms that one can even purport to *describe* the relativity of the various forms of life? The "deconstruction" of the inner/outer distinction can be realized through noting that the so-called outer perspective is, to the observer, no less an inner perspective than is the so-called inner perspective to the participant. That is, the observer *participates* in the "outer" perspective. (The fact/value and the data/theory dichotomies tumble down along with the distinction here at issue. What the observer observes is theory-laden.) So there is, perhaps, no non-question-begging reason that the participant should take her perspective any less *seriously* than does the observer. These considerations relativize the inner/outer distinction, and turn it back on the emotivists, postmoderns and ironists (unless they can successfully manage to take *nothing* seriously).

So the participant/observer distinction must be relativized. And even when taken seriously as relativized, we shall see presently that it still cannot be used to legislate *a priori* in a way that relativists will find useful.

To construe it as a relative distinction is to construe it as a distinction between, on the one hand, approaching a given form of life from the point of view of those who take it seriously and who, to some extent, derive their identity from it, and, on the other hand, approaching it from the point of view of participants from another form of life who neither take the given form of life seriously, nor find their identity informed by it. Those who follow the latter course are observers with respect to the first point of view, while they are participants with respect to the second, and, often but not always, the situation is symmetrical, in that participants with regard to the first viewpoint can be observers with regard to the second. We should not overlook the fact that one can also, of course, adopt the attitude of the observer towards aspects of one's own culture (criticisms of one's own practices demands as much). And, it is important to note, one may even adopt this attitude towards the very practices in which one is engaged. That is, one can participate *disingenuously*. One can be oriented by a pattern of meaning without being invested in it, for instance, while having a critical, cynical or ironic attitude towards it (see Note 54 of the preceding chapter). Such a situation might typically arise for instrumental or strategic reasons.

The distinction comes down to one between an unreflective relation to language games and a reflective awareness of the historicity of language games, including one's own. The tendency to absolutize the observer/participant distinction is isomorphic to the absolutizing of the reality/appearance distinction. The general detranscendentalizing temper of much of recent philosophy suggests that there is only a relative distinction in the latter case, one between what is stated in statements that would pass our best adjudicative tests, and what is stated in statements that would not, that is, a distinction between what is real and what is not *from our point of view, for us.*[28] That is to say that such a temper grants priority to the internal participant's point of view. The idea of an observer's point of view in the absolute sense is at best a regulative fiction.

Granting and, indeed, embracing the idea that all rationality is contextual, many have held that the only proper criteria for appraising a form of life are those drawn from *within* it, so that all non-question-begging criticisms will be internal or immanent criticisms. The inside/outside distinction invoked within this way of putting it is often used by relativists to settle the matter of what can be legitimately criticized and what cannot, arguing that the practices indigenous to a form of life can be rationally judged only in terms of standards internal to it, and that there can be no non-question-begging external judgments of the form of life as a whole. Even if, for the sake of discussion, we accept this restriction, we must face the problem of the *application* of this principle, the problem of identifying the relevant whole outside of which critical judgments are inevitably arbitrary and question-begging.

In what follows I shall argue that the celebrated distinction between reasoning internal to a form of life and reasoning that is external to such a life-world does not settle the issue as to whether a *given* form of life can be rationally evaluated as a whole, and thus that it will remain an open question in many cases whether a "totalizing" critique has overstepped its bounds. Few would disagree that, from *within* a form of life, we can make sense of a distinction between rationally based beliefs and what we just *happen* to believe, or between argumentative persuasion and power. But many would charge that, since there are no neutral standpoints for assessing rationality outside a given form of life, we cannot, in a non-question-begging way, assess a form of life as a whole from the outside. That is, we cannot mount a nonarbitrary critique *of* a form of life, as opposed to a critique from *within* a form of life. The metaphor of inside/outside upon which such a claim is based is seductive, perhaps too much so. For, in general, there will not obtain a "natural" boundary line such that the inside/outside distinction will have a univocal application. Forms of life are often nested or embedded within each other in such a way that what is external to one level is internal to another. Therefore it will be difficult to apply the distinction in practice, for one cannot, in general and in a nondisputable way, set the boundary line that separates the inner from the outer. One might think here of, for example, an ancient Greek city-state where there are more or less explicit norms enjoining persons to tell the whole truth. Imagine this city-state to be located on the Aegean, so that trade with its neighbors becomes an increasingly important element of its economic life. Given an increasing dependence upon barter, prudence might well dictate a relaxing of the commitment to tell the whole truth.[29] The point here is that, given that the form of life represented by the norms for truth-telling is embedded in a wider economic form of life, there is a standpoint internal to that wider form of life from which the former can be assessed as a whole.

Furthermore, whenever cultures interact over a period of time (which, thanks to modern technology and the electronic media, has always already occurred), it becomes very difficult to draw the boundary line separating them in such a way that one can indicate with precision and in a nondisputable way just what is internal and external relative to one of those cultures. Rather than a sharp dividing line here, we have what I would call a "zone of indeterminacy." Gadamer speaks here of a fusion of horizons where forms of life interpenetrate.[30] The inner/outer metaphor has an unproblematic application, in general, only in those contrary-to-fact instances of completely self-enclosed language games or forms of life.

Moreover, there are various levels of abstraction at which a given form of life can be described. As a consequence, what might be argued to be outside at one level of analysis may be understood to be inside at a more abstract level, thus permitting immanent critique. One can think of features that serve to constitute or to enframe a form of life or culture as formal features, where 'formal' refers to the most abstract constitutive structures of a culture, to the most abstract or general features of its self-constitution. A principle of equality might be one such feature in the case of modern democracies. Specific embodiments of such a principle can always be criticized in its name. Such formal features may be, like the principle of equality, explicit components of a culture's ideal self-image, but they need not be. Habermas's Piagetian notion of decentration, referring as it does to the differentiation of world concepts, their reflective employment, and the differentiation of validity claims, attitudes and forms of argumentation corresponding to them, is another sort of formal claim about the nature of modernity. Habermas's claims about what makes modernity what it is purport to offer a more comprehensive or general account of modernity than does, say, Weber's notion of modern rationality as purposive-rationality. And, on the basis of Habermas's claims, assuming they could be made good, a critique of the hegemony of purposive rationality could be mounted, even though, *pace* Habermas, it would not mean that his notion of rationality would be any the less just *our* rationality. In sum, even though the inside/outside distinction has its point as an analytic device, it often cannot, in a given case, be applied in a nondisputable manner, so it cannot, in a nondisputable way, demarcate the line on one side of which one can make sense of rational argumentation and on the other side of which one cannot.[31]

I have been making a case for the phenomenological priority of the participant's standpoint by pointing out that attempts to provide a "clean," antiseptically disingenuous account of a form of life are ineluctably "sullied" by the inescapability of taken-for-granted conventions of description, canons of rationality, criteria of significance and of sameness and difference, and so on. Like the search for a language that effaces itself as a language, the attempt to occupy the pure standpoint of the observer, where no unexamined directives for seeing things this way or that are taken for granted, must end in failure.

There is an analogy between skepticism in epistemology and nihilism in ethics. It is only against the backdrop of a *demand* for foundations that the failure to find them leads to skepticism or nihilism. Just as in nonfoundationalist epistemology we are warranted to assert a belief acquired through a reliable process, in the practical realm we may be warranted to act in accordance with norms as long as the consensus they express is in good order, for instance, as long as we can find ourselves in it or it seems to reflect a general interest, and, of course, as long as there is a consensus in the first place.

If, in the sense indicated above, the local is all we can hope for, then we should exhort ourselves to get on with the business of judging, evaluating, criticizing and so on, keeping our standards flexible and open to revision as our experience requires. Much as our acknowledging that we are always in the wrong before God would not, for the minister of Kierkegaard's *Either/Or*, be a reason for inaction, but would, on the contrary, free us to act, the acknowledgment of our irreparable finitude should not be cause for despair and paralysis. We, as moderns, being self-consciously aware of alternative points of view on rationality and morality, are peculiarly anxious over the question of a measure that would grant us self-assurance regarding our standpoint. Anxiety over the question of a reassuring measure is a form of cultural neurosis born of the loss of certainty. Once the veil has been lifted, and we are no longer able to take the "old tablets" at face value, Hegel's comments about the *aporias* of the epistemological project take on a peculiar resonance. In his critique of Kant, Hegel pointed out that we cannot assure ourselves of our standards for knowledge *before* we begin to know (for the examination that such an assurance would require would *itself presuppose* criteria). We have to just jump into the water, and start knowing. In the *course of our experience*, the standards will change, as will our judgments that are informed by those criteria.

We can read both Habermas and certain dominant strains of poststructuralism as victims of the anxiety I refer to above, Habermas because of his concern to establish *foundations* in order to fend off relativistic assaults, and poststructuralists because they have such a *demanding* sense of objective criteria, and so find all standards wanting, that is, merely local, and give up on objectivity altogether.

But, we may ask: Does the critique of what I would call philosophical nihilism presented in this section fully address the problem of nihilism? What can be the meaning of the exhortation to surmount our anxiety (and the *philosophical* problem of nihilism), given the lack of moral consensus which we face as moderns, and the consequent uncertainty we suffer over just *which* of the competing paradigms made available to us by our tradition ought to be accorded our allegiance? It is the absence of a moral consensus within our tradition that is perhaps fundamentally what holds out the threat of nihilism, more than the more artificial contrivance of philosophical nihilism.[32] How, for example, should we think about affirmative action, abortion, *in vitro* fertilization and so on? These concerns would render the solution to nihilism a practical rather than a philosophical task, the task of founding new forms of community.

So, even if we give up the project of seeking the stamp of approval from the "view from nowhere," we still need to adjudicate somehow the competing claims made from *within* our social and historical milieu. In the absence of credible means of performing such an adjudication, the undecidability associated with the values-perspective would be reinscribed within our (post)modern context. Quite apart, then, from the fact of the consonance of technological rationality (as a form of the will to power) and the values-perspective is the fact that this reinscription of the values-perspective would offer us precious little in the way of resources for criticizing technology or anything else of fundamental concern. A perhaps ironic consequence of the idea of tradition-constituted standards of rationality is that it seems to be a mark of our modernity that our standards of problem resolution are such that many if not most of our key questions cannot be settled rationally. And this is why a sense of community is so urgent for us now. But the question for us, given *our* standards of rationality, is, On what basis can such a community be established? What criteria would guide us in this task? And further, what is the potential of the *sittliche* account of rationality discussed in this section for allowing us to make sense of a notion of *critical* reflection that will do justice to the question, Is our community what it *ought* to be? These questions will be addressed in the next section of this chapter.

II

Poststructuralism, noncognitivism, pragmatism and the like are correct to say that there are no transcendental guarantees. The truth of this claim, however, does not render incoherent the idea of a nonarbitrary *critical* response to tradition. In pursuing this idea, I briefly consider here some of Rorty's recent remarks on community and solidarity, and I close this section with some critical remarks on the usefulness of the attempts of Habermas, Lovibond and MacIntyre to salvage a notion of rational critique, given their common acknowledgment of the historicity of our understanding.

Many who, like Richard Rorty, would probably accept the immanentist account of rationality outlined in the last section, and who would thus not consider themselves relativists in at least one widely accepted sense of the term, might nevertheless be skeptical of a notion of critical rationality empowered to call into question, in a non-question-begging way, the set of social practices in which we are implicated. I alluded earlier to a false dichotomy between pure objectivism and total relativism. I spoke of a situation where our alternatives are limited *either* to there being available a notion of rationality which can be fully justified, in terms of which competing notions drawn from the plurality of forms of life can be critically evaluated, *or* to our being forced to admit that all such standards are simply conventional through and through, and hence that each is refractory to nonarbitrary critique. I suggested that there is a tendency for Habermas's critical theory to choose one horn of this false dilemma. The pragmatism of Rorty, too, seems to assume that our options are limited to the two just mentioned. As a consequence, in order to avoid what he takes to be the untenable Habermasian quest for universally valid rules that are legislative for conversations about social life, Rorty tends to embrace the view that any coherent set of social practices is just a convention, just a language game that stands in need of no further justification (assuming that it is reasonably competitive in getting its adherents what they want).

I have offered reasons to doubt that Habermas's hoped for demonstration will be forthcoming. On the other hand, it does not seem satisfactory to adopt the pragmatist approach with its inability to do justice to the plausibility of critique. Rorty seems too complacent about the value of "our" Western liberal-democratic tradition. His notion of who "we" are is doubly problematic: first, it is not at all clear that the descriptor 'Western liberal intellectual' captures the enlightened self-understanding of all members of our polity; secondly, even if it did, Rorty's "we" has a *normative* function, and therefore cries out for some sort of justification. Given the importance that he gives to what he refers to as "our purposes," it becomes natural to ask, What's so great about *us*? It is not clear that the voices that would pose such a question could be taken seriously in the conversation that Rorty has begun. However, as I have suggested, the positions represented by Habermas and Rorty are not our only options, for between the extremes of holding reasons (for or against our form of life) to be conclusive and holding them to be irrelevant is a third position, where reasons are held to be relevant but not conclusive. Exploiting this third position makes it possible to retain much of the *critical* import of Habermas's work, while acknowledging the trenchant critiques, provided by Gadamer and Rorty, of his universalizing tendencies.

This way of putting our contemporary intellectual predicament suggests to me the fruitfulness of a response to it that invokes a form/content distinction. We can agree, with pragmatism and perhaps against Habermas, that the content of any form of life or language game is conventional and contingent, that all language games are objectively nonnecessary. But there are two plausible responses to this insight that there are no necessary language games. One, that of Rorty's pragmatist, is, "So *why not* the game that I happen to be playing?" If God is dead then everything is permitted. The other is, "So *why* this game that I am playing?" The latter response calls upon us to engage in justification and reason giving, to be compelled to make good the claim that the way we see things accords with the "good life." The motivation to embrace one response over the other is, I believe, largely rooted in the extrarational exigencies of present-day intellectual life. Those thinkers who adopt what I call the values-standpoint— the aesthetic reflective standpoint of the observer—can, through ironic distance, make a project of refusing to take seriously any validity claim in such a way as to render themselves immune to critique. Such thinkers cannot, of course, *argue* for their positions without the intellectual penalties of pragmatic self-contradiction or self-referential paradox. On the other hand, the thinker who takes claims to validity seriously has not foreclosed the possibility of rationally motivated critique oriented to intersubjective assent.

So the insight into the conventional nature of language games does not imply that we must surrender the notion of a formal space or dimension of experience within which we are encouraged to be unsettled about our perspectives—a dimension that would remain closed were we to focus exclusively upon the contingency of language games, without seriously asking: Might we be playing the "wrong" game? This space, wherein we may appeal to certain criterial properties of the "good life" even though we are unable to provide an explicit picture of it, would call us out of the language game that we happen to be playing without it being just another language game.[33] It would rather be a *virtual space* of alternative ways of seeing things, an outside that would allow us to think the possibility of taking our perspectives to task.[34] It would keep us open to taking seriously the conjecture that there is a disjunction between our own, admittedly contingent, ethical standpoint and the regulative ideal of the "good life," an ideal which is presupposed and anticipated in our reason-giving. Accordingly, I would argue that we can plausibly retain the ethical or moral *attitude* even while acknowledging the conventional nature of its *content*, and that, by stressing the tension between attitude and content, we need not give in to the tragic irony attendant upon the "all we've got are language games" view and its tendency to promote the notion that all such games are equally valid (or invalid).

Furthermore, even if we are reminded that what counts as the "better argument" is determined by context or tradition, we can still claim that, within any given regime of discourse or form of life, there is applicable a meaningful distinction between power and argumentative persuasion. And if a poststructuralist thinker like Foucault wants to claim that all discursive practices are inscribed in power and, at the same time, wishes to make meaningful *critical* claims about the embeddedness of regimes of discourse and practice in sites of power, then there must be presupposed a distinction between normatively acceptable power formations and those that are normatively unacceptable.[35] But *this* presupposed distinction has the status of what Foucault's genealogy would deconstruct, for such a distinction would inform a criterion that, like all criteria for him, is complicit with power. As Habermas suggests:

> [Foucault] contrasts his critique of power with the 'analysis of truth' in such a fashion that the former becomes deprived of the normative yardsticks that it would have to borrow from the latter. Perhaps the force of this contradiction caught up with Foucault, . . . drawing him again into the circle of the philosophical discourse of modernity which he thought he could explode.[36]

My suggestion is that we can reasonably understand the nonnecessity of language games as a *reason* to place a burden of justification on those who are implicated in a particular one. Sabina Lovibond, with her notion of moral complicity, puts well what I wish to urge here:

> It is our recognition of this fact, i.e., of the transience and replaceability of language-games, which confers upon our participation in the prevailing game a moral dimension that it did not previously possess. By acknowledging that we could do something other than what we actually do, we acknowledge the openness of our actual practice to a form of critical scrutiny which we could not previously have seen to be applicable to it. . . . [N]othing constrains our choice of how to live or what linguistic systems to maintain in use; and to those who recognize this, their participation in any existing way of life will henceforward appear under the aspect of moral *complicity*.[37]

The very fact that there are two possible attitudes to have towards one's practices—the accepting, "Why not?" and the questioning, "Why?"—once one has achieved a reflective awareness of the latter's historicity, *by itself* implies that one's relationship to those practices is of moral moment because it is a matter of choice. There is, then, the second-order moral issue of the choice between the two attitudes, as well as the first-order issue of rendering a critical judgment if one has adopted the moral attitude. Lovibond tries to make coherent the notion of a rational commitment to an avowedly contingent form of life from within what I have called the moral attitude.[38] I shall presently return to this and to a discussion of the criteria that enable such a commitment.

So the question, Am I playing the right game? is not only not incoherent, it is also quite natural. Accordingly, there is still room, the postmodernists notwithstanding, for the virtual space wherein we accept the burden of reason-giving, not only reasons drawn *from* our form of life but also reasons *for* (or against) our form of life. The context-boundedness of standards and norms does not prevent us from throwing our forms of life into question. The time has now perhaps come for an account of that virtual space in which such reason-giving takes its place.

Thomas McCarthy makes the rather bold claim that our practices of justification commit us to claims about the unconditionedness of our knowledge, despite the context-bound conditions of its generation.[39] Though all warranted claims to truth are made from within the context of some local adjudicative practice or other, we claim, fallibilistically, that our claims will withstand the rigors of *any* such practice or context. The claim to unconditionedness or to transcultural status allows us to use the idea of truth in a critical way to call such claims into question. As such, the notions of reason and truth serve as ideas with reference to which we can criticize the standards handed down to us, and, further, the notions of reason and truth cannot be reduced to any particular set of standards or warrants.[40] In other words, a warrantedly assertible vocabulary is not necessarily an ultimate or a most adequate vocabulary, though we may think so at a given time, and we know the difference. It is in this sense that truth cannot be reduced to any particular set of standards or warrants.

There are two observations that I would like to make about this briefly delineated account. They both have to do with what it does and does not provide. First, it does not provide a substantive account of transcultural notions of either truth or reason. It should rather be understood to invoke what I have called dimensions of experience which, like the concept of the "good life," are given substantive content through a *phronesis*-like application to particular contexts. Hence, in this sense, the meaning of such "transcendent" notions will be shaped to some degree by the context of their reception. Still, as I have noted, even such contextually fashioned notions can retain critical force. Even if 'true' means 'corresponds with scripture,' for example, or perhaps, better, even if the criterion of truth is such correspondence, one can still give priority to a demonstration of correspondence over coerced consensus, and one can, in the name of correspondence, criticize other claims to correspondence. Secondly, since it is a matter of some dispute whether the meaning of truth is historically contingent, the account cannot be understood necessarily to be legislative for *all* justificatory practices. That is, it is not indisputable that all cultures engaged in such practices make the claim to the *transcultural* status of what those practices warrant, although they do make a claim to its unconditioned status within a context or regime determined by the standards of reason and truth that they accept. Rather, what McCarthy provides is an insightful phenomenological description of *our* adjudicative practices, of what *we* intend or take ourselves to be doing when engaging in justificatory behavior. What is peculiar about us moderns is that our forms of justification are attempts to construct arguments that confer upon fallible claims an unconditioned, transcultural status. Perhaps it is only true for us that to say "*x* is true" means that we are warranted to assert that *anyone* would be warranted to assert *x*.

There *are* nonetheless some *general* phenomenological observations that can be made with regard to the rationality of justificatory practices. And the cogency of such observations does not depend upon our appealing to anything beyond the standards of rationality and/or the central vocabulary of a particular group. Rather, it depends simply upon our recognition that we can sometimes be brought to see that practices of justification that we may have heretofore relied upon may be arbitrary, to see that such practices may be untrustworthy. And there is no reason to think that others cannot be brought to see this as well. To *convince* someone of the arbitrariness of their practices of justification is *ipso facto* to provide them with a motivation to show some interest in the matter, is to provide them with a *reason* to consider alternatives.[41] I refer here to justificatory practices as being arbitrary in the sense that they turn out not to be truth-tracking or truth-sensitive in the way that members of a given community thought they were, where 'true' is to be understood to mean 'true within a given language.' By this I mean that there are cases where persons can be brought to see that there is no *intelligible* (to them) connection between, on the one hand, the reasonableness of their holding a particular claim or holding it to be true, and, on the other hand, the outcome of what they take to be procedures for evaluating it and other such claims. For they might be brought to see that those procedures are "loaded" in such a way that their outcome is prejudiced. By "loaded," I mean that the procedures, because of a flaw in their design, may yield an outcome that would support (or disconfirm) a claim even if the claim were false (or true), a flaw that could be detected and assessed from *within* the purview of the standards of rationality and/or central vocabulary of the group in question. This is a case where the outcome of a justificatory procedure will have been *exposed* as an artifact of the procedure and not of the procedure's truth-tracking sensitivity, and is therefore not to be taken as a reflection of the truth or falsity of what the claim asserts.

This is the sort of thing that can occur for us when an experimental design in the sciences is criticized. We assume that the experimental design itself, that is, independent of the hypothesized natural mechanism for which it is to serve as evidence, is indifferent or neutral with respect to its outcome, which outcome is taken to confirm or disconfirm a particular hypothetical claim. This supposition warrants our belief that the outcome will be sensitive to and only to whether or not the hypothetical claim is *true*. If it can be shown that there is a flaw inherent in the design, for example, that a relevant independent variable was not taken into account, a flaw that would predispose the apparatus to yield one verdict or the other independently of whether or not the hypothesized natural mechanism is operative, then we are entitled to say that the hypothetical claim was only *apparently* confirmed (or disconfirmed), even if *everyone* took it to have been *genuinely* confirmed (or disconfirmed). The experimental result did not *truly* reflect the presence (or absence) of a putative natural phenomenon or mechanism. For a simple, and simplified, example, consider the case of Aristarchus, the third-century BC Greek astronomer, who is reputed to have claimed that the earth revolved about the sun. Were this true, an apparent motion of the stars, called stellar parallax, should have been observed. None was, and the claim was taken to have been defeated. But this adjudicative procedure falsely presumed that the nearest stars were close enough for parallax to be observed. In other words, whether the earth revolved or not, this procedure, coupled with its assumptions, would yield a negative result. And we are entitled to say that the belief that the earth does not revolve about the sun, even if *universally* held by Aristarchus' contemporaries, was, *ceteris paribus*, false for them. (It should be noted that this line of argument implies, *pace* Rorty, that one does not have to be a Platonist in order to take the appearance/reality distinction seriously.)

And when a similar charge is brought against us, that is, the charge that our practices lack credibility, it will not automatically be merely a matter that can be shrugged off as a case of pitting someone else's vocabulary against ours, as is Rorty's wont, but, rather, a matter in which we, if we are at all cognitively serious, must take an interest. This is because there is implicit in the allegiance to justificatory practices the predisposition to believe that there *is* such an intelligible connection—that there is a rationally reconstructible relationship between the warranted assertion of a claim and the outcome of an assessment of that claim— or at least not to believe that there is not such a connection. Otherwise, why bother to engage in such practices?[42] That is to say that such intelligibility has, if you will, for "us" and for "them," the quiet force of a regulative ideal.

Let us speak more specifically about how this discussion should and should not inform an account of us moderns. What we take to be reasonable to believe is what passes our adjudicative tests. We believe that there is nothing about those tests that prejudices their ability to detect truth. Evidence to the contrary would lead us to repair those tests. That is, we believe there is an intelligible connection between our adjudicative practices and the trustworthiness of the verdicts that they warrant. McCarthy would claim that it follows that what those tests certify as true we believe to be unconditionally true. However, given the plausibility of the "nonconvergence" thesis, which recognizes the nonconvergent variability of categorial frameworks, and of the "underdetermination" thesis, which emphasizes the underdetermination of theory by data, this claim, even when understood as a particular phenomenological claim about us, should, perhaps, be further qualified. Perhaps the most that we are entitled to claim is that we are justified in believing that our truth claims will always be members of the set of claims that can be understood to be warrantedly assertible, given the categorial framework within which they are articulated.

At any rate, contextualists like Rorty, suspicious of appeals to the transcultural and the transcendent, or to the critical force of the ideas of truth or reason, might reply that they too can provide an account of the critique of ongoing practice, and that such an account need make no such appeal. If so, then a standard criticism of Rorty's pragmatism, namely, that it does not in any way countenance the critique of our practices, is misplaced. And indeed, as I hope to show, the problems in Rorty's position lie at another level of analysis.

Implicitly working with the metaphor of our language games and nondiscursive practices as tools for the realization of our basic values and purposes, Rorty could answer the challenge to provide an account of critique in a disarmingly simple way by pointing to the desideratum that our tools get us what we want, that they work. It is their failure to do so that motivates critical strategies of repair and/or replacement. He suggests that "the revolutionary [is] protesting in the name of the society itself against those aspects of the society which are unfaithful to its own self-image."[43] If, however, social institutions *are* working in this sense, then there is nothing much else to say. As Rorty puts it, ". . . the pragmatist cannot answer the question 'What is so special about Europe?' save by saying 'Do you have anything non-European to suggest which meets *our* European purposes better?'"[44]

But now the question becomes: What about the peculiar normative status that "our purposes" enjoys? Rorty's pragmatism perhaps countenances a critical transcendence of our language games and practices, but not of our purposes and not of "us."[45] What, if anything, prevents his being obliged to regard questions of the sort, Do we want what we ought to want? or, Are our purposes good ones? as straightforward category mistakes? Here is where the problems in Rorty's account lie. It is our philosophical impotence in the face of the "we" and its purposes that must give us pause.

So, in the last analysis, Rorty *does* subscribe to what I called earlier the "why not our practices and purposes?" school of thought. In what follows I should like, first, to suggest why we should not accept this *philosophical* position without qualification and, secondly, in light of that discussion, to raise questions about Rorty's move to deflect philosophical questions by his articulation of his *political* commitments, where the latter are expressed in the final vocabulary of liberalism.

Rorty is explicit about his opposition to the project of assessing the rationality of a language game as a whole, and suggests that, if we follow him along his pragmatist-historicist lines, it indeed becomes "impossible to ask the question 'Is ours a moral society?'"[46] Again, he would view the question as something of a category mistake. He bolsters his position by claiming that there is nothing "which stands to my community as my community stands to me, some larger community called 'humanity'."[47] Now, clearly there can be and often are larger communities which stand to our communities as our communities stand to us, larger communities or federations of communities to which ours belong. And, just as clearly, with respect to those larger communities a particular component community can be viewed as immoral, or as acting at cross-purposes to the larger whole. These considerations allow us to provide the following gloss of the question, 'Is ours a moral society?' It could be understood to mean, 'Are the self-image of our community and what it most deeply values consistent with the self-image and values of the inclusive wholes in which our community and its welfare are implicated?' Think of the Southern states of the U.S. prior to and during the Civil War. Not that I endorse without qualification this quasi-systems-theoretic approach, but, as I suggested earlier, such cases of nested forms of life provide instances of our being able to assess a community or language game as a whole, even our own, without violating internalist principles. Rorty seems to have too hermetic a notion of "our society."

Moreover, in line with this, we should not lose sight of the possibility that our purposes—what provides our identity for Rorty—can themselves be redescribed, relativized and expanded as a result of encounters with other societies, whether we are implicated in those societies or not. The "we," in the sense of a community held together by shared purposes, is capable of redescription, redescriptions suggested by other "we"s, other "we"s with whom we come into contact who offer not only alternative means to our ends but also redescriptions of our ends themselves. Of course judgment will always be required to distinguish between a *redescribed* end and a *different* end, though our ability to *recognize* an end as something with which we can identify will play an important role in making the distinction. As elsewhere, judgments of sameness and difference will depend upon both the altitude and the attitude from which a value is described. But the recognition of the fact that there are no *a priori* limits to the redescription of ends, that there is no *a priori* established line demarcating what is internal to a self-description versus what is external to a self-description, suggests that mutually recognized descriptions or self-images resulting from a "fusion of horizons" attest to the possibility of a contingently expandable sense of the "we." For example, liberals may find that their commitment to individual freedom can, from another angle of vision, be redescribed as a commitment to the idea of a self that is only contingently related to its community. The sense of what it is to be committed to liberalism will doubtlessly shift upon encountering a description of liberalism from within the horizon, say, of communitarianism or of Marxism.

Furthermore, there is no reason to think that we cannot actually *change* in certain ways without losing our identity in the process of such a fusion. Again, it will be a matter of judgment what counts as change and what counts as having lost identity. However, it makes sense to conceive of identity as a sort of cluster concept, in that few, if any, basic beliefs or professions of value, taken singly, are essential to an identity, although a large portion of such beliefs or professions of value must be maintained if a community is to retain its identity. So our identities need not be construed as being identical to our prevailing purposes. For example, the conception of equality associated with classical liberalism may prove too narrow for the final vocabulary that is to express the self-image of liberals who take seriously, say, the communitarian challenge. Or we may find liberalism itself too narrow a categorial scheme for an ultimate vocabulary that is to do justice to what we might come to recognize as criterial properties of the "good life."

What these remarks suggest to me is the possibility of an *historicist* notion of humanity as an unfinished project, as the result of historical negotiation. Here it is inviting to reinvoke the notion of a virtual space wherein we can be unsettled about our perspectives. One could say that Rorty's pragmatism does not give the possibility that such a space affords its due, the possibility of our assuming the burden of being unsettled about who we are, about how we represent ourselves to ourselves, about our self-image. This is the space of a virtual or ideal "we," of a regulative ideal that relativizes our own purposes. This allows us to appeal in a nonprovincial way, in a way not limited to the "we-intentions" of a particular group, to the human as a standard, to an achieved but revisable consensus, to a standard that is non-*aprioristic* and that is historically contingent.

The fusion of horizons, as understood here, is the product of a process that can be analyzed in the following way. The encounter with alien horizons can issue in an appreciation for another way of being human and for how our way appears from that perspective. It can perhaps issue in the forging of a common language, a language that is neither just "ours" nor just "theirs."[48] It is in terms of such a language that we can locate and triangulate each other's position in the space of human possibilities. Such an encounter, then, can give us a lively sense of alternatives, providing for us an expansion of the space of human possibilities, and can allow us as well to see the contours of our own perspective. The virtual space of the ideal "we" is, then, given content in such a hermeneutic encounter. But, we must also choose which possibilities to actualize, and that choice will be made in light of standards, that is, in light of criterial properties of the "good life" as we, by appealing to the "best" in us, see it. Such standards are historical products; so the hermeneutic encounter will allow for comparative evaluations of the newly revealed human possibilities in terms of tentatively consolidated but revisable standards. And the criterial properties of the "good life" may be altered for us in a number of ways as a result of such an encounter. The new culture may highlight features of the good life that may have been forgotten, marginalized or perhaps even never acknowledged by us. So both our vision of human possibilities and the standards for evaluating them get expanded. The "yet to come" of humanity as an unfinished project will then include both versions and criteria of the good life. Rorty's (and, for that matter, postmodernism's) distrust of such an appeal to the human arises from his understandable skepticism towards *essentialist* notions of humanity. But he errs in assuming that such essentialist notions are the only ones.[49]

Rorty tends to deflect criticism of the sort that I have been making, criticism departing from the questions, "What's so great about us?" or "What is so special about Europe?," by pointing to a particular "we," namely, the "we" with whom he identifies, the liberal "we." The liberal community is defined contrastively by, and owes its identity to, its allegiance to individual freedom as a central or core value. The peculiar nature of the liberal "we" is that it charges itself to constantly expand its sense of *us*.[50] By dedicating itself to inclusiveness, such a community fends off the charge that it is invidiously ethnocentric. Now, by Rorty's own lights, liberalism can justify itself only circularly, only to those who, like Rorty, value tolerance and other cosmopolitan virtues, to those who, like Rorty, believe that cruelty is the worst thing that we can do. An encomium to liberalism will be persuasive only to those who are, in a sense, already convinced. While denying the cogency of a purely rational defense of liberalism as a whole, Rorty attempts to remove the sting from this denial by claiming that liberalism is such that radical critique is unnecessary. He believes that the ideally liberal society is one in which the difference between the revolutionary and the reformer is canceled out.[51] I want presently to challenge this claim, but first I want to make more explicit what Rorty means by liberalism's demand for inclusiveness.

Though the liberal "we" is defined contrastively, its definition includes the stipulation that it expand itself by drawing into its ambit others, including those others who do not necessarily share the values of cosmopolitan liberals. The liberal "we" is the "we" that tolerates "them." Rorty suggests that the only way to perform such an expansion is to find particular and local descriptions under which we can see those others as being in the same fix that we are in. As suggested earlier, in part for Sartrean reasons, he is quite explicit in denying that the description, "the human condition," will do.[52] He would probably suggest instead that there may be a network of contrastive "us-descriptions" that can capture everyone, or almost everyone, while none would be *universalistic*. So liberalism's dedication "to enlarging itself, to creating an ever larger and more variegated *ethnos*"[53] is a dedication not to increasing the number of persons who share its "we-intentions," purposes and values (though it may wish to do so as well), but rather to increasing the number and variety of persons who can be seen to fall under descriptions of similarity, whether they share the liberal's fundamental values or not.[54] The core project of liberalism is to discover as many projects that we engage in with others as we can, core or otherwise, as a means of expanding the scope of our sympathy. So it is important to recognize explicitly that the expansion of the liberal "we" is *not* an expansion of the core sense of identity, nor is it a redescription or transformation of it, but it is, rather, the expansion of the set of those whom liberals care about. In this sense, liberalism's core sense of identity remains unchallenged.

Before commenting upon the claims that Rorty makes on behalf of his political commitments, two brief remarks of an immanent nature are in order. First, there is ineliminably affiliated with his view a presumption of universality of the sort that he explicitly eschews. Rorty believes the idea of moral progress to be a useful one and, further, that such progress consists in expanding human solidarity.[55] But if the liberal obligation is to identify with others, even if the only *psychological* means for doing so is to find *local* "us-descriptors," does not the obligation itself presuppose a universalistic commitment, that is, a commitment to the human community as a whole? What else could the obligation to *expand* the "us," no matter how widely our net has been cast, mean? Not only is Rorty making an empirical, hence defeasible, moral *psychological* claim about moral motivation without offering an argument for it (for example, why cannot "s/he is a fellow human being, in the same fix of facing natality, sexuality, and mortality as I," do as a motivation for moral sympathy?). But he, in fact, must presume something like a virtual human community (though not in the form that I have been discussing it). Why should we seek the us-descriptions that embrace others? Is it not because "we liberals" believe that they are "one of us human beings" and, like us, are capable of being humiliated? And is not the localized us-description merely a *device* for effecting the connection with them? The local solidarity of the us-description perhaps makes it easier for some of us to *recognize* fellow humanity. But is it not really *fellow humanity* that is the liberal's regulative ideal?

Further, our feeling the *pull* to widen the sense of the "we" depends upon taking seriously notions that Rorty finds anachronistic. Whence arises the predisposition to look for ways in which others resemble us (one of liberalism's primary self-assignments)? What are the reasons *internal* to the liberal form of life for not remaining content with a particular set of us-identifications? I believe that, *from the inside*, the slogan, "We have obligations to human beings simply as such," cannot be dismissively or skeptically understood as merely a means of reminding ourselves to expand the sense of "us" as far as we can.[56] Perhaps that is all that is "really" going on from the outside, but if anything, from the inside it is the other way around. If what I suggested in the last paragraph is true, the genuine liberal can no more view such a slogan as a *mere* device than she can view her very liberalism in such a way. Perhaps this is one of those junctures where Rorty's irony and his liberalism fail to cohere, much as did Sartre's existentialism with his Marxism.

Rorty regards the notion "human being simply as such" as a *focus imaginarius* that is salutary as long as it is recognized as being invented rather than discovered.[57] His further point is that we can now throw the latter (ladder?) notion away. In short, he wishes to remember without the mnemonic. I suppose that the most succinct way to put the difference between us here is that I think that reliable and sustained openness requires as a regulative ideal what he takes to be the mnemonic. In short, where are the mechanisms that would sustain the liberal self-doubt that he justifiably celebrates, the mechanisms that would keep the doubt in motion? Without such mechanisms, and he claims that we can do without them, his position comes distressingly close to a self-satisfied quietism awaiting the fortuitous appearance of a "stranger" or "poet" to prick its conscience.

I should now like to turn to a brief consideration of Rorty's claims for liberalism, that is, to whether it is the sort of political institution that affords us the luxury of canceling out the difference between the revolutionary and the reformer. It is in part an *empirical* question whether the political institutions embraced by the term 'liberal' can make good on this promise. A full-blown discussion of liberalism is beyond the scope of this study, but there is, of course, a rich and vast critical literature on this topic.[58] Another way of putting Rorty's point is to say that persuasion is all we need. He contrastively defines persuasion by opposing it to force, and takes the force/persuasion distinction to be isomorphic to changing a language game from its outside versus appealing to shared premises within the game. Given what I have said above about nesting, this distinction will, of course, have to be relativized; force from one perspective can be interpreted as persuasion from another (think of the history of the concept of "positive freedom"). The question remains, however, Are the basic premises of liberalism such that persuasion is all we need?

Further, parallel to the force/persuasion distinction for him is the deed/word contrast: the poets and revolutionaries are to "make life harder for others only by words, and not deeds."[59] That Rorty should hold to a strict line of demarcation here is not surprising, given his skepticism towards the usefulness of the notion of "ideology."[60] However, as Habermas and his otherwise arch-opponent, Foucault, would point out, words have not only meaning but also function. Regimes of discourse, language games and so on undergird, facilitate, enable, shape, and are at least partially constitutive of, practices; the words of those in power are deeds.[61] Those who control the "word," who control the terms of public discourse, inordinately influence public policy.

The question for us becomes: How would Rorty *recognize* a fundamental challenge to his liberalism? That is: What would he allow to count *against* the claim that liberalism is all we need, thus rendering it falsifiable? While he would, no doubt, quite correctly point out that, just as in science, there is no *a priori* way of telling whether a challenge can be met by reform or will ultimately call for the abandonment of a paradigm, he nevertheless understands liberalism in such a way that it is difficult to know what it would *mean* for a set of social conditions to require an alternative to it.[62] As Rorty seems to understand it, the rug is constantly pulled out from under the critics of liberalism, for liberalism is just, for him, the set of institutions whose intent is to redress the very grievances that would embarrass it.[63] And so what Rorty means by 'liberalism' is at times described at such a level of generality that it borders upon being vague and indefinite. As 'true' comes to mean for pragmatists 'what is good in the way of belief,' 'liberal' comes to mean 'what is good in the way of politics.' At this level of description, it becomes difficult to assign to the term much in the way of empirical content.[64]

While Rorty *does* address the importance of liberals being unsettled about the way they see things, that is, about who is being humiliated and how, he does not do justice to the issue of being unsettled about liberalism itself, about who "we liberals" are, about the final vocabulary in which "our" core values are expressed. My earlier remarks concerning the redescription and transformation of our purposes are apposite here. And when he suggests that the liberal *ironist* entertains "radical and continuing doubts" because she has been impressed by other final vocabularies, those doubts remain sealed off in such a way that they are not effective in challenging the vocabulary of liberalism (and I should say that this is not entirely a bad thing, given the purposes of the ironist). For the public/private split is invoked to insure that the redescriptions that issue from the ironist's doubt remain consistent with the purposes of liberalism.[65] In fine, assuming the seal between public and private holds, the liberal ironist's doubt does no publicly relevant work.

Perhaps, as I have suggested, the issue of falsifiability arises for Rorty, just as it does in science, because his claims lack sufficient empirical content. That is, perhaps his account of liberalism is not full and detailed enough. For example, when lauding the virtues and the effectiveness of persuasion in a liberal society, he does not confront the social fact of an institutionalized and systematically guaranteed differential access to the *means* of persuasion (although Rorty the man may not be insensitive to this issue, his *account* is). Is our society structured in such a way that we all have equal chances to make moves in our prevailing language game? Or to introduce others? Rorty appeals to the self-corrective features of science as a model for liberalism.[66] But liberalism is a *particular* political paradigm with substantive consequences, and they may be consequences which *structure in* obstacles to the removal of inequities that we all abhor.[67]

There is perhaps another source of Rorty's seeming indifference to the limits of liberalism. We might understand it in terms of some current thinking about the rationality of scientific change, which holds that the rejection of a theory is rational only if that theory fails to solve some of its salient problems and there is available a more successful competitor. Perhaps Rorty's complacency about liberalism derives in part from what he has called his failure of political imagination, from his inability to see beyond liberalism's limits, from his own admitted inability to imagine better goals than reform or better institutions than we have got.[68] The liberal ironist's ethnocentrism is nonfoundational, but her inability to see beyond the limits of what is admittedly not transcendentally guaranteed allows that ethnocentrism to function as if it were so guaranteed, as if it could not call itself and the institutions associated with it into question.[69] So, to return to the original framework in which this section was cast: given the cogency of a nonessentialist notion of humanity (humanity as an unfinished project), Rorty is caught in the false dichotomy of Humanity-cum-Reason *or* the *status quo ante* of a particular "we." He tends, though with some qualification, to opt for the latter.[70] And this tendency conveniently highlights, by contrast, the position on the issue of humanism that I wish to advocate here.

As I announced at its beginning, this chapter is intended as a defense of critical rationalism (as an aspect of the meaningful) against the nihilism of the values-perspective. I have sought to do so while acknowledging the challenge that such a defense must face from historicist insights. In concluding this chapter, I want to pursue the notion of humanity as an unfinished project, albeit in only a provisional way, by way of brief responses to the work of Lovibond, Habermas and MacIntyre.

An important issue remains to be addressed. It concerns the limits to the redescription and change mentioned in my discussion of an historicized notion of humanity. I have already (see p. 122 above) raised the issue of the criteriological considerations that would guide us in responding to the key question posed earlier in this chapter, namely: Are we playing the right game? As features of a framework that would accommodate both of these concerns, I propose the following notions: (1) the virtual "we" of a humanity that is a negotiated, unfinished project functioning as an *ideal* community, a notion that makes a virtue both of being open to and willing to take seriously the conjecture that there is a disjunction between one's own standpoint and the regulative ideal of the "good life," and of being critically respectful of the other; and (2) a Hegelian notion of *self-recognition* functioning as a boundary condition for the conversation wherein the negotiation takes place. Of course, what counts as the proper description of the self is open to contestable interpretation, and, as mentioned earlier, there can be contestable judgments about what counts as a modification of identity as opposed to an abdication of identity. The notion of self-recognition is meant to invoke a dimension of experience where the foregoing questions are pressed. Neither the "good life" nor identity is self-announcing. As an example using Rorty's idiom, consider the Afrikaners' notion of the "we," of their group self-consciousness. Clearly it is one in which black South Africans cannot find themselves. However, if the salient us-description could be renegotiated from an allegiance to apartheid to, say, being concerned with raising and supporting a family and caring for the economy and resources of one's native land, then, to switch idioms, a generalizable interest will have been brought to the fore.

Or, to take another example, consider gendered notions of the "we," in particular those aspects of it having to do with identity as moral agents or with identity insofar as it is informed by moral development. Carol Gilligan has persuasively argued that female moral development seems to be most adequately construed in terms of contextual notions such as those of equity, care and responsibility. By contrast, male development, at least in Western cultures, is often articulated in terms of noncontextual principles of abstract equality and notions of rights.[71] So we can think, on the one hand, of a "we" defined in terms of a concrete ethics of care, where social life is understood to be comprised of fields of concern that are internally related by care and an ethics of responsibility, and where the self is defined through relations with others, and, on the other hand, a "we" that owes its identity to a vocabulary centered around the notion of rights, where social reality is understood to consist of isolated atoms that are only externally related through contracts based upon rights. The notion of humanity as an unfinished, negotiated project would stand in tension with the "ghettoization" of moral identity, implying instead that, for example, notions of care would be appropriate, assuming that they are not already, for men as well as for women, and those of rights, for women as well as men.

That a genuine fusion of horizons is conceivable here, issuing in something new, as opposed to the assimilation of one "we" to another, or to an unmediated moral schizophrenia, is suggested by Ronald Dworkin's reading of "the right to equality." His reading *might* be a key to how we could effect the sublation, the preservation and combination, of the horizons of care and rights, of equity and equality, in such a way that we could see how a discursively achieved general agreement on this matter might look. I have in mind here his understanding of the right to equality, not as the right to equal treatment, but as the right to treatment as an equal, which is the right to be treated with the same concern and respect as anyone else.[72] Treatment of others as equals requires, on his terms, not an abstraction from, but a sensitivity to, the contexts and needs of others. The achievement of such a fusion of horizons would be a step towards the production of the sort of redescription of moral identity that I have in mind.[73]

So the idea of humanity as an unfinished project, or of the virtual "we," provides an orientation for what would otherwise be a directionless alteration of communal self-description, for what would otherwise be what I earlier called an abstract, empty freedom. But the question remains: What sorts of limits or controls prevent a "we," a "we" willing to take its part in the drama of humanity as an unfinished project, from being swept along and swallowed up in the rush to fuse horizons in such a way that it loses its identity or relinquishes what matters to it most? The Hegelian notions of self-recognition and alienation that Sabina Lovibond employs, and the resources for redescription that can be found in Habermas's conception of practical discourse, when the latter is shorn of its foundationalist pretensions, can be brought to bear in a helpful way here. As I pointed out in Chapter Six, though participation in practical discourse may result in the reconceptualization or redescription of what matters most to the parties in question, no one need accept a formulation in which she cannot *recognize* or find herself. So, taking the risk to genuinely raise the questions: Am I playing the right game? and, Are my purposes the right ones? need not entail the risk of losing oneself.

I mentioned earlier Lovibond's attempt to make plausible the idea of a rational commitment to an avowedly contingent form of life. She does so through exploiting a notion of reflective participation that would allow for an integration of the "inner" and "outer" perspectives.[74] She seeks to do justice both to the ironist's external awareness of the contingency of the *content* of a way of life and to the participant's investment in what I have referred to as the moral dimension of experience that is its *form*. She suggests that this can be effected to the extent that we can "find ourselves" in the institutional framework of a particular way of life:

> If we are to accomplish the desired integration, we need to be able to recognize the relevant institutions as an adequate expression of our 'true being', i.e. of the values and beliefs by which we define our identity. For the possibility of doing this can be equated with the possibility of regarding the prevailing form of life as *rational*: which is precisely what we must be able to do, if we are

> coherently to combine a practical commitment to that form of life with a reflective awareness of its replaceability by a different one.[75]

On the other hand, failure to find ourselves in a prevailing form of life, that is, feeling alienated from such a form of life, would be a basis for rational critique. Critique would arise then from the moment of alienation, from within a recognition that prevailing moral discourse may not provide the conceptual means for expressing what we want. We could say, in a way that would challenge the thoroughgoing "linguistic turn" of Rorty, that critique is not always generated in terms of an *existent* community, but rather that it can also seek to *create* a community.[76]

Now, there are, of course, ready objections to this way of putting the matter. Lovibond offers, as a critical standard for rational critique, the notion of our "true being." But what content can *this* notion be given, short of simply being categorized as "deviant," that is independent of the very language game (and its value commitments) under scrutiny, particularly if the culture in question is relatively homogeneous? Are not the desires that we take to be deserving of recognition those that have at some level been socially and culturally sanctioned? A denial here will quickly ensnare us in the problems that Herbert Marcuse had in distinguishing "true" from "false" needs, not that such a distinction cannot be redeemed, but once we acknowledge that needs are socially and historically conditioned, arguments have to be made that culture and history do not go "all the way down." I am suggesting that the notion of our true being or of our true identity may itself have an objectionably parochial content. But here one is entitled to ask, "Parochial from whose point of view, from God's?" I should like to say, "no," but, rather, that it may be parochial from the point of view of the virtual "we" of an historicized humanity. Lovibond seems to be aware of this problem, but it is not clear that her framework has the resources to overcome it. The evidence that she is aware of the issue is a distinction that she draws between having one's perspective determined by a local or empirical parochialism, and its being determined by our "defining situation" as human beings, that is, its being determined by a transcendental parochialism.[77] Through an invocation of a notion of Antonio Gramsci's, she herself speaks of a standard by reference to which what she calls empirical parochialism can be identified. She mentions Gramsci's notion of tying objectivity, as what I would call a regulative ideal, to the idea of the human race being *historically* unified in a single cultural system; this would mean that the struggle for objectivity, the struggle to free oneself from empirical parochialism, is the struggle for the cultural unification of humanity.[78]

Habermas's notion of practical discourse provides much of the conceptual wherewithal to avoid the parochialism that Lovibond rightly decries. To briefly recapitulate, what such discourse involves is a linguistic interpretation and reconceptualization of needs that is constrained by the necessity of self-recognition, and that is oriented towards a generalizable interest. The idea of a generalizable interest, forged through dialogue, is the key to warding off the parochialism to which Lovibond's framework is vulnerable, despite her best intentions. She acknowledges the problem, and seeks to address it through the idea of moral imagination. But, as Habermas suggests against Kant, this would give us access only to the *imaginary* other consistent with such a monological conception, not to the *real* other of the dialogical situation.[79] It is clearly salutary for Lovibond to invoke the notion of moral imagination, for she uses it to highlight what would take place in an ideal speech situation, namely, reconceptualizations that serve emancipative practice and in which one can find what one wants.[80] The problem is just that the idea of moral imagination does not seem to have what it takes to avoid being "locked up into oneself," to invoke the image that Hegel used to describe the plight in which Kantian morality left us. So what I have offered is a "friendly" objection, in that I believe that it contributes to the project for the sake of which Lovibond's distinction between empirical and transcendental parochialism appears to have been designed.

It should be mentioned that MacIntyre, too, offers an account of critical rationality within an historicist or contextualist framework. Though his central idea is quite compelling, we should be circumspect about what he has achieved. His account, while urging that there are no tradition-independent standards of judgment, is put forward, in part, as a response to the relativistic challenge, that is, to the claim that "if there is no rationality as such, then every set of standards has as much and as little claim to our allegiance as any other."[81] He understands the relativist challenge to rest upon a denial that rational debate between, and rational choice among, rival traditions is possible. It seems, therefore, that he construes his account as a response to a position like Rorty's.

For MacIntyre, rationality is to be sought in the way in which tradition-bound inquiry is pursued. He gives an account in terms of what, in Habermas's idiom, would be called learning processes, though for MacIntyre such processes are emphatically not tradition-invariant. They begin with the recognition of a problem from within the purview of a given tradition itself; the development or progress of that tradition is assessed in terms of its success in solving its problems. So we might speak of a learning process with respect to solutions to problems encountered by a particular tradition in accordance with the standards for problem solution of that tradition.

Traditions can not only undergo internal learning processes, but they can also learn from others, that is, they can discover conceptual resources in other cultures which, *by their own standards*, can contribute to the solution of their problems. This allows for an account of the rational critique *of* a tradition, insofar as the participants in a tradition in crisis can be compelled to acknowledge the superior rationality of the alien tradition, assuming that the problems whose solution it makes possible are sufficiently fundamental and central to the tradition in crisis.[82]

I believe this to be a sound account, but we should be clear about what it does and does not do. It has *not* shown that rival traditions can adjudicate disputes about the *standards* of rational justification themselves. A tradition can indeed be defeated by another tradition, but that very defeat, if it is to be considered a *rational* undoing, must be acknowledged in terms of the defeated tradition's own account and practices of rational justification (the moment of the "for us" is ineliminable). Since defeat is understood in terms of the standards and practices of a given tradition, the practices of rational justification themselves cannot be defeated in the same way. While it is true that standards of rationality can be construed as truth claims, it remains the case that it is only against their backdrop that success or failure at problem-solving can be assessed. The caveat that I have presented here is necessary because MacIntyre fails to distinguish consistently between the conceptual resources and claims of a tradition, on the one hand, and the standards of rationality that are both constituted by, and constitutive of, traditions, on the other.

This notwithstanding, MacIntyre attempts to undermine the relativist by arguing that there is no standpoint from which her challenge can be issued.[83] He suggests that the strongest case can be made for relativism in the circumstance where the rival traditions are all in good epistemological order. But in this case, the would-be relativist must be a member either of one of those traditions or of none at all. If a member of one, he claims, she would have no good reason to put her allegiance in question, and every reason for not doing so. Hence, she could not claim that every set of standards has as much and as little claim to allegiance as any other. The other alternative, being traditionless, is not a live option. But the situation that MacIntyre contrives seems a false dilemma, for, as Rorty and Lovibond insist, one can be aware of the contingency of one's commitments even as one ingenuously pursues them. While it may be true that MacIntyre's would-be relativist cannot claim that, *for her*, every set of standards is equally worthy of allegiance, she could consistently claim that there are no non-question-begging points of view from which standards can be distinguished in this respect. MacIntyre seems falsely to equate "allegiance to" with "belief in the transcendental necessity of."

In general, he wants to argue that relativism requires taking seriously a standpoint that cannot be occupied.[84] I myself advanced a kindred argument earlier in this chapter with respect to nihilism, a particular construal of "relativism." However, given MacIntyre's purposes, I have doubts about his claim's success in this setting. For since at least one philosophical position that he would, no doubt, consider a species of relativism—namely, the neopragmatism of Rorty— does *not* seem either to presuppose, or to be haunted by the loss of, the neutral aperspectival standpoint, MacIntyre's argument is only partially successful in responding in general to what he takes to be relativism. Consequently, it does not serve to distance him from thinkers such as Rorty in the way that he would presumably like it to.

This chapter has consisted of gestures in the direction of vindicating the critical standpoint of this book, namely, the standpoint of the meaningful, and also the idea of critically rational perspectives on the meaningful. The alternative, what I have called the values-perspective, is, I have argued, the result of an illegitimate absolutization of the external standpoint of the observer. It is in its wake that nihilism and weightlessness—"the unbearable lightness of being" characteristic of technology's functional degeneracy and of much of (post)modern life in general—follow. Ultimately, however, as I suggested near the end of the first section of this chapter, healing the rift between the internal and external perspectives is a practical task. And, as Richard Bernstein points out, matters of the utmost practical concern are implicated in the challenge to get "beyond objectivism and relativism." For at issue is the possibility of a practical judgment that is rooted in shared and sharable understandings of social life.[85] I am now in a position to say that what faces us is the task of uniting inner and outer by a commitment to and an orientation towards the notion of the virtual "we" of an historicized humanity; it is the task of forging forms of community that reflect what all could want.[86] It is a task that will require us to take seriously certain kinds of vocabularies and to reject others. Foremost among those to be taken seriously will be vocabularies that give a central place to notions such as self-recognition. We have neither Kantian nor Hegelian guarantees to grant us the solace of knowing that we of necessity, or ultimately, *must* take those vocabularies seriously. As a consequence, it is a challenge that can be either taken up or rejected, though I believe that it can be rejected only at our peril.

I end this lengthy interlude with brief remarks about what is involved in accepting or rejecting this challenge and about the forces that conspire against accepting it. The reflections of this chapter lead me to suggest that 'rational,' as a term of approval, should not have its use restricted to the assessment of a community's success in addressing its central concerns. Its use ought to be expanded to embrace as well the *concerns* or purposes that communities have, in the sense that we can speak of a rational concern as one that contributes to, or at least that does not detract from, the flourishing of the whole human community. This would mean that, all things being equal, a community that refused to acknowledge this would *ipso facto* remove itself from the community of morally rational societies.

The values-perspective of modern technology and the decentering gestures of contemporary projects of "deconstruction" conspire to undermine such an expansion of the province of rationality. Though many who would hitch their wagons to poststructuralism's (now waning) star would view our present inability to adjudicate competing answers to the issues that most concern us as liberation rather than as a crisis,[87] we can still hope to make sense of a notion of reason sufficiently robust to empower a moral and political practice that would make unnecessary the move to make a virtue of what is taken to be necessity.[88]

V
Conclusion

8

Technology and the Conversations of Modernity: Postmodernism, Technology, Ethics and Time

The preceding chapter was an extended meditation on some of the conceptual underpinnings of philosophical nihilism and of its close relation, relativism. Specifically, that chapter represents an attempt to vindicate the standpoint of the meaningful by clearing a rational space for a critique oriented by such a standard. Both nihilism and relativism are today associated with a social and cultural condition labeled 'postmodern' or with that subset of intellectual positions labeled 'poststructuralist.'[1] Hence the ultimate point of my critique in that chapter was to justify our continuing to take projects of critical rationality seriously—to justify the legitimacy of critical reason in the face of the poststructuralist or postmodern challenge. It makes a difference, of course, whether one understands the characteristics and tendencies commonly called to mind by these labels to be attributes of an historical condition or stage or, alternatively, to be those of a family of intellectual stances or sensibilities coexisting, however uneasily, with other, contrasting stances or sensibilities. However, what will interest me for now are those very characteristics and inclinations, be they of a really existing constellation of historical and cultural forces or of a consciousness that would celebrate those forces. My concern in this chapter is to draw the threads of my treatment of technology together with those of my allusions to postmodernism— arguably technology's current social context, at least in the West—to the end of making explicit some of the implications of my discussion for the conduct of a life and for the role of technology within it.

The technology of a given era must inevitably be understood against the background of its social context, a context wherein socialized desire—mediated in varying degrees by economic, military and political institutions—influences the rate and direction of technological development, even as technological development reacts back upon and informs that desire. Today that social context is said to be postmodern. Ours is the age of information and of the image, characteristics unthinkable without technology and which selectively reinforce certain lines of technological development. Many have commented upon the way in which "high-tech"—computer and communications technology—is implicated in the postmodern.[2] In the initial section of this chapter, I want to further that discussion, first by making explicit some of the elective affinities between technology and postmodernism, secondly, by suggesting how technology furnishes the infrastructure for postmodern society, and lastly, by arguing that a particular emerging technology, namely, Virtual Reality technology, is both an especially telling emblem of the postmodern and a particularly desirable commodity in postmodernity.

I

Modernity marks the stage at which totalizing worldviews rooted in religion and tradition lose their purchase on the European mind. Seized by the anxiety born of the fragmentation left in the wake of this loss, there nevertheless remained for some the conviction that some other sort of whole or totality (call it reason) could repair this spiritual wound, and do so in a way that would not require an impossible return to an earlier innocence. Hegel's great modernist project, to integrate rationally the various shapes of European consciousness into the meta-narrative of Spirit's coming to full understanding of itself, stands as testimony to that conviction. What gets called postmodernity, on the other hand, is the stage at which those who live modernity's fragmentary existence have given up the belief that *any* whole can soothe what ails us. All totalizing schemes and narratives have lost credibility, and there is no longer even any *sense* of what to look for to repair the lack.

Today, this issues in a pervasive normlessness and unrootedness which underwrite a reluctance, if not refusal, to take anything seriously for fear of being "taken in." The postmodern attitude is one of ironic, if not cynical, detachment, a detachment that characterizes our relationship to the world, to structures of meaning and to canons of rationality. This is not surprising, for when the critical spirit of modernity turns upon itself and consumes or exhausts itself in the process, as it has in the postmodern age, cynicism is virtually inescapable.

Holding the world at arms length in this way can also be seen as a response to the unsettling dread of being in time, in particular to being in what I have called external history. The cynical detachment and refusal to commit oneself characteristic of much of postmodernism can be seen, then, as a withholding of allegiance to anything as a way of anesthetizing oneself to loss.

The spirit of seriousness gives way to a spirit of play, where the aim becomes to dance lightly over the surface of things and of life, being distrustful of the deep and the heavy. This cynicism, irreverence and distrust, linked with the aesthetic spirit of play, lead to a fascination with surfaces, an inclination to see the world as something that exists only to gratify human desires, as a resource, and ultimately to seeing the world as a projection of those desires.[3] The world loses its weight as an Other.

Fredric Jameson, in a rich and highly suggestive essay, "Postmodernism, or the Cultural Logic of Late Capitalism," and subsequently in a book of the same title, offers a summary characterization of postmodernism as a fascination with surface, play and nonreferentiality, and as a cultural style that eschews the distinction between the serious and the nonserious, *truth and illusion*, and depth and surface.[4] To this catalogue Jameson would also add a crisis in historicity, Jean-François Lyotard would contribute an incredulity towards metanarratives of emancipation and of justification, and I would add perhaps a conflation of the distinction between meaning and value.[5]

The critique of the hermeneutic (of the notion of expressing an inside, of the notion of depth, of referentiality and so on) is the symptom of postmodernist culture that perhaps most clearly allies it with poststructuralist theory. The dismissal of the hermeneutic assumes four characteristic forms: a rejection of the essence/appearance distinction (ideology and false consciousness go along with it); of the latent/manifest distinction; of the authenticity/inauthenticity distinction (the disalienation/alienation distinction goes with it); and of that between the signified and the signifier.[6] This list includes the doublets that Foucault takes to be characteristic of humanism, and it thereby highlights postmodernism's alleged antihumanism. What replaces the depth models are conceptions of practices, discourses, textual play and language games.[7]

In a highly compact survey of the history of the sign, Jameson traces the trajectory of the notion of the sign, from an unproblematic relation to its referent at the dawn of capitalism, to its being disjoined from the referent and thereby enjoying a moment of autonomy and of critical distance in modernism, to the point at which the sign itself is rent asunder, the signifier being separated from the signified, where reference and reality disappear altogether, and even meaning is problematized. This last is the moment of the pure and random play of signifiers, the moment of postmodernism.[8]

In this movement, along with the distinctions rehearsed above, the distinction between the original and the copy also dissolves. The world becomes transformed into sheer images of itself, a pure shimmering surface betraying no depth and no real referent. This is the mark of the age of the simulacrum, the identical copy for which no original ever existed.[9] As one commentator remarks, postmodernism is the era of simulation, where reality is overtaken by its images.[10] As we shall see, postmodernism's emphasis upon simulacra goes hand in hand with such a society's effacement of the memory of original contexts of meaning.

The phenomenon of the simulacrum, perhaps theorized most famously by Jean Baudrillard, refers to a representation to which nothing real corresponds, to an image, to a virtual reality. In the case of a simulacrum, the real or the original to which it would otherwise, and in earlier eras did, refer is displaced by a model or code. Such a model or code is constructed in accordance with the requirement that it enable reproducibility, that it be a template for the reproduction of identical copies.[11] As Baudrillard suggests, the model is the "signifier of reference" that does not refer to anything real.[12] Perhaps the clearest example of such a nonreferential model is a computer program. It is a wholly contrived model or code for replication to which nothing real need correspond, for which no original need exist. The products of the processes directed by such codes or templates are dubbed 'simulacra.' Examples of simulacra range from photographic copies derived from altered photographs (altered through the use of airbrushing or developing techniques or through the juxtaposition of photographs taken at different times, for example) to, say, compact discs that are products of the integration of electronically altered and separately recorded (in time and space) musical tracks into a single album cut, where no "original" performance exists, to the "virtual reality" produced by Virtual Reality technology.

Produced by a code or a linguistic form that does not really refer but merely simulates reference, the simulacrum is the image or the reproduction that testifies to the short-circuiting of reference in postmodernity. For example, a TV ad, set in a locker room where athletes shower after a game, suggests through words and images that the use of a certain deodorant stick is the equivalent of masculinity; another ad links the wearing of a particular brand of jeans to youthful independence and indifference to convention.[13] The arbitrariness with which the floating signifier attaches to the commodity in the TV ad attests, in a radical form, to the disruption of the internal relationship between signifier and signified. Further, the ad seduces us into substituting the sign, the image, for the real thing. In allowing this substitution to determine our action, we thus lose the real. For example, the simulation of youthful indifference to convention in the form of wearing a particular brand of jeans must disappoint (the simulacrum is youthful unconventionality's *appearing* in the form of wearing the jeans), much as I have argued elsewhere that substituting value for meaning does. We don the jeans but remain the same bourgeois selves that we were before this gesture of reinvention.

Here, for Baudrillard, 'the code' refers to the collective language of commodity ads.[14] The linguistic practice governed by such a code is not a representational practice; its point is not to make truth claims about a world, but is rather to *construct* for us a world. To use Nelson Goodman's suggestive phrase, it is a "way of worldmaking" through arbitrary and unconventional juxtapositions of signifiers and meanings. The world thus made Baudrillard calls the "hyperreal." For Baudrillard, postmodern reality is hyperreality. 'Hyperreality' refers to the condition in which the real and the imaginary are confused, in which art is everywhere since artifice is at the very heart of reality.[15] (It is perhaps worth mentioning here that as a result, 'fiction' would signify an antiquated, modernist "aesthetic" category.) Within hyperreality the definition of the real becomes: *"that of which it is possible to give an equivalent reproduction."*[16] It is interesting to note here that this is the very notion of the real that is presupposed by arguments to the effect that technology can *replace* lost value when the environment is altered for the purpose of development.[17] That is, the reality of nature is held to be just that, and only that, that can be reproduced.

If it is merely the *appearance* of a thing that is important, then it can be exhaustively simulated, and the simulacrum entails no loss. This recalls my earlier observation that, if it is merely the end or the product of a practice that is important, then the values-perspective and the functional degeneracy that it permits, and indeed encourages, will entail no loss. The simulacrum fulfills technology's own time-contracting and value-decontextualizing criteria. In terms of my meaning/value distinction, the simulacrum can be understood as an instance of a value, for, in postmodernism, the simulacrum is shorn of its historical context, its context of origin, and of the context of practices from which it would ordinarily emerge. Examples of the first feature are to be found in postmodern architecture, of the second, perhaps in the simultaneous and ubiquitous availability of foods from all over the world, and perhaps in cultural festivals. In our time, even historical monuments are not immune to being assimilated to the realm of simulation. Jameson points out that the self-consciousness of modernity *as* modern, *as new,* presupposed the coexistence of the old, and that in the completion of modernity, a completion which for him defines postmodernity, the old (including nature itself) is completely displaced. As a consequence, he argues, in postmodernity, surviving historical monuments, all cleaned up and glittering, become simulacra of the past rather than indications of its survival.[18] I should want to suggest, then, that the simulacrum can be usefully understood as the postmodern realization of "value" or of what 'value' means in postmodernity. Hence this book's critique of the values-perspective is a critique of postmodern desire, is a critique of desire characterized as the desire for the simulacrum.

Much of what I say about the reign of value finds itself echoed in Baudrillard's discourse about simulacra, thereby supporting my claim that the simulacrum is the postmodern form of value. I think in particular of his description of hyperreality as the condition of "substituting signs of the real for the real itself," terms remarkably similar to my description of the substitution of values for meaning.[19] I have also tied the values-perspective to the perspective of technical control, and, again, a plausible case can be made for such a connection in the instance of the simulacrum.

As has already been suggested, postmodernity marks the collapse of a set of parallel distinctions: appearance/reality, counterfeit/origin(al), and illusion/truth. In the course of this book we have seen such distinctions challenged in the names of relativism, postmodernism and systems theory. In the case of the latter, systems theory, it is perhaps most clear that it is no longer a question of *representing* (the real or the original) but instead one of *working*, one of functional rationality, one of power.

And there is such a Nietzschean motif in Baudrillard's description of the postmodern condition. He speaks of a transition "[f]rom a capitalist-productivist society to a neocapitalist cybernetic order that aims now at total control."[20] And indeed, I have already alluded to the connection between the systems theory of Luhmann and the perspectivism of Nietzsche. The "code" for Baudrillard is a form of discourse that effects homogeneity and commensurability. For him, as for Lyotard, such discourses serve control.[21] One need only think here of Descartes' mechanistic world picture or, in general, of the physicalistic language of the natural sciences which represents phenomenal heterogeneity in terms of a commensurating discourse that, in Heidegger's terms, surveys all of reality at once, and permits the technological colonization of the world. In proclaiming that it is characteristic of technology to presume an ideal counterfeit of the world, Baudrillard speaks of "the demiurgic ambition to exorcise the natural substance of a thing in order to substitute a synthetic one."[22] Accordingly, the simulacrum is understood as enabling (technological) projects of control.

The discourses and practices that produce simulacra, like discourses of "truth" for Nietzsche and Foucault, and like "values" in general for Nietzsche, serve power. In a rather polemical critique of political surveys, polls and statistics, a critique that sees them all as constituted by a code insuring that they will never reveal new information, but only reproduce the assumptions that inform the questions, Baudrillard ties the response-fabricating character of such questions to (political) power.[23] One is left with a view of postmodern desire as the demiurgic desire (the *demiurgos*, that primordial practitioner of *techne*) to be the source, the origin of the "real," and to produce that "real" through codes generating the simulacrum (as perhaps an ersatz for the real object of desire, the infinitely displaced origin, the always already lost real?).

And if postmodern desire is the demiurgic desire to be the origin of the "real," a real produced through the ersatz of the simulacrum, then technology is strongly and definitively implicated. For, as I shall suggest presently, technology procures the simulacrum, thereby aiding and abetting control. Moreover, there are features of the postmodern context that contribute to an anxiety that *heightens* our concern about control. Disenchantment, secularization, incredulity towards metanarratives—these all put us face to face with a sense of *contingency* that heightens our insecurity, and inclines us ever more strongly to grasp for the means of controlling the future promised by technology. And the more conscious we become of both the real and a secured future spiralling out of our grasp, the more tenaciously we invest our hopes in technology (unless we choose to go back "behind" modernity and seek to fill our emptiness in some sort of religious or spiritual movement). But the real's always already lost status implicates such an investment in the vertigo of an Hegelian "bad infinite."[24]

While Baudrillard concentrates primarily on simulations, media, cybernetic control and so on, other theorists emphasize that many features of postmodern society can be traced to the economic imperatives of late capitalism. Discussions of postmodernism that highlight such connections help to flesh out a picture of contemporary technology's social context. This is particularly true of the accounts offered by David Harvey and Fredric Jameson. In such accounts, postmodernism is treated as the cultural superstructure of late capitalism. Such treatments, however, need not deny to postmodernism an internal logic which can in turn be served by postindustrial capitalism (on this, see the discussion at the end of this section).

Modern global capitalism, it is argued, is oriented to the production and consumption of images, of simulacra in the form of badges of prestige and the like. As Jameson alleges, in a postmodern symbiosis of the market and media, the marketplace is less one of physical commodities than of images.[25] Indeed, given modern technologies of reproduction which allow instantaneous communicability over space, images, because they are so ephemeral, are ideal commodities for an economic system that thrives on constantly accelerating turnover times.[26] In the TV ad, one sells, at the same time all over the world, romantic rescue or *machismo* or youth in the form of a commodity, so that, in the act of exchange, the consumer acquires the image of these states or qualities. It is the genius of MTV to capitalize on this phenomenon by devoting its programming almost exclusively to ads, dense with such images, for recordings. In such a symbiosis of market and media, the desire necessary to keep the consumer system going is summoned, strongly suggesting a convergence of postmodern desire and the requirements of capital.[27] Jameson argues that postmodernity marks the stage at which cultural production is integrated into commodity production, issuing in the transformation of the very sphere of culture.[28]

Among the consequences for postmodernism of the requirements of capital (in particular of the requirement for a general speedup in the turnover times of capital) are the "volatility and ephemerality of fashions, products, production techniques, labour processes, ideas and ideologies, values and established practices."[29] In such an instant and throwaway society, with its emphasis upon throwing away the established and on adopting the new and innovative, the postmodern "subject" is faced with a diversity of values within a fragmented society.[30]

As a result, the temporary becomes the hallmark of postmodern living. This, then, is our age, an age where there is a demand for a constant diet of the outré (be it sexual, aesthetic or technological) to which we respond with an increasingly exhausted indifference (there is no longer the background against which the novel can stand out), an age of Madonna, where the signal achievement is being famous for being famous (the simulacrum).[31] For us, it is neither the true, the good nor even the beautiful that engages; it is only the fascinating, the interesting.

Let us now explore further the relationship between postmodernism and irony, in order both to connect the discussion in Chapter Seven with that of poststructuralism, and to highlight some aspects of postmodernism's relationship to time. As I have already suggested, a fascination with surfaces and an allegiance to the idea that all of reality is a social and linguistic construction lead to ironic and ultimately cynical attitudes.[32]

As Paul de Man reminds us, irony is constituted by the relationship between a self that exists in a state of inauthenticity (a state of being self-unowned) and a self that exists only in the form of a language that asserts the knowledge of this inauthenticity, that is, the self in the form of a radical self-consciousness or state of having "stepped back."[33] If "inauthenticity" strikes our ear as too modernist in tone, consider irony as constituted by the relationship between a self that is engaged in taken-for-granted, but ultimately arbitrary and unjustifiable, practices and a self that exists only in the form of the knowledge of this condition, of this ungrounded engagement. De Man goes on to tie the ironic subject to the detached, disinterested observer.[34] This way of putting it can be readily understood to square both with the distinction between the internal and external standpoints discussed in the last chapter and with my reference to self-duplication at the beginning of Chapter Three, where I mention Kierkegaard's aesthete being an observer of her own life.

De Man cites Szondi to the effect that irony "measures whatever it encounters in the present by the yardstick of infinity and thus destroys it."[35] This, of course, accords well with my claims in the last chapter regarding poststructuralism's excessive demands. According to de Man, Schlegel refers to the infinity of the ironic process as freedom.[36] But it is an empty, dizzying freedom without guideposts. Consistent with my discussion of freedom as the absence of measure at the beginning of Chapter Three, we can see that the sequence of the ironic process is endless because it has no measure. It is useful, I believe, to think of postmodernist style as ironizing gone awry, where language is mentioned rather than used, as if all of our verbal activity, and hence lives, were to reside in quotes.[37]

The ironic standpoint of poststructuralism can be understood in its relationship to time. Indeed, one can usefully think of poststructuralism as a conception of the relationship of meaning (or Being) to time. The "metaphysics of presence," to which poststructuralism is opposed, presumes that meaning is given univocally, determinately and all at once. Derrida's notion of *différance* is a radicalization of Saussure's structuralist insight that meaning is determined by context (or a field of differences). The notion of *différance* presumes, since context is never given once and for all, that meaning is indefinitely deferred. The destabilization or the lack of closure of the system of differences leads to the *deferring* of meaning.[38] This firmly roots meaning in time (or, more precisely, to eternity).

The distinction between this approach to the problem of meaning, related to the ironist's suspension of any interpretive closure, hence of any determinate interpretation, and a Gadamerian view, which also, in a Heideggerian fashion, locates meaning in time, is that Derrida's view does not allow for the intelligibility of the notion of an accumulating unity of meaning, even as a regulative ideal. Accordingly, any interpretation will be equally far away from "there" as any

other; they are all infinitely far away. Meaning is radically dispersed and fragmented, putting us in mind of what I have called the values-perspective and its
concomitant omnidirectionality of aims and dispersal, its "spread-outness." But
we cannot have the concept of the fragmentary without the concept of the whole.
The standpoint from which we could perform the survey granting us unity and
closure of meaning is situated, therefore, at an *infinitely* receding horizon. Yet
it grants the measure for the claim of the indeterminacy of meaning.[39]

If what I suggest in Chapter Seven is true, namely, that poststructuralism
makes meaning radically problematic because of too demanding a sense of
objectivity, and that it remains haunted by this sense (the aperspectival is the
measure of the perspectival), then postmodernism is, or certainly may well be,
pace Lyotard, informed by a nostalgia for the whole. The image that captures
such a standpoint for Gadamerian hermeneutics, the standpoint of the unity of
meaning, would be a point that is approached by an asymptotic curve, a point
that, like Derrida's, is never reached, but one which renders intelligible the idea
of convergence as a regulative ideal, and hence, also, interpretive closure as a
cumulative and accumulating unity.[40]

Postmodernism's attitude towards time evinces an uneasiness with our finitude.
Its ironic displacement is symptomatic of a desire for the atemporal, for coincidence with the always already lost object of desire, and poststructuralism in
particular retains its nostalgia for objectivity.[41] Irony is the unhappy consciousness
of this impossible coincidence. Repulsed by the *de trop* of contingent historical
existence, the ironist takes flight and seeks security in a transcendent perch.
From her transcendent vantage point, the ironist can see all of history as a mere
passing show, as a made-up drama, an artifact, a perception which, because
history can be dismissed as a mere play(ing), removes the pain of time and the
frustration of actual life.[42] The groundlessness and arbitrariness of our practices,
their being cut off from their moorings and set adrift, "the unbearable lightness
of being"—this all comes into view from the perspective of the ironic posture,
the perspective from which we cannot bring off the willing suspension of disbelief.
Another, more dreadful, motive for the refusal to enter life is that, in doing so,
we risk going the way of all flesh in being subject to the tooth of time, in being
subject to loss and to death. The ironic stance betrays a desire to escape the, to
it, meaningless and ultimately absurd march of time.[43] The need for such an
escape from time and life is predicated upon an understanding of time that, in
this book, I have been at pains to displace, an understanding of temporality as
the essentially alienating time of external history. There is much in poststructuralism that is informed by a nostalgia for the atemporality of the objective standpoint,
a standpoint that is infinitely remote. I have argued that the nihilism associated
with poststructuralism arises from this nostalgia and from this desire.

As suggested in Chapter Five, Paul de Man relates ironic discourse to what
I refer to as the pointillism or parataxicality of a life lived in terms of external
history. As that chapter implies, de Man's distinction between the temporalities

of allegory and of irony can be instructively compared to my distinction between the time of meaning and the time of value, respectively. De Man, not surprisingly given his poststructuralist commitments, seems to think that the temporality of irony—in which time is reduced to the single isolated moment—comes closer to capturing actual human experience.[44] And the time-compression of irony finds itself reflected in postmodern society, which, driven in part by the imperatives of capitalism, is caught in a time-space contraction.[45] Postmodernism can be characterized as an attitude toward time or an experience of time that, because it cannot have the atemporal, places emphasis upon maximum intensity in time, not the living in time that would be a form of *praxis*, but a more passive fascination or playing which, according to Schiller, creates a timelessness within time. The result is a flashing pointillism, a lived experience as a series of disconnected intensities. Not being able to commit to a future or to take the past seriously, the postmodernist makes do with the present.

Much of what I have said about the fragmented and incoherent life-narrative of the technological subject and about its punctuate temporality finds an echo in accounts of the postmodern "subject" and its cultural products. Jameson speaks of the effaced temporality of postmodernism and of its literary theory.[46] For postmodernism's fragmented subject, experience is reduced to "a series of pure and unrelated presents."[47] Temporal existence without the flash of stimulation becomes meaningless. Another commentator speaks of our late capitalist society as one in which "[t]he need for novelty and fresh stimulation becomes more and more intense, intervening interludes of boredom increasingly intolerable."[48]

This image of the postmodern subject, constituted as a series of flashing intensities, is reinforced in a technologically charged way by Baudrillard's hyperbolic though evocative description of the subject as a kind of operator within communications networks, an operator without subjectivity, without interiority, who receives, transforms and transmits signals. In the era of hyperreality we become merely terminals of multiple information networks; we are constituted by our place in the circuit of information flows.[49] A telling shift, that: from Marx's notion of the individual as an ensemble of social relations to the idea of the individual as an intersection of information circuits!

I spoke earlier in this study about the breakdown of narrative resulting from an idealized time-contraction. In commentaries on the products of the postmodern subject, such images of fracture abound. Jameson speaks of the fragmentation and disintegration of narrative fabrics, and Harvey points to a time-compression so extreme that narrative cannot articulate events.[50]

Postmodernism's emphasis upon discontinuity and rupture militates against its appropriating the past as a living and animating endowment. The past becomes vaporized into an object of nostalgia, or into a mere resource—into a counterpoint to a no longer tenable belief in progress or into a source of material to be "aesthetically colonized." History itself is drawn into the framework of what Heidegger calls the technological disclosure of Being (*das Gestell*).

The idea of nostalgia is a useful one for illuminating postmodernism's relationship to time and, specifically, to the past. Though, as I shall presently indicate, it can be argued that nostalgia assumes a peculiar form in postmodernity, traces of the postmodern sensibility are clearly discernible in descriptions of our times that do not explicitly take the postmodern as such as their theme. One recent account of this sort is Christopher Lasch's. In a wide-ranging critique of the modern idea of progress and of its devaluation of limits, Lasch speaks of nostalgia as the result of the failure to realize the promise of progress, a failure made painfully evident by the cataclysmic events of our century.[51] To nostalgia, Lasch opposes the faculty of memory which, like repetition, provides a sense of continuity, and he commends remembrance as a mode that seeks to grasp the past's formative influence on the present.[52]

By contrast, nostalgia is the attitude we have towards the irretrievably lost, and it thereby presupposes an understanding of time as linear. Nostalgia is fixated on loss and the incommensurability of what is lost with the present. Memory, like repetition, emphasizes commensurability and continuity of past, present, future.[53] This sense of history, of continuity, is what is lost in postmodernity, according to Jameson. And the phenomenon of nostalgia can be connected with the disillusionment of poststructuralism: what is lost is something, as Jacques Lacan points out, that we never had. Lasch suggests that nostalgia's past is idealized, timeless, perfect; that is, it never was.[54] Nostalgia's past is the always already lost.

Nostalgia is a mode of dismissing the past, history and *time*. Lasch approvingly cites Samuel Taylor Coleridge's account of the distinction between the healing power of memory and a dismissive attitude toward the past. Those who dismiss the past, whether in rancor or nostalgia:

> are not good and wise enough to contemplate the Past in the Present, and so to produce by a virtuous and thoughtful sensibility that *continuity* in their self-consciousness, which nature has made the law of their animal life. . . . They exist in *fragments*, annihilated as to the Past, they are dead to the future. . . . [55] (emphases mine)

Lasch goes on to speak of nostalgia as the attitude of embittered adults who, feeling betrayed by the promise or the fruits of progress, *need* things to be a particular way. This calls to mind Kierkegaard's aesthete, dedicated as the aesthete is to enjoyment as opposed to effort. Lacking a tragic understanding of life, that is, not taking it as given that sacrifices and struggle will be required, that things will not be easy, that our efforts may and will fail, that there are no guarantees, such a (postmodern) personality becomes disillusioned, and removes herself, engaging perhaps in nostalgic fantasy. Nostalgia is a response to the loss of belief in the modernist metanarrative of progress. Nostalgia is memory's tune played in an ironic key. We can think of nostalgia, then, both as the attitude of the postmodern, haunted by the always already lost object, and as the attitude of the modern cosmopolitan who, finding that consumer satisfaction—because it is ephemeral, and the yearning for the new and different interminable—is never *finally* achievable, yearns for simpler desires and choices. This of course finds clear expression in, and is exploited by, TV commercials which promote a bewildering variety of products by invoking images of an idyllic past, of America as open and virginal, and of loving, welcoming, centered homes.

Optimism, Lasch suggests, undergirded by the belief in progress, is fragile, whereas hope, informed by a tragic sense of life, is more resilient.[56] What I have in this study called internal history or repetition does not become disillusioned, for it already has its object, that is, what is to be repeated, while one existing in external history is susceptible to disillusionment if the object is not attained or cannot be *finally* grasped. External history is, then, vulnerable to cynicism and detachment. This is why persons moved by repetition and who take their practices seriously are viewed as naive by those who adopt the values-perspective. But they *must* be viewed as naive *only* if one assumes that *only* "values" can guide or inform practices, and that struggle and effort are privative rather than constitutive.

Lasch's nostalgic subject's disillusionment presupposes her having accepted the promises of progress, and having experienced their going unfulfilled. As I have suggested, the poststructuralist sees everything as fragmentary, because none of it lives up to her (latent) desire for the whole. Everything in real time is deficient, for it fails to measure up to the atemporal, to the infinitely receding goal beyond time. In this way, the poststructuralist's disillusionment presupposes external history. By setting aside our allegiance to external history as the privileged model for construing our temporality, we could set aside a key precondition for postmodern disillusionment and nostalgia—bringing off, in effect, an end run around the postmodern problematic.

Nostalgia's profoundly unhistorical attitude represents the past as static and unchanging.[57] Nostalgia's idealized image of the past in its pristine purity is, then, a simulacrum of the past, an image whose original never was. When, as it has certainly become for the postmodernist, the object of nostalgia is a simulacrum, a text, the past as referent is bracketed.[58] The past, I would say, then becomes not a phenomenon referred to, as much as a *mode* of referring, not a thing seen, but a *style* of seeing. It gets reduced to being a frame through which a content is viewed. In the aesthetic practices of postmodernity, one can point to "framers" such as the art deco scripting of credits for a film, or scenes shot through a gauzed lens, as invitations to or codes indicating that we should adopt the nostalgia mode in our reception. These latter are specialized aesthetic practices, to be sure, but they conform to a specifically postmodern sensibility.

In this connection, Jameson distinguishes a properly modernist nostalgia from the postmodern backward longing. There is a *depth* to modernist nostalgia—the pain of experiencing a past that is beyond all but aesthetic retrieval. The postmodernist, at least in the *first* instance, does not feel this pain; she does not experience the loss. For the past just *is*, for her, its aesthetic rehabilitation. Its reality beyond its textuality has been suspended. Just as we get a simulacrum of reference with the code, with postmodernist nostalgia we get a simulacrum of (modernist) nostalgia. The nostalgia that is satisfied by an image is not "real" nostalgia, but a simulacrum of it. Having suspended belief in a transcendent real, the postmodern's nostalgia can only be either a nostalgia for the *belief* in a real past that has been lost, that is, a nostalgia for nostalgia, or a nostalgia for the image of the past. In either case, we are left with a simulacrum of nostalgia as characterizing a properly postmodern homesickness.[59]

One can see the nostalgia mode as a psychological response to the sensory overload, rapidly accelerating tempo and fragmentation of postmodern life, an experience which engenders a cultivation of blasé attitudes and a reversion to images of a lost past.[60] Images in general become the "illusory means whereby an individualistic society of transients sets forth its nostalgia for common values," for permanence, images projected via our disposal over sign systems.[61] Attempts to capture the past and tradition in this way end up as futile efforts whereby, to ring a change on Marx's phrase, all that is solid melts into simulacra, a transformation that I would understand in terms of a rupture in the internal relationship of meaning and value.

For all three commentators on postmodern times that I have considered thus far—Lasch, Jameson and Harvey—our relationship to the past has been somehow short-circuited via the nostalgia mode. Jameson understands this disappearance of the historical referent as betokening a crisis in historicity. In his estimation, the postmodern is a spatialized culture, a dehistoricized and dehistoricizing set of arrangements, a culture in which space "displaces" time.[62] This leads him to wonder whether temporality has any place at all in postmodernism, a cultural configuration which privileges the experience of a spatial present that is beyond past history and future destiny or projects. And if it does have a place, he believes, it would be only as an object of writing, rather than of a lived experience.[63] It seems to me that we can read the essentially atemporal processes of repetition by indeterminate negation that are characteristic of postmodernism, for instance, open-ended Derridean "readings," or the constant renarrativization of experimental video, as in effect a ceaseless running in place that gets us no closer to meaning (and no closer to death?). It is not without significance that these claims about the spatialization of time and the emphasis upon synchrony at the expense of diachrony recall my discussion in Chapter Four of the way in which the values-perspective of technology spatializes our experience.

Jameson suggests further that, with the death of the subject, of the individual, goes also the death of style, of characteristic expression. So the postmodern artist has only *past* styles to draw from; cultural production proceeds then by the imitation of past styles.[64] In the process, the past is typically shorn of its context and assimilated in its immediacy, achieving not the mediation but the effacement of historical distance and thus of temporality.[65] This is another form,

I believe, in which one can see in postmodernism, characterized as it is by a contemporaneous, synchronic juxtaposition of surfaces, a domination of spatial logic.

I would further argue that one can see, in the effacement of historical distance that goes with the imitation of past styles, a peculiarly postmodern form of historicism. This is evident in the ubiquitous presence of the ironic practice of quotation. In quoting preexisting texts, be they narratives or architectural spaces, a distance is achieved on them which enables an aesthetic play and contemplation. Consider in this regard Jameson's extended discussion of the Frank Gehry house in Santa Monica, California as an exemplary case of postmodern spatiality.[66] The house consists of an original structure—forming the core—which is a conventional frame dwelling of two stories, surrounded by a one-and-a-half-story-high wall of corrugated metal—forming the wrapper—so that the original extends upwards beyond the new structure. This house within a house, which defies us to orient ourselves unambiguously with respect to its inside and outside, has the effect of making of the original core of the house something of a museum piece, of inviting us to look at it as if it were framed by its "wrapper." But the house— core, wrapper and the space between them—is a dwelling in which people live. One can see the house as "quoting" its older, conventional part, a citing which has the effect of transforming the present reality of life in those rooms into an image of itself, into a simulacrum whereby the present is taken out of real history.[67] This is an example of what I would call postmodern irony, of placing the present in quotes, *mentioning* the presentness of the present, *dating* itself as present. This yields not the real present, the present of *use*, but the spectatorial image of it. It is as if to say, "this is *just* the way we do it *now*" (with no further commitment or judgment implied), or "this is *just* the way we or they *used* to do it." Here, for me, are expressed at once the irony, relativism and historicism of postmodernism.

Grasping the present as datable in this way betrays a distance on it, the sort of ironic distance that tears it from lived time and transforms it into the present *in vitro*—literally the present under glass, the already dead cadaver, the present as a thing. Is irony, then, an expression of the repetition compulsion enacted to remove the sting of death by beating it to the punch? For historicism, both the present and the past are dead; neither has a claim on us. They are simply concatenations of elements arrayed in a temporal museum, facts from which we have an aesthetic distance. The future does not escape this reification. Our contemporary present, replete with technological forecasts, "trends analysis" and books such as *Future Shock*, is one for which the future is defined as an extrapolation from the present. Our conception of the future becomes in this way a projection of what I have called technology's domesticative attitude toward time. As a result, the idea of the future as open is eclipsed. The resultant conception of the future construes it, to invoke an expression of Luhmann's that I alluded to earlier, as a "future present," a future which in a sense has already happened.

So the future, too, cedes its claim on us as a dimension for which we have responsibility. This reveals what is, for Jameson, the real crisis in historicity, for when the future is viewed in the way I have suggested, visions of it as radically transformed and different are blocked.[68] For the disengaged passivity of our times, neither past, present nor future commands a responsive and responsible attention.

It is not simply the case that modern technology is an enabling condition of postmodern society, or even only that technology is a central facet of the postmodern condition. In many ways, not the least of which is its providing fertile soil for technological surpassing, postmodernity is the radicalization or completion of the modernist project and its technological attitude towards reality. At the level of intellectual history, one can see this worked out in the move from Descartes, whose thought in many ways inaugurated modernity, to Nietzsche, widely credited with having provided the master inspiration for postmodernist and poststructuralist thought. Why was Descartes so concerned with certainty and with determining those things of which we can be certain, that is, mathematically representable facts? His interest is betrayed in the *Discourse on the Method*, namely, to render us the "masters and possessors of nature." This, then, strongly suggests a connection between what Heidegger calls the "world-as-picture," a conception that we owe to Descartes, and the "will to power," whose idea we owe to Nietzsche. The idea of the world-as-picture would, then, itself be understood as a *value* posited in the service of the will to mastery.

Heidegger goes on to trace the transformation from the Cartesian notion of the world as object (*Gegenstand*) to the modern technological understanding of the world as resource (*Bestand*), which issues in a world that is no more than a projection of human interests, a world from which Being has withdrawn, our own increasingly nihilistic world.[69] This is the world that gets experienced as "an unbearable lightness of being," an extraordinarily apt characterization of a society of images and simulacra. The internal connection between the technological attitude towards reality and our present condition allows Heidegger to think in one thought both the nihilism characteristic of our postmodern age and the dissolution of everything into standing reserve (*Bestand*) that is characteristic of our technological condition; it allowed me to draw the parallels that I did in Chapter Six between Heidegger's and Habermas's approaches to the fatal connection between technological rationality and the loss of meaning. Further, in Chapter Seven, I saw fit to connect both the technological attitude and certain aspects of the postmodern stance with the "values-perspective," with the standpoint of the disengaged, ironic aesthetic-observer. Clearly then there must be "elective affinities" between the technological and the postmodern. Let us now turn our attention to them.

The technological attitude and the postmodern bear similar relationships to metaphysics, to discourses of legitimation and of truth, to limits and, as my discussion above indicates, to time. The basis for these affinities is complexly determined. The similarities exist in part because the very understanding of what it is to be postmodern is shaped by technological discourses—the discourses of postindustrial society, of electronic reproduction, information technology, cybernetics and so on; in part because capitalism's own dynamic has influenced both the direction of technological development and the shape that postmodernity has assumed as technology reproduces the images that are constitutive of post-modernity and that are commodified in late capitalism; and in part because the postmodern fascination with surfaces and images functions as a demand, mediated by capitalism, for a certain direction of technological development, towards ever more versatile and effective production and reproduction of information and simulacra. There is, moreover, a deep affinity whereby both the technological and the postmodern attitudes towards reality project the latter as hostage to the will, whether we understand reality as that which is potentially useful or as that which has been constructed.[70]

With regard to metaphysics and to discourses of legitimation and of truth, postmodernism can be understood as the collapse of narratives of justification as distinct from narratives of genealogy, and hence as the silencing of questions of justification in favor of questions of genealogy. As a result, for it any sort of metaphysically informed critical distance has been abolished.[71] Postmodernism's hostility to metaphysics, on the one hand, and its receptivity to technology, on the other, have allowed it to come to pass that technology has reoccupied metaphysics' place. Echoing this claim, Lyotard alleges that, in the wake of the abandonment of metanarratives of liberation or emancipation, the justification of research and the validation for postmodern scientific discourse become per-formativity or power.[72] And performativity influences both denotative and pre-scriptive language games, discourses of truth and justice.[73] Recalling my earlier discussion of Luhmann's project, we may conclude that the truth/illusion distinc-tion has lost its purchase, both for technology's functional rationality and for postmodernism.

The suspicion of metanarratives, then, enables technology's illegitimate reoc-cupation of metaphysics' place. I speak of the reoccupation as illegitimate because such a reoccupation displaces the critical, ethical dimension, the dimension which makes a claim on us to play the "right" game, even as we recognize today that no noncontestable set of necessary and sufficient conditions can be placed on the content of such a dimension. Metaphysics' claims can be understood to be necessary and universal claims, in that they purport to describe the way that *all* must speak if reality is to be adequately represented; they prescribe a framework in terms of which reality as a whole can be apprehended. The hyperreality and textuality of postmodernism leave us only with weightless surfaces that are infinitely removed from their origins, and leave the real with no place to call home. Metaphysics ends because we can no longer make sense of the contrast between the real and its representations. There are only "representations" or texts. In the wake of our recognition of the radical contingency of such textual claims, technology has been allowed to become more and more universal, as everything is obliged more and more to come under its sway and yield to it. And, like the values-perspective of poststructuralism, technological rationality contributes to the evacuation of that dimension of experience within which, and perhaps only within which, it makes *sense* to ask: Are we playing the "wrong" game?[74] Technological rationality, tied as it is to the will to power, does not allow for that dimension's claim on us.

It should be noted that Lyotard's full account of postmodernism neither one-sidedly celebrates the technical goals of efficiency and performativity, nor does it, as is Baudrillard's wont, pessimistically surrender to their hegemony.[75] Instead, one could say that Lyotard also deploys a "normative" notion of postmodernity, one which envisions a postmodernity ever vigilant against any and every hegemonic, closed or commensurating discourse, where there is always available sufficient counterpower to keep the game open. Such a normative notion envisions metaphysics' replacement ultimately not by the hegemony of performativity, but by the pluralism of agonistics, paralogy and, to use Thomas Kuhn's idiom, constantly abnormal discourse, even *within* the sciences.[76]

So, while postmodernism shares with functional rationality a disrespect for constraints of a metaphysical provenance, it is not to be strictly identified with functionalist discourse. In fact, commensuration, systematicity and closure are the enemies for Lyotard. For him these are all tropes of terror. A Heideggerian reading of Lyotard would yield a picture in which performativity, in replacing metaphysics, becomes the last stage of metaphysics, that is, of hegemonic commensurating discourse. The point of the destabilizing dissensus of paralogy is to combat terror by constantly renegotiating the rules of the game.

I find Lyotard's argument against performativity here to be congenial, if a bit hyperbolic. We recall that what makes an action or interaction technological in the operative sense is, one, the separation of ends from means, and two, the rationalization of procedures for procuring the end. It is true that a vocabulary *limited* to notions of effectiveness, efficiency and so on in the procurement of ends does not have room for discourse that challenges those ends for other than strategic reasons. I would agree with Lyotard that this thereby endangers the diversity of interpretive voices that is constitutive of the human conversation. Everything gets seen in functional terms, and our ability to give expression to meaningful differences is constrained.

But in the name of whom or what can postmodernism assume a critical stance *vis-à-vis* technology? Certainly not in the name of the autonomous rational subject, as could modernism. Such a subject's claims to privacy, freedom and even to meaning and coherence—claims that form the basis for "modernist" critiques of technology—have no purchase in postmodernism's realm of decentered subjectivity. The weakness of Lyotard's position here is betrayed by his being equally critical of *all* so-called commensurating discourses, of Habermas's emancipatory vision of an ideal speech situation no less than of the reifying and, indeed, terrifying prospect of a society organized along the lines of systems theory. The "night in which all cows are black" into which all such discourses are indiscriminately cast by Lyotard's indeterminate negation is a realm where critical distinctions cannot be made. As a result, technology's performativity is arguably no worse than, is just as good as: (insert your favorite nonexplicitly postmodernist social theory). Any *systematic* critical posture towards technology or anything else would have to be rejected.[77]

To move on to the issue of limits, both the postmodernist and the technological attitude envision the vaporization of limits, of the resistance offered by reality and its otherness. The will or desire, in principle, seeks satisfaction. As the principle of projected satisfaction, the technological will cannot recognize the *rights* of resistance as a competing claim; it can thematize resistance only privatively, that is, only as something to be derealized. We have already seen this with respect to technology's attitude towards time. The technological form of life thus privileges nonresistant making, where, in the ideal limit, resistance is offered neither by nature, matter or time nor by traditional values.

As I have suggested in various ways throughout this study, we must be careful to ask: What, if anything, is lost when we uncritically project the ideal of nonresistant making, of a completely "user-friendly" world? What of the importance of the role of the "other," of resistance in the constitution of the self? Borgmann speaks of our technological commerce with reality in terms of disburdenment, or *disengagement* as opposed to engagement. He speaks of engaging forces that *center* and sustain life.[78] One need only compare the activity of reading a challenging novel to the passivity of watching TV, with the latter's consumption-oriented meanings, prepackaged and handed over. Baudrillard speaks of the decline of investment, of engagement with our bodies and even of direct social contact as work, leisure and social relations are more and more mediated by electronic commands and by communications networks in "cyberspace."[79] The instantaneity of postmodern communication allows us to seriously contemplate the idea of "stopping the clock," of taking "no time," an idea, given the underlying commodification of time, of getting something for nothing. Time comes to seem useless in its unfolding.[80] We come to experience it as contractable without loss. As argued in Chapter Five, whatever we gain in this way, we surely forfeit the meaning associated with such engagement and investment. We should not forbear to ask, What is given up in subjecting *tyche* or contingency to *techne*?

The Heideggerian discussion of technology, which holds technology to be a way of taking up with the world as standing reserve, where its Otherness disappears, can easily be linked to postmodernism.[81] In postmodernism, too, the sense of Otherness, of resistance, breaks down. It can be argued that, for postmodernism, there is a sense in which desire posits its object. Objectivity can be understood in this sense to be a projection of desire, can be understood as "always already" constructed. Desire posits what can be of value for it. Value thus has its foundation in freedom (though the self who has this freedom is dispersed and fragmented). Similiarly, the technological will projects its objects as means or as resources. In neither case is there a positive thematization of or respect for the real insofar as it is an Other to the technical will or to postmodern desire. As a result, from within both the postmodernist and the technological attitudes, the world is viewed either as a mere occasion for the unlimited satisfaction of desire, or as a resource for unlimited making.

The technological worldview thus envisions unlimited possibility. In this regard, Lasch speaks of the decisive coupling, in modernity and beyond, of an indefinite expansion and proliferation of desires, on the one hand, and of technology's provision of the means to satisfy them, on the other.[82]

Even if we were to grant that technology has no intrinsic ends, and therefore that it remains in thrall to the ends we set, it is nevertheless the case, as I have suggested in earlier chapters, that whatever does become an end of technology is transformed into what I have called a value. This uncouples the end from other concerns and liberates a "free play" in the complex of means and ends, unleashing the forces of innovation and enabling the surpassing of limits.[83]

In that technological rationality reinforces the suspicion of any constraints—cognitive or material—that would fetter an understanding bent upon control, it finds a willing accomplice in the normless and an-archic condition of postmodernity, which similarly threatens to discredit critical discourses that would circumscribe such a will to power. More generally, postmodernity can be thought of as the *realization* of the universalization of the technological attitude, as its completion. Postmodernity can be construed as the historical stage of the realization of technology's promise to eradicate limits and dissolve Otherness.[84] As I shall suggest presently, Virtual Reality technology is a key example here. Jameson, too, argues that postmodernism is the result of modernization's completion, which completion renders nature a thing of the past.[85] This suggests that postmodernism comes on the scene at a point where nature, our Other, is in danger of being thoroughly dominated and domesticated by technology. This stage, this enabling condition of postmodern practice, has been absorbed into postmodernism's self-understanding.

This discussion of elective affinities between technology and postmodernism suggests that we view technology as a characteristic part of the infrastructure of postmodern society. As the infrastructure for procuring the satisfaction of desire, technology—in concert with the capitalist organization of the processes of production, distribution and consumption—is the material basis of the proliferation of postmodern desire. Postmodernism's emphasis upon novelty colludes with capitalism's interest in proliferating and expanding desire and with the technological promise of satisfaction. The "good life" that technology, at least as it is now directed, tends to deliver is one of "endless novelty, change, and excitement,

. . . unlimited possiblity," in short, just the speedup of life that is characteristic of postmodernism.[86]

Interestingly enough, even though it is a central trait of postmodernity that the idea of progress in general has lost its purchase, the metanarrative of *technological* progress has been spared such an embarrassing fate. One way to put this point is to say that, insofar as the modern idea of progress was held to have its origin in a religious, specifically Christian and Judaic, notion of the necessary and inevitable completion of history, it, even though secularized, was held to be tainted by its religious provenance. It could thereby be dismissed because of its metaphysical underpinnings. This encouraged the widespread view that the modern age was therefore somehow illegitimate.[87] However, the possibility of indefinite scientific and technical advance was not questioned in this way. In fact, Hans Blumenberg has argued that what is *legitimate* in the modern idea of progress arose precisely from early modern experiences of scientific and technical advance, processes that seemed open-ended.[88]

Building upon Blumenberg's argument concerning the origins of the modern idea of progress, Lasch suggests that the expectation of indefinite scientific progress provided both intellectual and material sanction and encouragement for the proliferation of modern desire. Indefinite scientific progress formed the model for, and made possible the expansion of, capitalism's mechanism for satisfying desire. The resultant possibility of ever-increasing abundance in turn both authorized and abetted the expansion of desire. The insatiability of scientific curiosity and of desire form the basis for the modern idea of progress, where, in a movement whereby quality passes over into quantity, "progress" now means *material* advance.[89] And the proliferation of modern, or postmodern, desire has proceeded apace with the increasing technical possibility of its satisfaction. Technology's "will to surpass" is eminently suited to our desire for the new and innovative.[90]

Much has been made of the role of technological media in enabling the processes of reproduction that are emblematic of postmodernism.[91] In particular, technology procures the simulacra that orient postmodern desire. As already suggested, the simulacrum represents the characteristic separation of value from meaning in postmodernity. For example, technology procures, at the same time and in the same place, a bewildering variety of commodities and styles from all over the globe, but does so in such a way as to conceal any trace of origin, of the labor processes that produced them, or of the social relations implicated in their production, so that the world can be experienced vicariously as a simulacrum.[92] One might think of these commodities as being in a space where geographical and historical distance have been erased, a space of simultaneity, as if in a museum. As Gadamer suggests in his critique of the "aesthetic consciousness," they consequently lose their place and the world to which they belong.[93] And one could expand this consideration to bring it to bear upon postmodernism's embrace of "difference." While, to be sure, in many ways a salutary commitment, in that it challenges ethnocentrism, provincialism and the like, there is nevertheless the danger of fetishizing difference *qua* difference, given postmodernism's ironic stance. That is, difference threatens to degenerate into being a merely formal matter, a matter of form, because content is not taken seriously. In the embrace of "the different," the postmodernist may find herself having constructed an imaginary museum of difference, where things are all *indifferently* different, the same in their difference.

As one, in the mode of technology, pursues the end associated with a practice rather than the goods internal to it, one finds oneself in pursuit of the end shorn from the context of the practice. For example, consider as a goal having the experience of the cathedral of Notre Dame in Paris. If the end can be procured without "going through the trouble" of getting there and of taking the time to get there, then all to the better. The ability to procure the simulacrum of Notre Dame would fill the bill, and, increasingly, what is called Virtual Reality technology, now in its infancy, promises to provide such a simulation.[94]

Virtual Reality technology (hereinafter referred to as VR) promises to make arcane philosophical scenarios such as Descartes' dream, or the brain-in-a-vat so beloved by analytic philosophers, less fanciful. 'Virtual reality' refers to a three-dimensional, computer-generated simulation of reality, with visual, aural and tactile dimensions, that produces an environment in which a user can be completely immersed, and with which she can interact. Referred to by many of its adherents as a three-dimensional "consensual hallucination," VR is a technology that permits data or information to be visualized, heard and felt, as software transforms information to simulate a real environment.[95]

VR is the result of the attempt to create a communication medium that is phenomenologically engulfing yet unobtrusive. By mounting, directly on the head, goggles equipped with a pair of small video monitors with the appropriate optics, a stereoscopic image is produced before the eyes. This image is continuously updated and adjusted by the computer so that the visual stimuli are altered in the appropriate way as the observer moves her head. In this way, one finds oneself completely surrounded by a stable, three-dimensional world. This virtual world can either be generated in "real time," the time of action, by the computer, or it can be preprocessed and stored in the computer's memory, or it can actually *exist* elsewhere and be encoded or "videographed" and transmitted to the user in stereo, digital form (in the last two cases the process is often referred to as "telepresence").

In addition to the goggles, one may wear stereo headphones. They too produce stimuli that respond to head movement, so that an "acoustically correct" aural environment is added to the visual. One may wear special "data" gloves, or even an entire bodysuit, wired with position and motion transducers to transmit to others—and to represent to oneself—one's image and activity in the virtual world. An image of the glove can be displayed in the scene, which is adjusted as the user moves her hand or fingers, enabling her to interact via the computer with objects in the virtual world, for example, to pick up a virtual plate from a virtual table by grasping it.

Moreover, the gloves and bodysuit may be enhanced so that they provide the correct tactile feedback, enabling one to feel the "presence" of virtual objects. Such gloves not only convey information from the user to the computer, but contain devices—such as an array of blunt pins—that can produce pressure on the skin. Under computer control such appliances can produce an approximation to the pressure on hand and fingers that one should experience when, say, picking up a virtual plate with one's virtual hand. Work is underway at the Massachusetts Institute of Technology to model the very texture of objects.[96] Lastly, at least at this writing, the effect of being in another place can be further enhanced by providing kinesthetic feedback. Special treadmills, for example, can help to simulate the feeling of walking up stairs in a virtual environment. Collectively, these devices constitute a medium that, more than any other, facilitates a willing suspension of disbelief.[97]

The effects that I have described have already been achieved, but as yet systems are relatively crude, and the illusion is imperfect. However, the technology has progressed to the point at which VR has been exploited already in military applications, in the fields of art, aerospace technology, medicine, entertainment, architecture, education and chemistry. For example, using Computer Aided Design (CAD), an architect can specify the plans of a building and incorporate them into a computer program that will generate a three-dimensional simulation of the building that the architect can inspect by walking through it before actual construction, allowing a modification of the plans, if necessary, before construction. VR has both expected and already realized uses in the manufacturing process, for example, by providing a template for fitting airplane parts together, or aiding in the synthesis of drugs by enabling a chemist to locate the optimum relative binding positions of molecules, using large-scale virtual molecules and force feedback to simulate intermolecular forces of attraction and repulsion.[98] In medicine, organs and organ systems can be simulated to train surgeons.[99] Artists are experimenting with three-dimensional graphic design.[100] And, although it may take ten to twenty years to create a truly lifelike virtual tactile experience, not surprisingly AT&T is working on a system that will actually enable us to "reach out and touch someone."[101] Of course, virtual sex is not far behind, and is in fact envisioned in the cyberpunk novel credited with inspiring much VR research, William Gibson's *Neuromancer*.[102]

One might think of VR as, to use the words of one of its pioneers, the "ultimate gadget," the very "culmination of gadgetry."[103] When we don the gear that transmits the designed information environment, we, like Alice stepping through the looking glass, exploit a newly found power to improvise reality, to synthesize it as a projection of our appetites and desires, to surround ourselves with a pure product of our freedom. And it can be done instantly, at the speed of light; we do not have to wait.

Moreover, within cyberspace, the space of Virtual Reality, the concept of distance is optional; locomotion and relocation are independent of time and space.[104] Because access to a particular "location" need not be linear, cyberspace does not, in principle, require movement from one location to another. In the virtual world, we can enjoy a Godlike *instant* access.[105] And, because such an experience is computer-generated, it can be "saved" in the computer's memory and retrieved at will, so that its sensory aspects can be explicitly and fully shared with others. Those features of our experience can be fully externalized, so that, in yet another way, technology complements the postmodern, here in challenging the barrier between the inside and the outside.

I would argue that the new technology of Virtual Reality carries to its logical conclusion postmodernism's fascination with surfaces. The virtual experience is a pure experience of a surface world. There is reason to think that Baudrillard would be sympathetic to what I claim here. For he implies a connection between Virtual Reality technology and a postmodern society of simulation when he points out, in a discussion of the postmodern scene, that "simulators of leisure or of vacations in the home—like flight simulators for airplane pilots—[have] become conceivable."[106] Such a possibility would allow us literally to remain distant from the object, say, Notre Dame, and its origins. We could even "improve" it. If such possibilities—in concert with seemingly ubiquitous theme parks and their analogues—could make the "real" things gratuitous or inconsequential, then we would find ourselves having literally ushered in the epoch of the hyperreal.

Indeed, Virtual Reality, images generated by codes inscribed in software, is a textbook example of a simulacrum. Its advocates and chroniclers explicitly invoke the notion of the hyperreal—the realm of simulation generated by models of a real without origin or reality—to describe it.[107] Such engineered or technologically generated reality stands as a metaphor for the technologically procured simulacrum. In separating the end from the practices and effort typically associated with it, Virtual Reality technology represents a logical extension of the values-perspective, and is the logical completion of the process of substituting the sign for the real. This postmodern technology is a *symbol* of postmodernity itself.[108] There is, after all, in postmodernity a perception that all of experience is a humanly constructed surface. Moreover, many believe that Virtual Reality's cyberspace instantiates "the collapse of the boundaries between the social and technological, biology and machine, natural and artificial that are part of the postmodern imaginary."[109]

Moreover, Virtual Reality technology, though of course only in a virtual way, will greatly facilitate the "schizophrenia" that is valorized in postmodernity. "Who" people are typically implies some consistency, but in cyberspace people are free to adopt an ambiguous form or, indeed, multiple personae.[110] And, presumably, one will eventually be able to rent or purchase software that will produce desired body image(s), ushering in an era of "schizophrenia as commodity fetish."[111]

Further, the simulacrum or image produced by VR is *controllable*, and not subject to the messiness or unruliness of *time*. Virtual Reality technology allows us an ironic, aestheticized distance on experience, and the control that goes with it. Jaron Lanier, one of the acknowledged pioneers in the field, in fact touts the potential of this technology to enable us to "organize and use experience."[112] Experience becomes something that can be stored in a computer file.[113] This makes possible the disposing over and play(ing) with experience that testify to its having become weightless. At the same time that we are granted this aesthetic and technical power over our experience, we find that that experience can be reified into a commodity that can be bought and sold. Moreover, this technology allows us to assume the standpoint of another participant in a virtual drama and to "replay" for ourselves our history from that perspective. How better to facilitate becoming an observer of one's own life, or in Baudrillard's terms, a satellite of oneself? Further, in virtual space, subjectivity will no longer be uniquely linked to a particular perspective, for we can all literally occupy precisely the *same* perspective.

We are completely free to dispose over time—we can reverse an experience, maintain it in an indefinite present, vicariously even reverse segments of our lives. Because the interaction is stored in the computer's memory, we can literally repeat a segment of our lives—any series of events may be stored as a recorded memory and "relived" later, both by oneself and others, with all the fidelity of the original experience. Further, one can interact with this memory, thus "altering the past." "Cutting and splicing," we can reconfigure time. The past and present in such a virtual world can be given equal status and be coexperienced.[114] The spatialized time effected here is a captured, controlled and domesticated time. All of these consequences of substituting information for human experience put one in mind of my earlier discussion of the symbolic valence of word processors with respect to nihilism and immortality.[115]

One can think of postmodern living as, in a sense, a matter of not having fully suspended disbelief. The significance of Virtual Reality technology in postmodernity might well then not be—the technologists' ambitions notwithstanding—to persuade us to suspend disbelief, or certainly not only that. It might be, rather, to offer up a reality which, since the "original" does not enjoy our full investment, is no less convincing than the "original," and which would thereby be closer to being ontologically "on all fours" with the latter. The power, potential and significance of Virtual Reality technology is its ability to offer us, then, a "real" experience that we can control and manipulate. The postmodern subject, because it theorizes itself and its world as simulacra, as texts, prior to any explicit technological fabrication, has less to lose in stepping through the looking glass and entering the world of Virtual Reality. Such a subject is already virtualized, volatilized and fragmented. I have spoken of the postmodernist stance as one of having already stepped back from experience, or of hovering above experience. In postmodernity, experience is *already* a virtual reality. Hence my speaking of Virtual Reality technology not only as a culmination of development in information technology and a characteristic postmodern technology, but also as a symbol of postmodernity itself.

And what is the nature of experience on the other side of the mirror? Perhaps most conspicuous is the fact that one is no longer "weighed down" by one's body. One's representation in virtual space, one's virtual self, need not be embodied. One can be a floating point of view.[116] As cyberspace supplants physical space—as it is doing already with on-line telephone communication, E-mail and so on—we break free of the constraints of bodily existence. Computer networks bracket the body either by omitting it or by simulating it, thus freeing us from the restrictions imposed by our physical identity. We can either ignore or create the body that appears in cyberspace, placing us in complete control of the body that we wish to reveal.[117] Rather than thematizing the body as enabling human experience, the cyberspace experience thematizes the body as a prison. Heim cites a telling passage from Gibson's *Neuromancer*. Speaking of a "cyber-naut" who had been barred from reentering cyberspace, Gibson writes:

> For Case, who'd lived for the bodiless exultation of cyberspace, it was the Fall. In the bars he'd frequented as a cowboy hotshot, the elite stance involved a certain relaxed contempt for the flesh. The body was meat. Case fell into the prison of his own flesh.[118]

Baudrillard too, we recall, speaks of a coming scene where high technology makes possible a freedom from an increasingly gratuitous body.

We might well ask, in passing, What happens to the dialectic of social recognition as a result of the re-presentations of telepresence? What of recognition in the new, much-heralded communities carved out of cyberspace, where E-mail's rationalization of communication is already supplanting face-to-face interaction and the normative features that arise therefrom? In the Hegelian narrative, recognition is supposed to confirm self-certainty. But if what gets recognized by the other is my *constructed* identity, which lacks the vulnerability of my primary identity, then what is thereby recognized by the other does not confirm me but only my ideal construction of myself. But even that does not get confirmed, for the other knows it is only a persona. Such representations would be met by attitudes ranging from a suspension of belief to outright cynicism. Social interaction in such a space might well lose its validating dimension, at least as we know it.[119]

With a Platonic-Cartesian disdain for the body goes a celebration of effortless, resistanceless teleportation. Movement in cyberspace feels like moving through a frictionless, timeless medium; everything exists implicitly all at once.[120] Reality offers no resistance, as our desires can be fulfilled at the speed of light with the touch of a button. It is as if we would *have* to jettison the body in this frictionless world, for otherwise the will, encountering no resistance, would figuratively be thrown off balance by its own weight.

I should like to close this discussion of Virtual Reality technology with a brief reflection on the obvious fact that it lacks historicity. My concern here is not so much with its technical uses for *modeling* the real, as in contexts of computer-aided design and manufacture, much of which is quite salutary. My uneasiness has more to do with the technology's projected *substitutive* uses, with its insertion into the life-world. What is lost, for example, when we substitute the ersatz Notre Dame of Virtual Reality, no matter how convincing, for the real cathedral? What informs our experience of the latter? Is it not in large measure that structure's and its site's embodiment of a response to an aesthetic and architectural problem-atic of a particular time and to a set of then-contending social and cultural forces? Is it not just a fact that we are inclined or predisposed to value some things, in part, because of their origins?

Certainly at least initially plausible arguments have been advanced to the effect that we can partially explain the significance of certain sorts of objects in terms of their origins, in terms of the kinds of processes that brought them into being.[121] This is particularly true of repudiated fakes and forgeries in the art world, and trivially true of objects whose significance consists virtually entirely in the fact that they were produced in a certain way or came from a particular place, for example, specimens of volcanic rock or of moon rock. Part of what it is to value an original work of art, apart from intrinsic, formal aesthetic characteristics, is being able to connect it in a continuous way with a particular biography, and thus to be able to behold something produced by that life in response to the aesthetic problems that it faced in a particular historical and cultural setting. Our *assuming* that this is what we are beholding informs our experience of the work. So we might understand the significance of a natural setting or of a work of art to be determined by both its intrinsic properties and by what I shall call its narrative connections. Insofar as a narrative connection with a particular origin or with a particular sort of process is a significant component of the importance a thing has for us, Virtual Reality cannot fully satisfy unless we are deceived, and perhaps not even then.

And if we discover that we have been deceived, we are distressed, because we took our encounter with the work to be one not only with its purely formal, phenomenal properties, properties which are there for us in the present, or in the relatively shallow time span requisite to engage us with the working of the work, properties that *perhaps* can, in principle, be reproduced without loss. We are distressed because we took that encounter also to be one with the *trace* of a particular artist's grappling with a particular set of problems, or, in the case of architecture, also with the trace of contending social and cultural forces within the life of a people. These are the kinds of connections that we feel are disrupted by the fake. Genuine works are condensations of ways of addressing concerns and of responding to constellations of forces. Those concerns and those forces transcend the work, which testifies to them, which puts us in touch with them. Is this not part of the work's referential status? The fake bears false witness to this Other, to this life and to those forces which are not ours. The fake, being evidence only of an attempt to reproduce, points only to itself or to reproduction itself. So when we are made aware that we have to do with a fake or a reproduction, no matter how faithfully it seems executed, the experience *cannot* have the same meaning for us. And not only for reasons of sentimentality or, perhaps, of injured pride, but because from then on we can never be certain that what we took to be its "referential" features were not mere *artifacts* of the process of reproduction, that is, that what we took seriously was not merely an accident of the reproduction itself.

Now, of course postmodernism's celebrated "death of the subject" and its characteristic indifference to the difference between the virtual and the "real," between counterfeits and originals, problematizes this emphasis upon pedigree. This is, in part, why I suggested earlier that virtual experience has its purchase in postmodernity. Further, it can be argued that reproduction itself is precisely the form that characteristically postmodern traces will assume. Hence the simulacrum would be seen as the product of the working out of a peculiarly postmodern problematic with regard to reference (that is, where the referent is understood as just another text), and could therefore be regarded as a "genuine" trace. Moreover, strictly speaking, the simulacrum is not a fake, since where it reigns the original/copy distinction has lost its purchase (postmodernism represents the limit case where the ontological difference between reproduction and duplication vanishes). Hence, from the standpoint of postmodernism, my remarks valorizing narrative connections with origins must seem external, if not question-begging, observations. But is it not part of our historicity and of what it means for us to be finite to be thus narratively put in touch with that which is not purely a product of *our* freedom, to be put in touch with that which we cannot prescribe but with which we must come to terms, be it nature or history, to confront an Other that cannot be vaporized by our digitalizing gaze?[122]

Further, what of the goods internal to the activity of travel when Notre Dame is summoned at the flick of a switch? Will they not have been forfeited, even though the end will have been achieved? Instantaneous teleportive "trips" perhaps have beginnings and ends; journeys, on the other hand, have stops. Such quick trips are never quick enough. On journeys, there is always more time. And quite apart from what I have said in earlier chapters about the significance of the time of action, there is considerable evidence that the more time and trouble expended to procure a good, the more it is appreciated. One could engineer a repair of *this* loss only at the embarrassment of rendering the device that reproduces the effort gratuitous, unless we are whisked away to a place that we are currently physically unable to reach. For the condition of the value of VR technology in such substitutive contexts is that there be a discernible improvement in accessibility. And, to be sure, one can easily envision the value of such technology in procuring "the next best thing to being there" for those who, for whatever reason, are unable to travel. (The next best, however, entails loss, though of course it, like all losses, has to be seen in context with likely benefits.) And who would gainsay the didactic benefits of VR recreations in educational settings? However, as we virtualize and display, say, historical scenes for educational purposes, will not an inquiry-productive ambiguity be removed? For we may, and children certainly will, be inclined to take the simulacrum as an accurate representation of the event, and hence to see no need for further suspicion and question, no need to dig deeper. Removing the ambiguity of the written text is not an unalloyed good. Lastly, what will it mean to be able to repeat an experience at one's whim, as often as one likes? Like words too often repeated, such an experience stands in danger of losing its meaning.

All that I have urged about giving the time or history of an action its due goes to pointing to the loss incurred when the end becomes the master value and emphasis is placed upon achieving it in as little time as possible. The fake and the simulacrum cannot reproduce what is lost in the temporal-historical dimension.

Jameson characterizes the postmodern as an era where there are no more monumental works, but instead a *ceaseless* reshuffling of fragments of preexistent texts.[123] This characterizes, in a quite literal way, not only the possibilities ushered in by word processing technology and its tendency to make of our documents what I would call the "always already rewritten," but also the current hyperbole about the end of the novel and of the author.[124] Earlier I referred to video art and its structure of trumping displacements which, though they must be displayed diachronically, are meant to be conceived synchronically, much like the self-cancelling structure of irony according to de Man. Given what I have already said about irony, we are led to ask: Is there something in postmodernism, with its ceaseless repetition of difference and its trumping and reshuffling, that aims at cheating death by "stopping the clock," by removing us from time?

High modernism's acts of establishment produced "monumental works," works that staked claims in the space of meaning, and they were received as such. In staking claims, in hazarding determinate or definitive utterances, such works took positions, positions which excluded other, incompatible, positions. This renders such works highly vulnerable to contestation, and allows us to understand the anxiety often associated with their production. By understanding such works and their claims as *mere* "texts" whose content becomes almost a matter of indifference (their meaning is indeterminate), and by making of them ingredients in an indefinitely reconfigured and "reshuffled" collage or pastiche ("hypertext" word processor programs can provide concrete realizations of this), postmodernism guards itself against that vulnerability. It immunizes itself to the anxiety attendant to making a claim and, through its potentially infinite re-playing, to the anxiety that goes with facing death. Postmodernism is in this sense risk-aversive, and its technology is complicit in this aversion, an aversion that reverberates all the way from the rarefied air of semantics to the all too dense soil of history and mortality.

II

Throughout this book I have sought to examine the implications of technological rationality for our ability to find our lives meaningful and rationally defensible. I have sought to offer a critical analysis of the way in which technology has inclined us to think of ourselves and of our practices. I now want to raise the question: What is to be done?

How should a life in which technology has been assigned its proper place be conducted? For us, unable to count on securing the measure that would guide such conduct in a self-subsistent, independently existing order, to raise such questions is to inquire after the possibilities for a postmetaphysical ethics (conduct of life) and the role of technology in it. In this regard, there are at least six intelligible responses and/or aspects of a response to our encounter with time in its uncertainty and unruliness. One is the attempt to close risks off through technology. A second is to give in to risks with the cynical detachment and disingenuousness characteristic of postmodernism, being careful not to grant our allegiance to anything as a way of anesthesizing ourselves to loss. A third, mentioned in Chapter Four in terms of an "ethics of resolve," is to face the risk, take risks and resolve to hold the course, relinquishing the demand for assurances and guarantees, be they Platonic or religious, and focusing upon how our this-worldly concerns can endow our lives with meaning. A fourth is a Schopenhauer-ian resignation and pessimism, tempered only by the palliative of an ersatz satisfaction in the aesthetic experience. A fifth is a Nietzschean celebration of the loss of a synoptic whole and the freedom that its loss gives us to fashion ourselves. And last, a profession of faith *à la* Josiah Royce.[125]

I commend the third response, an ethics of resolve. To recapitulate: it is important from the outset to distinguish an "ethics of resolve" from the connotations of willful self-assertion (or of a disguised reassertion of the "will to power") that Heidegger's '*Entschlossenheit*' may have for some. I understand an ethics of resolve to be informed by an attitude towards time that is open to time's flow and that sees as its task the maintenance of integrity within the flux. Its concern is not to domesticate time but, in accepting the challenge thrown down by time, to forge, reveal and confirm the self in relation to others. Though it, unlike some of the other responses, offers no promise of shelter from the vagaries of temporal existence, it is perhaps the response that places us in the least fragile condition. For resolve, like hope and unlike optimism, has an internal history, is an engagement of the will, is a determination of the will. And resolve is to be distinguished not only from optimism, as we saw earlier in this chapter, but also from faith, acquiescence and acceptance. I shall presently be speaking of resolve in connection with the idea of preserving the integrity of practices from the hegemony of technological rationalization. This is in turn a way of preserving meaningfulness, a *sine qua non* of the good life.

I have made much of the importance of meaningful differences, and have argued that the discourse of technology constrains our ability to give expression to meaningful differences and to articulate a story that would allow us to see our lives as a whole as meaningful. As we adopt technological attitudes toward ourselves and our practices, our action more and more assumes the form of alienated labor, where we view our work only as a means to a good life increasingly identified with leisure and consumerism, forgetting the importance of choices that make a meaningful difference to a meaningful life.[126]

Technology is eminently able to provide for us a *state* of satisfaction, no matter how ephemeral. Historically, as it has become more proficient in doing so, we have been encouraged, and have increasingly tended, to emphasize as significant the end-state of satisfaction to the exclusion of seeing as significant what has been demoted to the status of *merely means*. (Much of our encouragement has come from the advertising industry, capitalist ideologues and other promoters of what Habermas and Daniel Bell call social modernity.) As indicated in Chapter Two, we collectively alienate our values insofar as they become technology's ends, ends of a rationalized practice oriented towards efficiency. Part of our task is to reclaim those ends, reclaiming them as values that help give shape and coherence to our meaningful practices. But how do we respond to the undeniable fact of the increasing marginalization of meaningful practices? How can they be made, in Borgmann's terms, "focal" again without running afoul of what I shall call the "aesthetic retrieval of meaning?"

The paradox of the aesthetic retrieval of meaning is that the project to *create* meaningful practices in order to repair or respond to our nihilistic condition is itself a capitulation to the means-ends schema of technological rationality. For such a project runs the risk of our viewing those practices as *arbitrary instruments* (to restore lost meaning). Many of the so-called "New Age" practices, with their simulacra of Native American and Egyptian rituals and so on, seem to be implicated in just such a paradox, a paradox that even Borgmann's analysis does not escape.[127]

Insofar as we view such practices as arbitrary creations or as *mere* instruments, they will not work. For with no further foundation than having been freely and wholly contingently chosen, they could with equal reason be rejected. Accordingly, we could greet the meaningful differences that they would engender with an ironic indifference. And this is the aporetic condition of modernity.[128] In a thoroughly disenchanted world, where meaning has been lost to us, it would seem that it could be regained only as the product of a conscious, creative, *willful*, and therefore ultimately arbitrary choice. Postmodernity can be seen as acknowledging this dilemma and resolving it by making its peace with the indeterminacy of meaning.

Only if our concern were with subjective states of an agent would a view of such practices as mere instruments be adequate to its task. That is, only if an end-state of private satisfaction or pleasure were the sought-after goal would such a view not undermine the role that such practices are to play. But this is, of course, precisely the technological understanding of our relation to our practices that we are here seeking to subvert. Such a separation of the end from the means is *ipso facto* a capitulation to the logic of purposive rationality. With no loss, such practices could be viewed as arbitrary and eminently replaceable by functional equivalents. On the other hand, if understanding such practices as having been created out of whole cloth subverts their role as enabling meaningful differences, then, unless there are *already* meaningful practices that have not yet wholly lost their salience for us, or that are not wholly beyond being recuperated from their inconspicuousness, meaningful differences that claim us will not be available. So, if meaning is to be possible, there must already be available to us meaningful practices, practices which in some sense have not yet fully relinquished their claim on us. There is a circle here.[129] Meaning cannot be engineered.[130] If our world were completely bereft of meaningful practices, practices whose significance cannot be duplicated by a functional equivalent, as opposed to a world in which such practices have only been marginalized, then meaning would not be possible. Must meaning then not be, in some sense, found and not made?

Structures of meaning (and canons of rationality) must in a sense already be there for us. And they *are*, even if only at the margins. Technological consciousness and postmodern sensibility are complicit in the marginalization of meaningful practices. So it is from the margins that we must seek transformative potential. Neither technological rationalization nor the postmodern project is yet absolutely pervasive, even in the West.[131] Accordingly, the reflections in this essay should be taken as cautionary reminders, as opposed to claims about the inevitability of our plight.

I suggested in Chapter Seven that our lives are already meaningful. It is now time to answer the question: What are the implications of that chapter's critique of philosophical nihilism and its establishment of the philosophical possibility of critique for what concerns us here, namely, a critical response to technology? First, by challenging the distinction between the participant and the observer, the chapter's critique corrects the self-misunderstanding on the part of a technological consciousness that would overlook its own situatedness, its own participation in taken-for-granted meaning contexts, language games, and practices of time-contraction, of domestication and of functional equivalence, that is, its own finitude. Such a recognition is likely to temper the inclination to regard other contexts of meaning as necessarily invidiously arbitrary.

Secondly, and more importantly here, while combatting this false self-understanding, the analysis in Chapter Seven at the same time represents a challenge to the world picture that those very language games and practices encourage, to the world picture underwritten by the technological attitude. This technological world picture—in authorizing and encouraging abstraction from contexts of meaning and in not acknowledging its own situatedness—predisposes us to disparage such contexts and the practices that thrive therein, and to view them as mere *constraints*, as opposed to as enabling conditions, constraints from which we should seek to emancipate ourselves. This picture relocates the source of values from such structures of meaning to such a "liberated" subject, and encourages an alienated self-understanding on our part. This picture, which brings into focus and privileges the practices of temporal domestication and so on, at the same time marginalizes and seduces us into forgetting other, meaningful practices to which we have access, practices which situate us in a meaningful order and therefore in an ordering of values not to be understood to be wholly of our own making. The picture leads us to overlook, to lose consciousness of, what we stand to lose from the spread of practices of technological rationalization (some of those losses were discussed in Chapter Five). Breaking the hold that such a nihilistic technological picture has on us—the picture of a disengaged subject freely positing values, where the legitimacy of the values derives solely from having been so posited—would help to make more lively for us the significance of those marginalized and all-but-forgotten practices.

Thirdly, insofar as this picture views critical standards derisively as arbitrary products of the will, and takes the project of critique (be it of technology or of any other object of human concern) to be a *merely* subjective enterprise, its dismantling warrants the *appeal* to structures of meaning and to ideals of rationality in carrying forward a philosophical assessment of technology. So here the argument of Chapter Seven can be understood as a metaargument, demonstrating that the standpoint of the meaningful is not invidiously arbitrary, and therefore that the enterprise of rational critique cannot be dismissed as a *mere* perspective. *Insofar* as the rejection of constraints on technology is justified by or based upon the assumption of an invidious distinction between the point of view of the values-perspective's observer and that of other practices, Chapter Seven's undermining of that distinction also undermines a basis for technology's rejection of such constraints. That is, they cannot be rejected by the institution of technology as "mere" values.

But technology occludes our awareness of this. The technological picture occludes a view of things that allows us to make *sense* of *finding* meaning in life, of being claimed by something independently of an investment of our will in it or independently of subjective states of satisfaction. I shall shortly suggest how such a nonsubjective ordering of value can emerge from practices and from practical commitments in which we find ourselves already engaged. However, such practices and commitments, if seen at all in this picture, get dismissed as merely arbitrary. But, as I have argued, though these practices and the forms of life in which they figure are nonnecessary, it would be wrong to understand them as necessarily arbitrary in an invidious sense, as if there were something else that they should aspire to be.

As pointed out in Chapter Three, human interests and concerns make it possible for there to be meaning in the world. From such fundamental interests arise the practices which in turn anchor the logical spaces or dimensions of experience within which things can have value. Neither the interests nor the meanings they enable are objectively necessary. But to call them arbitrary is again to suggest the picture of a disengaged subject, logically prior to its commitments, who *subsequently* introduces meaning into the world through sheerly willful commitments. But this cannot be an adequate description of how life becomes meaningful. For the world as viewed under the descriptions available to such a disengaged subject could make no claim on it. Hence we cannot start with the world as a pure object confronting a fully autonomous, disinterested subject and generate an account of a human experience of the world. Under such conditions, there would be, as David Wiggins puts it, "nothing which it is humanly possible to care about."[132] There would be no reason for anything in the world to matter, for us to greet anything with anything other than indifference. So this picture cannot make sense of life's having meaning. It is phenomenologically inadequate. So, again, if we are to make adequate sense of the meaning life can have, we must defer to a view in which meaning is already there, though perhaps glimpsed only through a glass darkly. And the technological picture cum the idea of technological rationality cloud the glass by understanding ends ultimately to be arbitrary products of the will, to be sheer preferences, and by understanding only means and the exclusively strategic assessment of ends to be legitimate objects of reason.

That meaning is *ultimately* nonnecessary—that it is made, however gradually and unconsciously, rather than found lying "objectively" there—does not imply that it is invidiously arbitrary, nor does it imply that we cannot *find* things and actions to be meaningful. The making associated with a framework of meaning—a framework that lets there be meaning—is largely communal, and can be thought of as the development and maintenance of a form of life. The making associated with such a frame is a necessary condition for anything mattering in a specifically human way. And experiencing the world through such frameworks allows us to understand value properties "not as created but as *lit up*" by the focus that such frames underwrite.[133] In such a way we can see the world as a place where we can *find* meaning.

Through its own domesticative practices, technology effects a shift in our attention away from practices that would make a meaningful difference. In sum, technology and its associated world picture tend to bracket "thicker" notions of meaning, what in Chapters Three through Five were called those prereflective meanings associated with the idea of repetition, and they are guilty of a self-misunderstanding with regard to a thinner "transcendental" notion.

I want now to turn to the issue of generating ethical norms from experience or practice. Let us briefly consider how such norms arise from the practices associated with our worldly involvements. The point will be to come to perceive, to put ourselves in the position to perceive, how the practices and projects in which we are already engaged, for example, parenting, friendship, communication, and loving, generate their own norms. For example, the project of love demands that the beloved's love be offered freely. There are thus, intrinsic to such a project, norms prohibiting the strategic manipulation of the beloved.[134]

Conversation, itself a meaningful practice and one of the many practices that are constitutive of the practice of friendship, offers another example. When conversations are rationalized for the purpose of giving and eliciting information only, a tendency some studies link to "computer-compulsive" persons,[135] then one forfeits other goods internal to that practice, for example, self-expression, sharing, creating and enjoying the creation of a relationship, and so on. Though we may well hesitate to regard this as an ethically objectionable violation of a norm, we would certainly regard it as an impoverishment of a practice. A relationship or a friendship is the sort of thing that can be effected in and through conversing itself. However, when even *such* a relationship is separated out as an *end* or as an explicit *aim*, then conversation is vulnerable to being transformed into a *strategy* for achieving that end. And when this occurs, conversation's significance as a mode of self-expression, as an occasion for aesthetic delight and enjoyment, for sharing, and, because it gets experienced in *common*, for effecting and reinforcing solidarity, is lost. When the relationship *per se* becomes a separated goal, as it might, for example, for a salesperson attempting to establish rapport with a potential client, or in the case of a "pickup" line, then that goal directs or steers, in a "feedback"-related way, the behavior. And the test that such conversing was not engaged in for the goods internal to it is that once the goal is achieved, the conversation is "switched off." One might speak of this in terms of manipulating a person into a relationship, rather than of fostering a relationship. And it is telling that this is a view of language emphasized by Kierkegaard's seducer and in Sartre's analysis of "being with others." (Now, this of course is not to deny that there are situations where it is perfectly legitimate to engage in such "strategic" conversation, for instance, when a therapist is attempting to establish a relationship with a client. But this is a *specialized* use of conversation, insulated from the life-world, and presumably *consensually* pursued by client and therapist.) And, of course, relationships and friendships can *themselves* be rationalized and made strategic for the procurement of other goods, for instance, job advancement. (This would be another example of what I meant when, in Chapter Four, I claimed that when ends become worldless, they can collapse into means.) And, when done, we forfeit the goods internal to friendship and, indeed, violate the integrity of that practice, insofar as it is treated merely as an instrument of expediency. We would, clearly, not be oriented by a concern to do the "best" by our friend for the sake of so doing.[136]

Once we have oriented our sight toward this aspect of our experience, we will recognize how values can be internally connected to meaningful practices. Certain ways of being, technology's purposively rationalized approaches among them, can be seen to *violate* the integrity of experiences and practices. Hence, the notion of the *integrity of a practice* will mark a dimension within which norms will find a place. The idea of the integrity of a practice is linked to an ethics of resolve, in that both reject the imperatives of domesticating time and of bracketing historicity in the interest of expediency.[137] I referred obliquely to this idea earlier when, in Chapter Six, I discussed Habermas's notion of the colonization of the life-world by systemic mechanisms. Though Habermas does not explicitly use 'integrity' in his discussion, it seems to capture what he is getting at. My commentary on his discussion suggested that the interactive dimension, the dimension of both cultural and linguistic meaning, is compromised by such technical incursions.

A practice can be said to have integrity to the degree that the internal relation between the ends or values that it seeks to achieve and the meaning that gives it a point is respected. The notion of integrity here provides a framework for norms, in that normative pressure is brought to bear by the requirement that the end that a practice seeks to achieve be so related. "I work for Aetna, but I am a nurse first," though uttered by an actor in a TV commercial, is nicely expressive of the sensibility that I am commending here.

This is not meant to imply that there is only one way to pursue a practice. But social and cultural templates for roles set limits on the interpretations that get "lived out" as we fulfill the roles associated with meaningful practices. So, with the roles come norms such that our failure to satisfy those norms can be publicly recognized and assessed. Nor, of course, as I have argued at length, does it imply that all the norms governing our practices are immune to criticism.

Health care practices provide telling examples of end-oriented thinking where ends or goals are separated from the dimension of meaning and the integrity of a practice can be said to have been violated. For example, an exclusive concern with the prolongation of life for its own sake, without due attention to how the surplus days of the elderly will be meaningful, is particularly illustrative.

Acknowledging the inadequacy of the picture that opposes an autonomous self to an objective world, nursing professors Patricia Benner and Judith Wrubel endorse the position advocated in this book in holding that we are always already constituted by concern, a concern that lets worldly things and events matter.[138] In keeping with this, they draw a distinction between illness and disease. Illness is understood as the human *experience* of loss or of dysfunction, while disease is understood as the manifestation of aberration at the tissue, cellular or organ levels.[139] They go on to draw a distinction between, on the one hand, caring practices, practices that acknowledge the dimensions of embodiment, concern and meaning, and, on the other, purely technological or strategic interventions that, bypassing those dimensions, are oriented exclusively by the goal or value of eradicating disease.[140] The latter strategic interventions are underwritten by an abstraction of physiological conditions from contexts of meaning. In their view, caring practices must acknowledge situational meanings, must acknowledge why a particular dysfunction matters to a particular patient. Ultimately, caring requires an ability to engage in a conversation framed in terms of a vocabulary drawn from the patient's field of meaning.

Benner and Wrubel hold that the practice of nursing, when most effective, is a caring practice. It includes among its aims attaining an understanding of how the patient "lives" her illness (so that one can respond to *that* in one's practice) and allowing the patient to feel understood. The promotion of this latter feeling is a good inherent to this practice, a good that is not likely to be procured by a functional replacement. The pursuit of these aims requires that the nurse adopt an *ethical* attitude towards the patient in that the latter must be treated as a subject who is a potential partner in conversation, occupying the center of a field of meaning, a subject who inhabits a world. The nurse must thus be attuned to the dimension of mattering. Consequently the integrity of nursing practice requires an ethics of care and responsiveness.[141] Or, put in a more Aristotelian vocabulary, being guided by such an ethics is a virtue in a nurse.

The point is that nursing practice seeks not only to cure disease, but also to be responsive to the situated meanings of persons. So caring responses to the stress of illness are predicated upon a view of stress as a disruption in the world of a worldly subject, as a disruption of meaning and smooth functioning, rather than a view of it as signaling the frustration of a purely goal-directed, productivist self, a self standing in external history over against an alien and alienating world.[142] An exclusively medical or technological response, one that treats the disease or physiological anomaly only, would constitute a corruption of caring practices and a violation of, or would at least manifest an indifference towards, the patient's subjectivity. For example, the "same" sensation can be lived or experienced in different ways depending upon its significance, and responding only to the sensation can miss the point. The pain associated with cancer treatment is not as distressing as the pain associated with signs of recurrence.[143]

Benner and Wrubel recognize that they are waving the banner of a marginalized practice, for medicine is increasingly technology driven. It is almost as if, as Richard Rorty suggested in conversation, patients existed for the sake of amortizing the technology, which technology is purchased in the hope of giving a hospital a competitive advantage in attracting patients. As an example, a friend of mine, for whom daily athletic activity is extremely important, injured his ankle while playing basketball. Though indications were that his problem could quite easily have been diagnosed by a more traditional medical examination, MRI, or "magnetic resonance imaging," was prescribed. This state-of-the-art technology required a specially trained technician to decipher the results of the procedure. Since one could not easily be found, the diagnosis was postponed by several days, thus postponing treatment and the time at which my friend could resume his active life. What mattered to him ended up being subordinated to the requirements of the technology.[144]

Purely technological procedures impoverish or corrupt both what Borgmann calls focal practices and what can be called the human practices. By the former, I refer to practices that are valued not only for what they procure but also for the goods internal to them, for example, their centering and focusing properties, or the ways in which we get implicated in the process of performing them. By the latter, I mean expert and nonexpert practices whose field of application is human subjectivity or intersubjectivity, and whose effectiveness arguably therefore depends upon a responsiveness to embodied and situational meanings.[145] And of course these two sorts of practice overlap.[146] Among the goods internal to, or meaningful effects of, a practice are the effects that flow from the practice's engagement with situational and prereflective meanings. And when such engagement occurs, a practice implicates us even more; it has more "weight." And certainly, our quotidian interests and concerns provide the context or occasion for some of our most meaningful focal practices. For example, one need think only of how our concernful awareness of our need for nurture and of our mortality provide the occasions for the culture of the table and funeral rituals, respectively.

In the human practices in general, effective practice requires attentiveness to how the various strategies associated with those practices, and the correlative goals of those strategies, are lived. This is another way of stressing the significance of the internal relation of meaning to value, a relation requisite to effective parenting, friendship and so on. Only if we think of such practices as purely technological interventions that mediate between an autonomous self and its goals, ends or values, interventions that mediate without implicating that self, can those practices be understood to be displaceable and rendered marginal without loss. But if we understand how we are meaningfully engaged with and by them, we see that loss will always be the price of displacement.

Once we orient our sight toward this aspect of our experience, we will recognize how meaningful practices, while neither transcendental nor necessary, provide us with the conceptual and moral resources from which to criticize both technology and other potentially distortive social arrangements and practices. For a final example of such a potentially distortive understanding—and, indeed, here a productivist technological understanding—of the practice of caring, witness recent corporate policy prohibiting discrimination against gays, not out of a concern for respect or even for rights, but on the grounds that homosexuals will feel more relaxed about sharing their personal lives and will, as a consequence, be less anxious and therefore more *productive*. Compassion and how it can work for you!

The ethics that I have adumbrated in this essay is one that is reflective of our being-in-time and of the uncertainty and unruliness of that situation. To live postmetaphysically is to live without surety, is to face the risky. Being able to appeal neither to metaphysics' redemptive transfiguration of the temporal nor to its sanction of a disdainful neglect of the timely, we are left to face time without mitigation. Technology wants to arrest the flow, to stop or freeze the flux. I have spoken of repetition as an openness to the flux, but with a keel to prevent capsizing and to allow us to stay the course. The point has been to display the rationality of *investment* without *certainty*. To live with resolve is to recognize that our timely existence need not be cause for despair, and that something of significance stands to be lost if we overvalue the project to disarm contingency.

I wish now to dispel the notion that the critique of technology articulated in this study is a blanket condemnation of modernity. I shall do so in terms of a brief response to the sort of backward-looking, antimodernist intervention that one encounters in the recent work of Christopher Lasch. Recent antimodernist interventions, such as Lasch's *The True and Only Heaven: Progress and its Critics*, express a justifiable concern about unlimited technological progress and the indefinite expansion of material needs. Lasch responds to these developments by advocating the importance of accepting limits. I too raise this issue in my discussion of technology and postmodernism. However, as much as it behooves us to pause to listen to these voices, analyses like Lasch's are quite problematic. For what is to count as a limit is not self-announcing. Lasch, for example, offers no criterion for applying his advice. How are we to determine what the limits are? Further, he seems not to recognize that limits or fate, or what counts as either, are both historically and, very significantly, *politically* conditioned. Hence, presumably not all limits deserve to be respected. How do we distinguish those that should be from those that should not be? His analysis therefore, it seems, is informed by a false dichotomy: either we surrender to fate *or* we capitulate to a fetishization of control; either we accept the blind workings of nature *or* we view every aspect of life as subject to choice.

Lasch ends up by uncritically, and in my view unjustifiably, privileging work-ing-class perspectives and values, the worldview of what was called "the silent majority." He thinks, for example, that what is largely at issue in the abortion debate is two attitudes towards the future—fate versus control, acceptance versus planning.[147] But that one cannot plan everything does not imply that one cannot, or should not, plan some things. Here he loads the dice. Why assume that pro-choice partisans are driven *only* by the standard of competitive advantage? Furthermore, that there are limits does not imply that we know where they are, and that we should accept everything that contingently happens to happen. That is, it is a matter for reasoned debate just which limits should be respected and which should not be.

Lasch understands the modern project to consist in the substitution of human choice for the blind workings of nature.[148] And this is, of course, true. If neoconservatives applaud what Daniel Bell and Habermas refer to as social modernity but reject cultural modernity, then Lasch, perhaps more consistently, rejects both. He seems to assume that cultural modernism necessarily leads to seeing the world merely as a resource for the satisfaction of our rapacious materialism. But, as Habermas would argue, this is not neccessary. The Enlightenment project can develop along an alternative track, for instance, towards communicative rather than the monological rationality of postmodernity. Lasch's logic entombs us squarely, it seems, in Weber's iron cage.[149] Why cannot the West, at least in principle, hold up enlightened and critical culture as an exemplary form of life without holding up its standard of living as such an example? Why cannot the critical temperament be directed at consumptive life-styles, for example? In fact, does not Lasch's own practice provide us with an example of just that?

Progressive optimism, Lasch holds, rests upon a denial of the *natural* limits of human power and freedom.[150] But again, such limits are historically and technologically determined. For instance, new sources of energy or more economical ways to use the old are certainly conceivable.[151] As a consequence, such limits cannot be posited *a priori* in order to say what *cannot* be done.[152]

We have arrived at a juncture where it is helpful to ask: Should we continue to pursue the hermeneutic directions opened up by Heidegger and Gadamer, in the manner of Chapters Four and Five, which emphasized the fact that technology puts repetition out of play, which opposed repetition to rupture, the meaning perspective and continuity in time to the values-perspective and discontinuity in time? Or should we be critical of technological rationality because of its tendency to repress noncoerced argumentative discourse about practical questions as opposed to technical ones? The *aporias* that Habermas's project faces notwithstanding, it does challenge us to discriminate rationally between the meaningful that is good and that which is not. Hence my earlier claim that Habermas wins the Habermas-Gadamer debate phenomenologically (in capturing the nature of the *experience*—at least *our* experience?—of ethical deliberation) and Gadamer wins ontologically (in pointing out the conditionedness of that deliberation).

I would like to bring the two positions into a dialectical juxtaposition by thematizing a final Scylla and Charybdis I should like to steer between, having introduced Lasch's discussion of limits and fate. I commend a position that places the burden of proof on both extremes (on pure traditionalism, on the one hand, and on the modernist rejection of tradition, on the other), a burden which requires that each show its credentials, that each display its *bona fides*. This would be a position that thus interrogates both extremes and thereby carves out for itself a middle space, confirming Lasch's dichotomy as a false one. It would be a determinate negation of both social modernity and Lasch's populism. In this way, one could point in a responsible fashion to both the danger and the legitimacy of technology. A notion of repetition-cum-critical innovation—alluded to, albeit briefly, in Chapter Four—would, at least in an abstract way, capture this middle position. There is little that is *a priori* in these matters. The proper admixture of repetition and critique is a matter for judgment and conversation. The idea of a reflective equilibrium commends itself here, where it is a matter of being intelligibly connected with the old but seeking to hear what the new has to say, where old and new issue each other reciprocal rejoinders. And indeed, judgment and conversation are ineliminable, but if my position is to be a determinate one, one ought to be able to infer guidelines from it. The guidelines would be the set of questions that emerge from the interrogation of the extremes, and they would converge upon such questions as: *What level of instrumentalization and of technical rationalization is necessary or consistent, under existing though contestable conditions of natural or quasinatural adversity and scarcity, with a socially emancipated life, meaningfully lived?* It is precisely the spirit of such questions that I sought to capture in my notion of humanity as a conversationally negotiated project and by commending meaningfulness, self-recognition and the representation of general interests as candidates for its criterial properties. Taking such questions seriously should help us to determine which practices and social issues should be submitted to technological rationalization, and to what extent, and which should not. It should further sensitize us to some of the trade-offs we may face insofar as certain issues *are* treated technologically.

At issue in discussions guided by such questions will be decisions regarding the relative proportion of *techne, praxis* and play in such a life. The examination of a life might look to how these various modes and the temporalities corresponding to them are interrelated within a life and, indeed, within a society. Is one mode present disproportionately, for example, or is one missing altogether? Here, for example, we can begin to highlight the *legitimacy* of the postmodernist sensibility as it informs aesthetic expressiveness and play. Or the examination can have to do with one of these dimensions or modalities itself. For example, the modality of *praxis* gives rise to the question: Is this the kind of being I want to be; is this the shape I want my life to assume? When we tell stories about our lives, those stories will be woven from the threads provided by these three modalities.

The sort of conversation that I envision would not, therefore, lead to rampant, uncritical technophobia, for under certain conditions of natural adversity we might well want *more* scientific-technical progress, for instance, a cure for cancer, for AIDS and so on. But even here, as I have already suggested, we must attend not only to the pursuit of health defined in purely physiological terms but also to the caring practices and the concern for the wholeness of a life that would place that pursuit in perspective.

This would place us at odds, then, not with domesticative technology *per se*, but with its hegemony. Moreover, if, as I suggest in Chapter Two, all technologies have their origin in intersubjective values, and those values come to include the metavalues associated with what Habermas calls "technology as ideology," then an alteration in those metavalues could lead to an alteration in the direction of technical development.[153] The new role of technology would then ideally be the outcome of something like a consensus arising from a discursive will formation, ever vigilant to uncover and criticize sources of domination and distortion, and, of course, also committed to discuss what should *count* as domination and distortion, given communitarian insights. Questions of the sort that I have alluded to define the boundaries for the contestation of what is to be done, a conversational contestation calling upon all of our powers of judgment. Our times demand nothing less.

Notes

Chapter 1

1. Heidegger, "The Word of Nietzsche: 'God is Dead'," in *The Question Concerning Technology and Other Essays*, trans. William Lovitt (New York: Harper, 1977), pp. 53–112; and Albert Borgmann, *Technology and the Character of Contemporary Life: A Philosophical Inquiry* (Chicago: University of Chicago Press, 1984), pp. 79–81.

2. *Cf.* for example, Mark Poster, *The Mode of Information* (Chicago: University of Chicago Press, 1990), pp. 8, 12.

3. Heidegger, "The Word of Nietzsche," pp. 71–72.

4. *Ibid.*, p. 75.

5. Constance Penley and Andrew Ross, eds. *Technoculture* (Minneapolis: University of Minnesota Press, 1991), p. xii.

6. See Andrew Feenberg, *Critical Theory of Technology* (New York: Oxford University Press, 1991), p. 4; and Jane Flax, *Psychoanalysis, Feminism and Postmodernism in the Contemporary West* (Berkeley: University of California Press, 1990), p. 33.

Chapter 2

1. See Albert Borgmann, *Technology and the Character of Contemporary Life: A Philosophical Inquiry* (Chicago: University of Chicago Press, 1984), pp. 9–12. Borgmann does not think, however, that these views exhaust the plausible positions on the issue. There are intermediate views between these. For example, some writers in the Marxian-inspired tradition of critical theory are inclined to adopt an historicized noninstrumentalist view.

2. There is a considerable and growing literature challenging the idea of technological determinism. This is especially so in the case of works emphasizing the social construction of technology. See, for example, W. E. Bijker *et al.*, eds., *The Social Construction of Technological Systems* (Cambridge: MIT Press, 1987); and

D. MacKenzie and J. Wajcman, eds., *The Social Shaping of Technology* (Philadelphia: Open University Press, 1985).

3. Mark Zvelebil, "Clues to Recent Human Evolution from Specialized Technologies," *Nature* 307, No. 5949, January 26, 1984, p. 314, cited in Thomas DeGregori, *A Theory of Technology* (Ames: Iowa State University Press, 1985), p. 14.

4. See also DeGregori, pp. 14f.

5. DeGregori, p. 16. The three distinctive aspects of technology just mentioned will be the basis for distinguishing technology from science, *praxis* and art, respectively.

6. *Ibid.*, p. 37.

7. See Melvin Kranzberg and Carroll Pursell, eds., *Technology in Western Civilization*, vol. 2, (New York: Oxford University Press, 1967), p. 18.

8. See, for example, Marike Finlay, "William Leiss on Technology: A Foucauldian and Habermasian Reading," *Canadian Journal of Political and Social Theory* 10 (1986), pp. 174–195; and Finlay, "Technology as Practice and So What About Emancipatory Interest?" *Canadian Journal of Political and Social Theory* 11 (1987), pp. 198–214. See also MacKenzie and Wajcman, *op. cit.* I disagree sharply, however, with Finlay's assumption that any attempt to formulate and abstract a set of features common to various social embodiments of technology is a form of illegitimate essentializing, of hypostasizing such a set, of holding it to have an independent existence. Pointing to the social construction of processes of technological labor under conditions of capitalist production, for example, does not invalidate my claim about relatively invariant features that manifest themselves at an appropriate level of description. What the claim of social constructionism does here is to point out that the ends that technology serves are sometimes what Habermas would call "nongeneralizable," i.e., socially or politically biased, values. That is, sometimes the point of a technology is not only to produce a product more efficiently, but also to monitor and control the worker during its production, i.e., to produce a particular social relation.

9. On such matters, see Finlay, *op. cit.*; Constance Penley and Andrew Ross, *Technoculture* (Minneapolis: University of Minnesota Press, 1991); and Andrew Feenberg, *A Critical Theory of Technology* (Oxford: Oxford University Press, 1991).

10. See Mario Bunge, "Toward a Philosophy of Technology," in *Philosophy and Technology: Readings in the Philosophical Problems of Technology*, eds., Introduction by Carl Mitcham and Robert Mackey (New York: The Free Press, 1972), pp. 68–70.

11. Bunge, p. 63.

12. It is important to acknowledge here the widespread challenge to the view that technology is simply applied science in the sense of technological advance requiring scientific discovery, or in the sense of technological development's stimulus necessarily coming from scientific discovery. Technological advance, it is argued, can occur without any *additional* scientific knowledge being introduced into its cognitive base, be that knowledge previously known but not yet applied, or new. For example, witness the world-historical innovations of mass production and the concept of interchangeable parts. Further, scholars point to instances of technological develop-

ment being stimulated not by an opportunity to develop applications suggested by a prior scientific advance, but rather by needs within a given technological system. See, for example, Thomas Parke Hughes, "The Science-Technology Interaction: the Case of High-Voltage Power Transmission Systems," *Technology and Culture* 17 (1976), pp. 646–659. The point of view that I am advancing in the text does not conflict with the position indicated here, for when a technological advance is predicated neither upon a scientific advance nor upon the application of science already known, then either the system in which it constitutes an advance is based upon science, or both the advance and the system are the results of the application of scientific method.

13. Hughes, p. 651; and Otto Mayr, "The Science-Technology Relationship as a Historiographical Problem," *Technology and Culture* 17 (1976), p. 667. Further complicating this problem is the fact that what, at a given time, is taken to be the science-technology distinction may be in part a social construction, or may be determined by what society judges to be practical and irrelevant to practice at a given time. See Nathan Reingold and Arthur Molella, "Introduction" to papers reprinted from "The Interaction of Science and Technology in the Industrial Age," *Technology and Culture* 17 (1976), p. 629; and Otto Mayr, p. 664.

14. See "Discussion of Paper by Thomas Hughes," *Technology and Culture, op. cit.*, p. 660. As Hughes' discussion of F. W. Peek's research into the nature of lightning indicates, aspects of a research technologist's activity can genuinely be labeled 'scientific' (Hughes, p. 656). However, I would argue that typically the extent of the research technologist's forays towards the "science" end of the spectrum is a function of what her practical project requires. In Peek's case, the project required the simulation of lightning in order to test various components of transmission lines. I would suggest then that a technologist's position on the spectrum is determined on a "need to know" basis, which is a function of practical exigency.

15. Those who would reject the salience of the cognitive/practical distinction here— and that would include both those whose view of science is informed by some version of instrumentalism or pragmatism and those influenced by some trends within the Frankfurt School of Critical Theory or in the thought of Husserl, Heidegger and Max Scheler—and who would claim that science itself is but a device for technical control and manipulation, face the challenge of giving an adequate account of the different criteria of success that characterize what are generally acknowledged to be the distinguishable enterprises of science and technology. Though social values may influence what gets brought under scientific scrutiny, the purely scientific will is ultimately "disinterested," in the specific sense that it is not wed to a particular experimental outcome. For it, the "pressures of life" are bracketed or neutralized (though they may not be for an individual scientist). The technological will is not disinterested in this sense. Even fundamental engineering research—basic scientific research with an eye to practical payoff—is committed to finding corroborated scientific claims that may prove *useful* (see Joseph Agassi, "Between Science and Technology," *Philosophy of Science* 47 (March 1980), p. 93). If we, with Karl Popper, agree that science progresses by, and ultimately seeks, falsifications or refutations, then we can distinguish the criteria of scientific success from even those of fundamental engineering research. The commitment to truth on the part of the

scientific community is sufficiently strong (at least in principle and ideally) to redeem the self-negation of a refutation. Though a postempiricist such as Thomas Kuhn might contest this claim, my point is that at least it can be *argued* in the case of science, because of its cognitive commitment. But it cannot be argued in the case of technology, because of its commitment to success in reliably altering the world. While refutations are cognitive achievements, and are for this reason "suffered" by science, they signify failure in the practical arena (See Karl R. Popper, *Conjectures and Refutations: The Growth of Scientific Knowledge* (London: Routledge, 1963), pp. 112–114; and Agassi, pp. 94–98).

Tendencies to conflate science and technology are often predicated upon an uncritical identification of truth and usefulness. For example, often the distinction is not made between the success of laboratory operations and the success of practical operations in the overdetermined world outside the laboratory. The practical, real-world success or failure of a scientific theory is not, in general, an index of its truth, or even of its warranted assertibility. There are many cases of false scientific theories being of great practical use. One need think only of the usefulness of Ptolemaic cosmography for navigational calculations. Or of N. A. Otto's successful internal combustion engine, which turned out to be based upon false theoretical assumptions (see Lynwood Bryant, "The Silent Otto," *Technology and Culture* 7 (1966), pp. 184–200). There are a number of reasons for this: (1) either the false part of the theory is not used in the deduction that informs the technological application, or the false part has no practical consequences; (2) because the emphasis in technology is upon using knowledge to achieve a real-world goal rather than on "stepping back" in order to achieve cognitive security, the levels of precision demanded in practice are often far lower than that demanded in scientific research, where precision is an element of a theory's falsifiability; and (3) in real situations, relevant variables are seldom adequately known and precisely controlled, for in the domain of practice, timely and effective action is much too strongly urged to permit the detailed study necessary to isolate and assess relevant independent variables (see Bunge, pp. 65–66). Theory choice in science, no matter how little it is algorithmically governed or how much it is value-laden, remains an epistemic affair. Technology's concern with extraepistemic values such as reliability, safety, standardization and speed, at the possible expense of depth, scope, accuracy, and fruitfulness for further research programs, makes its criteria of success rather different from those of science (see Bunge, p. 76). An epistemically promising new theory may well be rejected in favor of a less promising but less risky alternative.

Even if one argues, as is Habermas's wont, that the technical interest underlies science's projection of its object domain, we can still acknowledge the distinction of the two enterprises at the level of their self-understanding, a distinction that accounts for different criteria of success and hence observable differences in institutional dynamics. This is a distinction that our universities neglect at their peril in the current rush towards corporate sponsorship of research. For a fuller discussion of some of the issues broached here, see my "Critical Remarks Concerning Marcuse's Notion of Science," *Philosophy of the Social Sciences* 13 (1983), pp. 451–463.

16.   See Henryk Skolimowski, "The Structure of Thinking in Technology," in *Philosophy and Technology*, p. 44.

17. See Jacques Ellul, *The Technological Society*, trans. John Wilkinson, Introduction by Robert K. Merton (New York: Vintage, 1967), pp. 79–146. One must be wary, however, of Ellul's striking tendency to hypostasize technology as an independent force. See also John Kenneth Galbraith, *The New Industrial State* (New York: New American Library, 1968), and *Economics and the Public Purpose* (New York: New American Library, 1975).

18. Ellul, p. 74. It is often useful to distinguish the three terms 'technique,' 'the technical,' and 'technology' in the following manner: 'technique' refers to action which is concerned with effectiveness in the achievement of a given goal but not necessarily with efficiency; 'the technical' refers to that which concerns itself with goal-oriented action in general, where the consideration of efficiency is constitutive; 'technology' refers to that specification of the technical in which effectiveness and efficiency are grounded by science.

19. If the quantity of labor displaced by a technical improvement is not greater than or equal to the labor congealed in that improvement, then it is not profitable to adopt it. Karl Marx, *Capital: A Critique of Political Economy*, trans. Samuel Moore and Edward Aveling, ed. Frederick Engels, vol. 1: *The Process of Capitalist Production* (New York: International Publishers, 1967), p. 392.

20. *Cf.* Karl Marx, *The Grundrisse*, trans. and ed. David McLellan (New York: Harper and Row, Harper Torchbooks, 1971), p. 143; and Ellul, p. 82.

21. See Ellul, pp. 81–82, 133.

22. Ferenc Feher, Agnes Heller and Gyorgy Markus, *Dictatorship over Needs: An Analysis of Soviet Societies* (Oxford: Basil Blackwell, 1983), p. 230.

23. Friedrich Klemm, *A History of Western Technology* (New York: Charles Scribner's Sons, 1959), p. 325.

24. From Lenin's letter to the Chairman of the Electrification Commission, 14 March, 1920, cited in Klemm, p. 325. See also Ellul, pp. 144, 290.

25. Ellul, pp. 245f. See Langdon Winner, *Autonomous Technology: Technics-Out-of-Control as a Theme in Political Thought* (Cambridge: MIT Press, 1977) for a critical analysis of this position.

26. Feher *et al.*, p. 230. Ellul's and Feher *et al.*'s claims are expressions of what has come to be called a "convergence theory," some versions of which enjoy a virtual consensus among social scientists. Underlying this dominant view of the "imperatives of modernization" is the assumption that technology has its own autonomous logic of development and that recipient social systems are bent to technology's imperatives in such a way that those systems will ultimately converge upon similar trajectories of development (see Feenberg, p. 119). The theory then implies that technological development in communist societies will converge with the Western model. The stagnation and collapse of communist economies is taken as empirical evidence for this thesis, for the "imperatives of modernization" require that those societies adopt more and more Western models of social organization in order to realize industrial technology's potential, just as, for the same reasons, Western societies adopt elements of regulation and planning (Feenberg, pp. 120, 121; and see also, Albert Borgmann's "Introduction" to *Europe, America and Technology: Philosophical*

Perspectives, ed. Paul T. Durbin (Dordrecht: Kluwer Academic Publishers, 1991)). Both advocates of social constructivist studies of technology and critical theorists such as Feenberg reject such analyses, arguing that it is not technology *per se* that accounts for the observed convergence but rather the adoption by socialist societies of a *particular form* of technology from the West, a capitalistic form embodying an authoritarian culture of work (Feenberg, p. 132). Hence, political values are held to be accountable for convergence rather than technological imperatives. While I am sympathetic to such attempts to demonstrate the plausibility of combining progressive social transformation with technological progress, and I think that surely Ellul's claims are too broad and sweeping as framed, I am nevertheless not convinced by strategies such as Feenberg's. Those who, like Feenberg, would historicize "technology" and "efficiency," and who would thus reject wholesale Ellul's talk about a single "technical phenomenon," have at least the following three challenges to meet. First, to demonstrate that convergent social institutions result from a "capitalistically coded" technology and not from technology *per se*, one needs a notion of the form those institutions would assume absent a capitalistically coded industrial system. But given that, *ex hypothesi*, there are no going examples of noncapitalistically coded industrial systems whose associated social institutions we can inspect, the confirmation of such an historicist claim is fraught with considerable methodological challenges if it is not to be circular or question-begging. Secondly, even if what is taken to be technology today *is* socially and culturally coded for capitalism and is not, therefore, the only form that technology *can* assume, it would seem that capitalism's increasingly global reach would leave very little room for anything other than a marginal status for technology coded in other ways. What, in the Hegelian sense, are the "real possibilities" of alternatives now? Thirdly, and most important for my project, it remains to be shown that we cannot speak coherently of a formal technological "residue" that survives transformations in social and cultural codes and, further, that such a residue does not itself have implications of import. (What I refer to as the "domestication of time" is an example of such an implication.) Feenberg, for instance, grants that means-end rationality is such an "unsurpassable dimension" of modern industrialism (p. 126).

27. See Feenberg, p. 121.

28. Ellul, p. 80.

29. "Edges Fray on Volvo's Brave New Humanistic World," *New York Times*, July 7, 1991.

30. "Comparative Evaluation of Streptokinase and r-TPA to Reduce Myocardial Damage in Acute Myocardial Infarction: An Echographic Study," *Journal of the American Medical Association*, vol. 265, No. 24, (June 26, 1991), p. 3232. There is another current example from the field of cardiology. It has been a subject of some controversy whether a very expensive procedure known as the excimer laser angioplasty is really more effective at relieving vascular constriction than the much less expensive conventional balloon angioplasty. It has been argued that the laser procedure helps less than 5% of patients. But see Litvak *et al.*, "Laser Coronary Angioplasty," *American Journal of Cardiology*, vol. 66 (November 1, 1990), p. 1027, cited in *American Family Physician*, vol. 43, No. 3, pp. 1044–1045. In general (at least until quite recently), medicine in the U.S. has been a particularly telling example

of an institution driven almost exclusively by technologial rationality. I return to this in Chapter Eight.

31. See DeGregori, p. 39. See also Thomas P. Hughes, "The Evolution of Large Technological Systems," in *The Social Construction of Technological Systems*.

32. The first expression is, of course, derived from the translated title of Ellul's book, while the second refers to an essay by Jürgen Habermas.

33. Lewis Mumford, *Technics and Civilization* (New York: Harcourt, Brace and World, 1963), pp. 14–18.

34. Frederick W. Taylor, *The Principles of Scientific Management* (New York, 1911). See also Kranzberg and Pursell, pp. 52–55.

35. Ellul, p. 137.

36. See Klemm, p. 88; and Daniel Boorstin, *The Discoverers* (New York: Random House, 1983), pp. 36–46.

37. In his *The Culture of Time and Space: 1880–1918* (Cambridge: Harvard University Press, 1983), pp. 110–111, Stephen Kern discusses the ways in which the rapid rise in the use of pocket watches in the last decades of the nineteenth century markedly increased the sense of calculability and predictability in human relations.

38. E. P. Thompson, "Time, Work-Discipline, and Industrial Capitalism," in *Classes, Power, and Conflict*, ed. by Anthony Giddens and David Held (Berkeley: University of California Press, 1982), p. 306. It is remarkable how psychological disturbances can, because of their very extremity, distill basic human concerns into a markedly pure form. My wife, a psychotherapist, tells of a client who refused to wear a watch, for it was, to her, a dreadful reminder that time is running out.

39. See also Klemm, pp. 195–196, concerning the influence on technological development of seventeenth-century Protestant aversion to the wasting of time, to the loss of even one minute.

40. Borgmann, p. 191.

41. Anthony Giddens speaks of capitalism's role—because of its imperative to increase surplus value and its requirement that qualitatively different kinds of labor be rendered commensurable—in the demand that socially necessary labor time be reduced and that time be an objective and neutral medium in terms of which qualitatively different kinds of labor can be compared (*A Contemporary Critique of Historical Materialism* (Berkeley and Los Angeles: University of California Press, 1981)). However, we must keep in mind that the Galilean achievement of an objective notion of time, independent of the rhythms of lived human experience, predates industrial capitalism, as does, as Giddens acknowledges, the idea of linear time, which owes its origin in part to Christianity (pp. 132–133). What we should say, perhaps, is that the notion of linear, objective time is an enabling condition of capitalism (as it is also of modern technology) which in turn emphasizes and privileges such a notion to the exclusion of other ways of understanding time. Further, in keeping with the view that technology does not take its *arche* from capitalism alone, we might say that technology is a more than "willing carrier" of capitalism's attitude toward time. Hence, it might be said that in capitalist societies,

technology's imperative to contract time is overdetermined. In such cases, the will to time contraction can be linked both to a deep-seated, species-wide, anthropological interest arising from the awareness of our finitude, as well as to capitalism's own concerns.

Chapter 3

1. Mary Hesse, "In Defense of Objectivity," in *Revolutions and Reconstructions in the Philosophy of Science* (Bloomington: Indiana University Press, 1980).

2. See Richard Rorty, *Philosophy and the Mirror of Nature* (Princeton: Princeton University Press, 1979); and Hans Küng, *Does God Exist?*, trans. Edward Quinn (Garden City: Doubleday, 1980). Karl Pavlovic, in "Science and Autonomy: The Prospects for Hermeneutic Science," *Man and World* 14 (1981), pp. 127–140, also advances an argument for methodological commonality.

3. One thinks here of the writers associated with the Frankfurt School, particularly of Herbert Marcuse (Jürgen Habermas is a notable exception). Because such writers tend to reject science too sweepingly, their discussions are tantamount to a Hegelian indeterminate negation, and consequently lack power.

4. One might also think of Hegel's notion of experience in the Introduction to the *Phenomenology of Spirit*. Both the criteria and the validity claims discussed there are part of a form of life, and in the course of experience, both undergo transformations. I return to these themes in Chapter Seven.

5. I have already suggested, and will argue at greater length in chapters to come, that an adequate understanding of values entails thematizing their internal connection to structures of meaning.

6. Though as I argued in the last chapter, we should be very wary of *reducing* science to this. Less contentiously, we might say that science embodies a view of experience that is commensurate with a mathematical projection of nature, a projection which yields enormous cognitive dividends.

7. Throughout the discussion in this paragraph and the next, the reader might keep in mind an example of some sort of prereflectively meaningful action that takes place against a background of *unarticulated* cultural assumptions or claims, assumptions from which the action derives its meaning even though the agents typically are not explicitly aware of them. For instance, consider the action of helping one's neighbor paint her house against the background assumption of communalism, or the action of not helping one's neighbor against the background assumption of individualism.

8. There are obvious affinities between this view of experience and the model provided by Hegel's speculative notion of experience, whereby moments of a particular whole become articulated and reintegrated; however, I hold experience to be open-ended.

9. Gadamer opposes the metaphorical relationship which structures ordinary language to the subsumptive relationship which, he claims, is characteristic of the scientific organization of experience, and, on that basis, he draws a distinction between ordinary and scientific experience (*Truth and Method* (New York: Seabury Press, 1975), pp. 314ff, 392). The recent work of Hesse and Kuhn serves to question the

validity of that opposition when applied to science and therefore also the distinction between hermeneutic and scientific experience that is based on it (Mary Hesse, "The Explanatory Function of Metaphor," in *Revolutions and Reconstructions in the Philosophy of Science*; and Thomas Kuhn, "Second Thoughts on Paradigms," in *The Essential Tension* (Chicago: University of Chicago Press, 1977)). While it may be misguided to draw a distinction between scientific and hermeneutic activity, as Gadamer does, on *that* basis, I shall argue that it can and must be drawn on another basis.

10. I say 'more or less' because some of that analysis, particularly the discussion of the analytic-synthetic aspects of experience, constitutes somewhat of a departure from what the tradition of philosophical hermeneutics offers. I certainly do believe, however, that it is very much in the spirit of a hermeneutic account of experience.

11. Martin Heidegger, "The Age of the World Picture," in *The Question Concerning Technology and Other Essays*, trans. and Introduction by William Lovitt (New York: Harper and Row, 1977), p. 127.

12. Karl-Otto Apel and Habermas can be seen as suggesting, from the point of view of a philosophical anthropology, a basis for this *a priori* by claiming that the methodology and the character of the object domain of modern natural science are rooted in an interest in control over objectified natural processes. (See the discussion in Chapter Two, especially Note 15, for an indication of some of the complexities involved in positions such as Apel's and Habermas's.)

13. A further example of the relationship between the first two levels is provided by the discovery of Neptune and the explanation of the precession of Mercury's perihelion. The first-level hypothetical predictions of Uranus's orbit, drawn from Newtonian theory, were falsified by the observation of irregularities or perturbations in its orbit. Astronomers, however, did not thereby give up Newtonian theory, a second-level commitment. Instead, they hypothesized, using Newtonian celestial mechanics, that there was a disturbing astronomical body, with certain specifiable properties, that was responsible for Uranus's perturbed motion. This hypothesis led to the discovery of Neptune, the guilty planet. In this case, expectations were disappointed at the first level as a result of an anomalous experience, but not at the second. The case of Mercury's orbit, on the other hand, provides an example of a shift of commitments at the second level. Astronomers were consistently unable to explain the shift of Mercury's perihelion (the point in its orbit nearest to the sun) through an appeal to Newtonian theory. It was not until Newtonian mechanics had been supplanted by Einstein's General Theory of Relativity, or not until a shift of commitments had taken place at the second level of my scheme, that this phenomenon could be explained.

14. Of course, the process of acquiring scientific competence involves the development of the ability to see similarities between problems in one's discipline, the acquisition of experimental and/or theoretical techniques and the learning of various other research practices. None of these competencies is developed solely through the learning and application of formal rules (see Kuhn, "Second Thoughts on Paradigms"; and Michael Polanyi, *Personal Knowledge* (Chicago: University of Chicago Press, 1958)). One might want to regard this nonformal aspect of scientific socializa-

tion as being prereflective in some sense. However, this skill acquisition takes place within the frame provided by the two reductions, a frame which excludes those prereflective meanings in which our cultural self-interpretations are embodied.

15. In addition to the reductions discussed in the text, Galilean science inaugurated other such prejudgments, among them the stipulations that no attempt to explain using teleological expressions has any place in science, and that the concept of space is of something geometrical and not differentiated qualitatively.

16. Heidegger, "Science and Reflection," in *The Question Concerning Technology* pp. 168–169. The conceptual structure represented by my three-level scheme suggests philosophically important differences between the transition from Aristotelian to, say, Galilean physics (a movement involving a shift of commitments at the third level), on the one hand, and the transitions from Galilean through Newtonian to Einsteinian physics (movements involving a shift of commitments at the second level), on the other. The device of the three-layered view brings into sharper focus than do the writings of Kuhn, Toulmin and so on the differences between the transition *to* modern science and those *within* modern science.

17. *Ibid.*, p. 169.

18. *Ibid.*, p. 168.

19. See Karsten Harries, "Copernican Reflections," *Inquiry* 23, pp. 253–269.

20. The scientific neutralization of prereflective meanings has further implications. It threatens to marginalize the richness of the interpretive frameworks available for understanding our lives and therefore the richness of our lives themselves. There can be no final appropriation of the meaning of experience; just as there cannot be a once-and-for-all interpretation of a text or a last historian. My experience is a text, as I suggested above, but it is one that is being continually written. It is a text in the making. This endows it with an openness over and above even that of a completed text or historical epoch. The latter are, in a sense, definite and finished but open to an indefinite number of appropriate interpretations or appropriations. Experience, then, has the openness of being incomplete as well as that of being open to interpretation. (I return to this in Chapter Five, when I discuss some disanalogies between life and texts.) The meanings which I extract from my experience contribute to and point to, intend, an always incompletely realized sense of my life which furnishes me with further anticipations for interpretation. In the sense, then, in which it *might* be reasonable to speak of a perfect knowledge of nature, it would *not* be reasonable to speak of a perfect knowledge of a text, or of history, or of a perfect appropriation of the meaning of experience. (Interestingly, some very influential contemporary physicists hold on to the dream of a Final Theory uniting the four fundamental forces of nature; see Steven Weinberg, *Dreams of a Final Theory* (New York: Pantheon, 1993); and the reservations voiced by Roger Penrose in "Nature's Biggest Secret," *The New York Review of Books*, October 21, 1993, pp. 78–82.) Gadamer expresses this by claiming that inquiry into the meaning of a text or historical inquiry cannot be regarded as inquiry guided by an object (in itself) in the way that natural scientific inquiry arguably *can* be so seen (even if that object is at best a regulative ideal for science, and despite the complications introduced by the so-called nonconvergence thesis, the belief that succeeding scien-

tific paradigms represent radical, if not incommensurable, shifts from, rather than progressive developments of, preceding frameworks). One thinks here of Mary Hesse's own call for "perfect metaphors" to serve the purpose of theoretical explanation. She expresses that call in terms reminiscent of our discussion of objectivity as a regulative ideal for science: "the (perhaps unattainable) aim to find a 'perfect metaphor'" (Hesse, "The Explanatory Function of Metaphor," p. 119). One might regard the ideal of the perfect metaphor as the postempiricist counterpart of the ideal of objectivity, an ideal in terms of which science could be regarded as research guided by an object. But Hesse's metaphor is a metaphor with a difference. To illustrate one implication of this: while one and the same instance of love might, in ordinary language, be fruitfully referred to metaphorically as both young and old—young because of its vital and robust nature, old because of its being experienced as having been somehow ordained from the beginning of time—the existence of contradictory metaphorical characterizations in science demands adjudication.

As I have emphasized, the methodological requirements of science demand that the knowledge-productive preunderstandings of meaning of which I have spoken be taken out of play. It is they which render discourse about a matter, in Richard Rorty's terms, incommensurable. (Rorty's notion of incommensurable discourse is, however, problematic. Such discourse is, for him, defined as discourse where no agreement upon a mechanism for resolving disputes exists (*Philosophy and the Mirror of Nature*, p. 316). But such discourse, if it is to be between self-enclosed language games, stands in danger of being not the conversation which Rorty describes it as, but a series of monologues. For instance, in the case of literary interpretation, unless there is some notion of a text which transcends any particular understanding, the conversation will be incoherent. Lacking such a notion, there would be no link between the utterances of the participants, and the conversation would dissolve into monologue. Without an outside measure, we could not make sense of *a* conversation. See also the discussion of Rorty in Chapter Seven below.) Insofar as these preunderstandings are in part responsible for the openness of the meaning of experience, science's suppression of them in the interest of a univocal ideal of objectivity must limit the variety and scope of the self-understanding available to us, were we to assume a scientific attitude toward our experience.

21. I return in Chapter Seven to this idea of hermeneutic horizons being risked and challenged in the interest of embodying the "good life" when I discuss the idea of "humanity as an unfinished project."

22. On the limits of the predictive capability of a science of humanity, see Pavlovic, "Science and Autonomy."

23. Rorty, *Philosophy and the Mirror of Nature,* p. 355. Rorty would, however, want to make rather less of this fact than I would. See Charles Taylor's "Understanding in Human Science," *Review of Metaphysics* 34 (September 1980), pp. 25–38, for an account of scientific language that independently supports the view that I have argued for here.

24. In the published article from which this chapter was adapted, I explore some of the implications of this chapter's discussion for the so-called *Methodenstreit* centering upon the distinctiveness of the human sciences *vis-à-vis* the natural sciences (see

"Science, Language and Experience: Reflections on the Nature of Self-Understanding," *Man and World* 16 [1983], pp. 25–41).

Chapter 4

1. See Heidegger, "The Question Concerning Technology," in *The Question Concerning Technology and Other Essays*, trans. William Lovitt (New York: Harper, 1977).

2. Hannah Arendt, *The Human Condition* (Chicago: University of Chicago Press, 1958), p. 154.

3. Cf. also Hegel's critique of the Enlightenment notion of utility (*die Nützlichkeit*) in the *Phenomenology of Spirit*.

4. Martin Heidegger, *Being and Time*, trans. Macquarrie and Robinson (New York: Harper and Row, 1962), pp. 116–120. Our options here are the following: if we restrict rationality to means-end rationality, then the evaluation of our actions and of things will be either impossible, because of the infinite regress, or arbitrary. In the latter case, as David Wiggins points out in "Truth, Invention and the Meaning of Life," *Proceedings of the British Academy* (1976), if value is constituted by our desires, simply as such (as the arbitrary product of our will), there can be no compellingly valid reason why we should want one thing or want to do one thing rather than another. As a consequence we might ask, What difference does it make, then, what we choose? And, further, what is to prevent us from lapsing into an inert condition, the condition of nihilism, in which no choice seems worth making?

5. See, for example, Jürgen Habermas, "Technology and Science as 'Ideology,'" in *Toward a Rational Society*, trans. Jeremy J. Shapiro (Boston: Beacon Press, 1970).

6. We might say that the *meaning* of helping a neighbor paint her house is in enacting, sustaining, extending, reinforcing and reaffirming communal notions of solidarity. The *value* that it serves is, of course, getting the house painted.

7. See, for example, Albert Borgmann, *Technology and the Character of Contemporary Life: A Philosophical Inquiry* (Chicago: University of Chicago Press, 1984), p. 202.

8. See Charles Taylor, "Interpretation and the Science of Man," *Review of Metaphysics* 25 (1971), pp. 18–19.

9. Taylor, p. 22.

10. Taylor, pp. 27, 29–30. See also Peter Winch, "The Idea of a Social Science," in *The Idea of a Social Science and its Relation to Philosophy* (London: Routledge and Kegan Paul, 1958).

11. Karsten Harries, *The Broken Frame* (Washington, D.C.: Catholic University of America Press, 1989).

12. The Platonic idea of the Good as a standard in terms of which political life was to be fashioned and the fitness of a political structure *measured* signals a technical understanding of politics, both because of Plato's incorporation of the principle of *techne*, and also through its emphasis upon a spatialized standard of reference or goal (from which a given state of affairs can be measurably more or less "far away.")

13. See Borgmann, pp. 80–81; and also Heidegger's claim that "[v]alue stands in

intimate relation to a so-much, to quantity and number. Hence values are related to a 'numerical and mensural scale' (*Will to Power*, Aph. 710, 1888)," ("The Word of Nietzsche," in *The Question Concerning Technology*, p. 71). See also Langdon Winner's notion of "reverse adaptation," a feature of technological culture which requires "the adjustment of human ends to match the character of the available means" (Winner, *Autonomous Technology: Technics-Out-of-Control as a Theme in Political Thought* (Cambridge: MIT Press, 1977), pp. 229, 234).

14. The distinction that I draw here between *praxis*, or symbolic action, and *techne*, or technical action, is similar in many respects to the distinction Arendt makes between action and work (*The Human Condition*, pp. 177, 180, 191, 206–207) and to the contrast that Habermas, himself influenced by Arendt in this respect, draws between communicative interaction, on the one hand, and purposive-rational and strategic action, on the other ("Technology and Science as 'Ideology,'" pp. 91 ff).

15. Søren Kierkegaard, *Either/Or*, vol. II, trans. David F. Swenson and Lillian Marvin Swenson (Princeton: Princeton University Press, 1959), p. 136.

16. *Ibid.*, p. 135.

17. On the "ethics of satisfaction," see Karsten Harries's "Death and Utopia: Towards a Critique of the Ethics of Satisfaction," *Research in Phenomenology* 7 (1977), pp. 138–152; and my "Marcuse, Time and Technique: Concerning the Rational Foundations of Critical Theory," *The Philosophical Forum* 17 (1986), pp. 246–249.

18. *Either/Or*, vol. II, p. 136.

19. See Søren Kierkegaard, *Repetition: An Essay in Experimental Psychology*, trans. Walter Lowrie (New York: Harper and Row, 1964).

20. See John Caputo, "Hermeneutics as the Recovery of Man," *Man and World* 15 (1982), pp. 346–347. By the terms 'singleness,' 'identity' and 'continuity,' I do not intend to connote a notion of personal identity that entails homogeneity and stasis. This issue is taken up explicitly in Chapter Seven's discussion of humanity as an unfinished, negotiated project. What I am trying to highlight here is the idea of integrity.

21. Kierkegaard, *Repetition*, pp. 136–137. See also Marsha Abrams, "Coping with Loss in the Human Sciences: A Reading at the Intersection of Psychoanalysis and Hermeneutics," *Diacritics* 23.1 (1993), pp. 67–82.

22. It is not irrelevant to note that the end or goal, the criterion for, and hence the meaning of, *techne* or making is available beforehand, fully determinate and *a priori*. Just as in the case of Plato's blueprint for the ideal society, time plays no part here, is not constitutive. If what is made can be understood, to some extent, *a priori*, what is done can only be understood retrospectively and always from within a hermeneutic situation produced by an effective history, where time is constitutive.

23. See *Either/Or*, vol II, p. 140.

24. For a discussion of what I call the "time of the apparatus," see Robert Brumbaugh's *Unreality and Time* (Albany: State University of New York Press, 1984), pp. 54,

121, 134. We must, of course, be careful about ascribing intentionality to a project or enterprise, particularly when those who are engaged in that enterprise do not necessarily adopt the attitudes imputed to the enterprise as a whole. But, as I suggested in Chapter Two, even though individuals may be motivated purely by intellectual curiosity, one might argue that the enterprise in which they are engaged has a point or a meaning that may transcend them.

25. See Heidegger, *Being and Time*, pp. 458, 463–471.

26. The time of science is linear, i.e., topologically open, and homogeneous. To the extent that the term 'causality' is used legitimately in science, one is committed to a notion of time-order. In the analogies of experience Kant, following Leibniz, maintains that temporal judgments follow from causal judgments: ". . . it is the concept of the *relation of cause and effect*, the former of which determines the latter in time, as its consequence." (Immanuel Kant, *Critique of Pure Reason*, trans. Norman Kemp Smith (New York: St. Martin's Press, 1965), p. 219). Hence the notion of causality implies the necessary determination of events with respect to temporal order. The relationship between temporal determination and factual judgments is also brought out in the work of Max Weber, in which the assertion of necessary connections between events in temporal series is a methodological presupposition of any "causally working empirical science." (Max Weber, *The Methodology of the Social Sciences*, trans. and eds. Edward A. Shils and Henry A. Finch (New York: The Free Press, 1949), p. 187). For Weber, factual judgments refer to events which are embedded in a temporal series and which can be related through a causal nexus. Causality implies temporal ordering:

> . . . the expression in question must always and without exception mean only this: that certain components of the reality which preceded the result in time, isolated conceptually, *generally* in accordance with general empirical rules, favor a result of the type in question (*Ibid.*)

Now if we take the before-after relation for granted, as the foregoing suggests, and make some plausible assumptions which may be seen as properties of the relation "before," then time cannot be topologically closed, i.e., circular.
The assumptions are:

> 1. Of any two events, either one is before the other or they are simultaneous.
> 2. If A is before B and B is before C, then A is before C.
> 3. No event is before itself.

(Bas. C. van Fraassen, *An Introduction to the Philosophy of Time and Space* (New York: Random House, 1970), p. 61).

This is easily illustrated by considering a circle the points on which represent moments of time. All moments on the circle are before themselves, contradicting the assumption that no event may be before itself, and it is not the case that the temporal ordering, with respect to before and after, of any two events is unambiguous. The relations "before" and "between" would not make sense within a circular theory of time. Accordingly, the time of science has the topological structure of the straight line.

The above argument rests upon the assumption that the notion of causality implies the temporal priority of causes to effects. This assumption, however, does not enjoy the unanimous endorsement of philosophers of science. For example, Mario Bunge denies it in maintaining that the causal principle, as he formulates it, does not contain the idea of temporal priority. (Mario Augusto Bunge, *Causality: The Place of the Causal Principle in Modern Science* (Cambridge: Harvard University Press, 1959), p. 63). However, the linearity of scientific time can be established independently of the notion of causality by noting that physics takes real numbers to be the values of the time variable and lets them vary from minus infinity to plus infinity (van Fraassen, p. 60). If the values assigned to temporal events are real numbers, and time is assumed to be unbounded, i.e., to range from minus infinity to plus infinity, then the topological structure of time is that of the real line. I am saying that the before-after relation is taken for granted in science and, for the reasons cited above, scientific time is linear time.

27. Mircea Eliade, *Cosmos and History. The Myth of the Eternal Return*, trans. Willard R. Trask (New York: Harper and Row, Harper Torchbooks, 1959), p. 154.

28. See Hans Blumenberg's *The Legitimacy of the Modern Age* (Cambridge: MIT Press, 1983), for a penetrating discussion of the genesis of the modern "idea of progress."

29. See Jacques Ellul, *The Technological Society*, trans. John Wilkinson, Introduction by Robert K. Merton (New York: Vintage, 1967), p. 321. See also Herbert Marcuse, *One Dimensional Man* (Boston: Beacon Press, 1964).

30. See Marcuse, *One Dimensional Man*, p. 157. See also my "Marcuse, Time and Technique." Marx has noted that:

> Through the subordination of man to the machine the situation arises in which men are effaced by their labour, in which the pendulum of the clock has become as accurate a measure of the relative activity of two workers as it is of the speed of two locomotives. Therefore, we should not say that one man's hour is worth another man's hour, but rather that one man during an hour is worth just as much as another man during an hour. Time is everything, man is nothing; he is at most the incarnation of time. Quality no longer matters. Quantity alone decides everything.

(Karl Marx, *The Poverty of Philosophy* (Moscow: Foreign Languages Publishing House, n.d.), pp. 58–59, quoted in Georg Lukács, *History and Class Consciousness: Studies in Marxist Dialectics* (Cambridge: MIT Press, 1971), pp. 89–90).

31. Habermas, "On Theory and Praxis in our Scientific Civilization," in *Theory and Practice*, trans. John Viertel (Boston: Beacon Press, 1979), p. 275, and "Technology and Science as 'Ideology,'" p. 106.

32. Ervin Laszlo, *A Strategy for the Future: The Systems Approach to World Order* (New York: George Braziller, 1974), p. 176.

33. See Arendt, *The Human Condition*, pp. 40–45, on the distinction between action and behavior.

34. See also Jean-François Lyotard, *The Postmodern Condition: A Report on Knowledge*, trans. Bennington and Massumi (Minneapolis: University of Minnesota Press, 1984). I return to these themes in Chapter Six's discussion of Niklus Luhmann's systems theory.

35. Heidegger, *Being and Time*, p. 438.

36. *Ibid.*

37. Calvin O. Schrag, *Communicative Praxis and the Space of Subjectivity* (Blooming-ton: Indiana University Press, 1986), p. 208. See also Heidegger, *Being and Time*, p. 449.

38. Arendt, *The Human Condition*, p. 178.

39. See Arendt, p. 98, for relevant discussion of labor and work.

40. Heidegger, *Being and Time*, p. 438.

41. See also Schrag, pp. 57, 62, 64–66.

42. Heidegger, *Being and Time*, pp. 442–443.

43. *Ibid.*, p. 437.

44. *Ibid.*, p. 448.

45. Alasdair MacIntyre, *After Virtue: A Study in Moral Theory* (Notre Dame: University of Notre Dame Press, 1981), p. 191.

46. *Ibid.*, p. 202.

47. See Paul Ricoeur, "The Human Experience of Time and Narrative," *Research in Phenomenology* 7 (1977), p. 29.

48. MacIntyre, p. 203.

49. Ricoeur, "The Human Experience of Time and Narrative," pp. 30–32.

Chapter 5

1. Langdon Winner, *Autonomous Technology: Technics-Out-of-Control as a Theme in Political Thought* (Cambridge: MIT Press, 1977), p. 315.

2. Stephen Kern speaks of a "mania for speed and smashing records" (*The Culture of Time and Space: 1880–1918* (Cambridge: Harvard University Press, 1983), p. 110).

3. Although, as Max Weber suggests, "[a] work of art which is genuine 'fulfillment' is never surpassed; it will never be antiquated" (Max Weber, "Science as a Vocation," in Gerth and Mills, eds., *From Max Weber: Essays in Sociology* (New York: Oxford University Press, 1974), p. 138).

4. Arendt, *The Human Condition* (Chicago: University of Chicago Press, 1958), p. 236.

5. See MacIntyre's discussion of goods internal to a practice on pp. 175–183 of his *After Virtue: A Study in Moral Theory* (Notre Dame: University of Notre Dame Press, 1981) for other examples of effects that actions of themselves have on us.

6. David Carr, *Time, Narrative and History* (Bloomington: Indiana University Press, 1986), pp. 45–49, 97.

7. Shoshana Zuboff, in *In the Age of the Smart Machine: The Future of Work and Power* (New York: Basic Books, 1988), pp. 71–73, discusses the effects of industrial computerization's disruption of the *embodied* nature of work.

8. See Borgmann's discussion of "focal practices" in *Technology and the Character of Contemporary Life: A Philosophical Inquiry* (Chicago: University of Chicago

Press, 1984), pp. 196–210, for a fuller discussion of the sort of practice I have in mind here.

9. See, for example, David Carr, *Time, Narrative and History*; McIntyre, *After Virtue*; Jerome Bruner, "Life as Narrative," *Social Research*, 54 (1987), pp. 11–32; and Alexander Nehamas, *Nietzsche: Life as Literature* (Cambridge: Harvard University Press, 1985).

10. Moreover, it may well be true, even apart from their setting in a temporal environment, that the *internal* temporal structure of actions can be explicated, as Carr suggests, in a narrative fashion, that is, in terms of a narrative beginning, middle and end. However, this temporal explication would not thereby assign narrative significance to the action itself, but, rather, only to the component aspects of the action, the subactions.

11. Paul Ricoeur, *Time and Narrative*, vol. 1, trans. Kathleen McLaughlin and David Pellauer (Chicago: University of Chicago Press, 1984), p. x.

12. By 'reduction of meaning to value,' I refer to the collapsing of a dialectical structure of mutual implication, a structure in which, in an Hegelian sense, values are understood as *moments* of meaning. As I suggested in the previous chapter, values properly understood are seen to stand in an *internal* relationship to structures of meaning. What gets criticized in this essay as the "values-perspective," or as an illegitimate reduction of meaning to value, is not, therefore, a rejection of the notion of "value" *per se*, but rather of the tendency to treat values *in isolation* from and in place of the structures of meaning that alone give them point. Such an illegitimate collapsing and substitution occurs whenever the end of a meaningful practice is exclusively privileged *vis-à-vis* the practice itself.

13. We find a literary equivalent to such a self in Paul de Man's discussion of irony and an anthropological realization of it in Clifford Geertz's discussion of the Balinese and their cockfights. In *Blindness and Insight: Essays in the Rhetoric of Contemporary Criticism* (New York: Oxford University Press, 1971), de Man contrasts the temporal structures of allegory and irony in terms remarkably similar to those of our discussion thus far. De Man ties allegory to narrative and both of these to the "unveiling of an authentically temporal destiny" (p. 190). Opposed to what I referred to in the last chapter as the temporality of the system, that is, a spatial temporality of simultaneity, where the intervention of time is merely a contingency, de Man suggests that "in the world of allegory, time is the originary constitutive category." He further understands the meaning of the allegorical sign in terms of repetition (pp. 190–191). Allegory is explicitly wed to narrative, where there is a spreading out along the axis of an imaginary time in order to give *duration*. This temporal structure is contrasted with that of irony. The latter takes place instantaneously, rapidly, suddenly, in one moment, as if it were an explosion. He speaks of ironic works as growing shorter and shorter, and climaxing in the single brief moment of a final *pointe*. Time is reduced to a single moment, and existence becomes a discontinuous, staccatolike succession of isolated moments (pp. 206–208).

In "Deep Play: Notes on the Balinese Cockfight," from his *The Interpretation of Culture* (New York: Basic Books, 1973), Geertz discusses the punctuate temporality of Balinese life and its reflection in the temporal structure of the cockfight. Here, again in terms that are remarkably similar to mine, he refers to a present that is severed into a "string of flashes," of "disconnected quanta," a present that is an "on-off pulsation of meaning and vacuity" (p. 445).

14. See Carr's discussion of Dilthey's investigation, in the latter's *Gesammelte Schriften*, vol. VII, of the notion of the "coherence of life," *Time, Narrative and History*, pp. 75–77.

15. Carr, p. 96.

16. See Carr, p. 88. At this point in Carr's treatment, what began as a phenomenology of experience has shifted to being a phenomenology of *moral* experience.

17. Heidegger, *Being and Time*, p. 427.

18. *Ibid.*, p. 437.

19. *Ibid.*, pp. 442–443.

20. Carr, p. 93.

21. Barbara Herrnstein Smith, *Poetic Closure: A Study of How Poems End* (Chicago: University of Chicago Press, 1968), p. 35.

22. *Ibid.*, p. 36.

23. Ricoeur, *Time and Narrative*, vol. 2, p. 22.

24. That our always being in the middle, in the midst, of life suggests that life lacks closure is interestingly analogous to some reflections of an important thinker who helped effect the transition to modern ways of thinking. Nicholas of Cusa, in the late fifteenth century, entertained a thought experiment that led him to connect the idea of an infinite universe to the notion that, as a consequence, there is no privileged center, that the center is everywhere. See Karsten Harries, "The Infinite Sphere: Comments on the History of a Metaphor," *The Journal of the History of Philosophy* 13 (1975), pp. 5–15.

25. Hypothetical projections of closure can be related to what, in his celebrated "death analysis," Heidegger referred to as "being-towards-the-end" (*Sein zum Ende*). David Carr, whose work has been frequently invoked in this chapter, acknowledges that life lacks the closure of other sorts of narrative (Carr, pp. 78–79). However, while avoiding this ontological impasse, Carr's discussion leads to an epistemological *aporia*. He is eager to avoid positions, such as those of Sartre, Hayden White and Louis O. Mink, positions that maintain that narrative accounts are necessarily in some sense false because they have a structure utterly unlike the events they depict. Carr counters that, to the contrary, the events of our lives and in the life of our communities are *already* narratively structured prior to the accounts rendered by specialists such as historians (*ibid.*, p. 9). For him, narrative structure is the fundamental stratum of our lives. He claims that "there is nothing below [narrative structure]," that life is thus a matter of interpretation all the way down (*ibid.*, p. 66).

Narrative is constitutive of experience in that events, experiences and actions appear for us only as narrativized or through a story. But what about conflicting stories? How do we adjudicate them? In speaking of events that are lived in terms of one story being alternatively lived in terms of another story, Carr evokes images of the Gestalt switches of which Kuhn was so fond (see *ibid.*, p. 76). How, then, setting aside questions of coherence, can narratives be true (or false), and what can they be true *to*? With revisions viewed in terms of Gestalt switches, how do we make sense of a *cumulative* augmentation of self-knowledge, of a *deeper* understanding of who we are, as opposed to *different* and perhaps "incommensurable" understandings? Carr's account must address these questions because, unlike the poststructuralist narrativists, Carr takes seriously the interest in truth and objectivity (*ibid.*, pp. 98–99, 171–172). Yet he offers us no account, especially important given his emphasis upon narrative interpretation, of how they are to be attained or, for that matter, reason to believe they are attainable. He claims that the past, what really happened, acts as a constraint upon narrative production (*ibid.*, pp. 98–99, 171). But having already gone so far as to say that there is nothing outside narrative structure makes it difficult for him to respond to a claim put forward by a fellow narrativist, Alexander Nehamas, who suggests that the past is not self-announcing: ". . . it is not easy to say exactly what *the* past is in the first place. The events of the past are necessarily located through and within a narrative, and different narratives can generate quite different events" (Nehamas, p. 160). Or stated within a somewhat different idiom, past actions, events and experiences *are* actions, events and experiences for us only under some description or other. The problem arises from the necessity of establishing, in a non-question-begging way, the "proper" description of such past events in a manner that could privilege one description of what would constrain narrative willfulness over its competitors. So, despite the illumination that Carr's discussion provides, more needs to be said about how we would go about fixing the limits beyond which a constraining past would be violated and false narratives produced.

Chapter 6

1. See Martin Heidegger, *Nietzsche*, vol. IV, trans. David Farrell Krell (San Francisco: Harper and Row, 1984), and "The Question Concerning Technology," in *The Question Concerning Technology and Other Essays*, trans. William Lovitt (New York: Harper and Row, 1977). See also, in this connection, Husserl's *The Crisis of European Sciences and Transcendental Phenomenology*, trans. David Carr (Evanston: Northwestern University Press, 1970).

2. Heidegger, *Nietzsche*, vol. IV, pp. 63, 68.

3. This line of thought has been developed as a critique of Nietzsche by Alisdair MacIntyre in *After Virtue: A Study in Moral Theory* (Notre Dame: University of Notre Dame Press, 1981).

4. See Heidegger, "The Word of Nietzsche: 'God is Dead,'" in *The Question Concerning Technology*, pp. 102–103.

5. Heidegger's interpretation of Nietzsche as a metaphysician is, of course, controversial.

6. Heidegger, *Nietzsche*, vol. IV, p. 201.

7. Habermas, *The Philosophical Discourse of Modernity: Twelve Lectures*, trans. Frederick Lawrence (Cambridge: MIT Press, 1987), pp. 353–354, 371–372, 420–421.

8. See Melvin Kranzberg and Carroll W. Pursell, eds. *Technology in Western Civilization*, vol. II (New York: Oxford University Press, 1967), p. 20; and Charles Susskind, *Understanding Technology* (Baltimore: Johns Hopkins University Press, 1973), p. 70.

9. Niklas Luhmann, "Weltzeit und Systemgeschichte," in *Soziologie und Sozialgeschichte* (Stuttgart, 1971), p. 100f, cited in Algis Mickunas, "Human Action and Historical Time," *Research in Phenomenology* 6 (1976), p. 53.

10. See also what Georg Lukács says about the fate of the subject under the purposive rationality of capitalism in his important essay "Reification and the Consciousness of the Proletariat," in Lukács, *History and Class Consciousness: Studies in Marxist Dialectics* (Cambridge: MIT Press, 1971).

11. Habermas, "Technology and Science as 'Ideology'," in *Toward a Rational Society*, trans. Jeremy J. Shapiro (Boston: Beacon Press, 1970), pp. 105–106.

12. Habermas, *The Philosophical Discourse of Modernity*, pp. 371–372.

13. The themes of independence from the flux of time and control of the future are echoed in the work of Luhmann. He speaks of systems theory's interest in the "technical neutralization of history" as well as of technology's "defuturization of the future." The technical neutralization of history would mean a functional independence from the past as a source of meaning, an independence achieved through the development of functional equivalents to history, i.e., other systems mechanisms for guiding choices in the present (Luhmann, *The Differentiation of Society*, trans. Stephen Holmes and Charles Larmore (New York: Columbia University Press, 1982), pp. 281, 316–320). I return to the issue of time later in this chapter.

14. By "perspectivism" I mean the view, attributed to Nietzsche, that no particular point of view, value orientation, etc. is privileged over all others, as far as putting us in touch with the "real world" is concerned. See Nehamas, *Nietzsche: Life as Literature* (Cambridge: Harvard University Press, 1985), p. 49.

15. Habermas, "Technology and Science as 'Ideology'," esp. pp. 118–119.

16. See Max Weber, "Science as a Vocation," in *From Max Weber: Essays in Sociology*, trans. and eds. H. H. Gerth and C. Wright Mills (New York: Oxford University Press, 1946), pp. 143–152.

17. Sabina Lovibond, *Realism and Imagination in Ethics* (Minneapolis: University of Minnesota Press, 1983), p. 94.

18. Weber, "Science as a Vocation," pp. 147–148.

19. Habermas, *The Philosophical Discourse of Modernity*, pp. 113f; and Seyla Benhabib, *Critique, Norm and Utopia: A Study of the Foundations of Critical Theory* (New York: Columbia University Press, 1986), p. 260. "Subject-centered reason" or the "philosophy of the subject" denotes a conception of reason that presupposes the subject-object relationship to be fundamental, and that is constituted by two equiprimordial forms of that relationship: one where a knowing subject represents the object and one where an acting subject transforms the object (*The Philosophical Discourse of Modernity*, p. 63).

20. Habermas, *The Theory of Communicative Action*, vol. 2, trans. Thomas McCarthy (Boston: Beacon Press, 1987), pp. 134, 138.

21. *Ibid.*, pp. 124–125.

22. *Ibid.*, p. 117.

23. *Ibid.*, p. 138.

24. Benhabib, *Critique, Norm and Utopia*, p. 239.

25. Habermas, *The Theory of Communicative Action*, vol. 2, p. 117; and "A Reply to My Critics," in *Habermas: Critical Debates*, eds. J. B. Thompson and David Held (Cambridge, MA: MIT Press, 1982), p. 279.

26. Habermas, *The Theory of Communicative Action*, vol. 2, p. 117. See also excursus following, in Chapter Seven.

27. Habermas, "Science and Technology as 'Ideology'," p. 92.

28. *Ibid.*

29. Habermas, "A Reply to My Critics," p. 281, and *The Theory of Communicative Action*, vol. 2, p. 234.

30. Habermas, *The Theory of Communicative Action*, vol. 2, p. 117.

31. *Ibid.*

32. *Ibid.*, pp. 232–234; and Benhabib, pp. 230–231.

33. Habermas, *The Theory of Communicative Action*, vol. 1, trans. Thomas McCarthy (Boston: Beacon Press, 1984), p. 34.

34. Habermas, *The Theory of Communicative Action*, vol. 2, p. 137; and Benhabib, p. 239.

35. Habermas, *The Theory of Communicative Action*, vol. 1, pp. 17–18.

36. *Ibid.*, pp. 49ff., 69–70.

37. Habermas, "Towards a Theory of Communicative Competence," in *Recent Sociology*, ed. Hans Peter Dreitzel, No. 2 (New York: Macmillan, 1970), p. 143.

38. Habermas, *Legitimation Crisis*, trans. Thomas McCarthy (Boston: Beacon Press, 1975), p. 110.

39. *Ibid.*, pp. 113–114.

40. *Ibid.*, p. 108.

41. Habermas, "A Reply to My Critics," p. 257.

42. Habermas, "A Postscript to *Knowledge and Human Interests*," *Philosophy of the Social Sciences* 3 (1973), p. 177.

43. Habermas, *Legitimation Crisis*, p. 108.

44. For a fuller discussion of Habermas's notion of practical discourse and its ability to accommodate "questions of difference," see my "On Habermas and Particularity: Is There Room for Race and Sex on the Glassy Plains of Ideal Discourse?" *Praxis International* 6 (1986), pp. 328–340.

45. Habermas, *The Theory of Communicative Action*, vol. 2, p. 333.

46. Benhabib, p. 246.

47. Habermas, *The Theory of Communicative Action*, vol. 2, p. 186.

48. *Ibid.*, pp. 280–281, 325.

49. *Ibid.*, p. 183.

50. *Ibid.*, p. 186.

51. *Ibid.*, pp. 196, 356–357.

52. *Ibid.*, p. 143.

53. Benhabib, p. 249.

54. Here I differ with Benhabib, who claims that there can be no "administrative production of meaning." She argues that, in order for patterns of meaning to be functional or to motivate action in a system, those who subscribe to such patterns must find them plausible. Such patterns cannot be simply imposed because they must present credentials that will warrant the conviction and command the assent of participants (p. 249). It is true that there are certain beliefs or patterns of meaning that are located at a sufficiently fundamental level in our cognitive architecture that we cannot see how we could simultaneously doubt them while understanding our lives to be ordered and to make sense, e.g., a belief in God for some or in the laws of logic for others. Such beliefs or patterns of meaning would have a transcendental-functional status. They could not function if we withheld assent. But not all patterns of meaning require our allegiance in order to be functional. We can draw a distinction between ingenuous and disingenuous subscription to or participation in patterns of meaning. One can be oriented by such a pattern without being invested in its truth or plausibility. For example, the performative pattern of meaning can orient or motivate the actions of employees as long as they are convinced that conformity to such a pattern will get them what they want (see Habermas, *The Theory of Communicative Action*, vol. 2, p. 356; and Niklas Luhmann, *The Differentiation of Society*, p. 45). Such an instrumental relationship to a pattern of meaning will allow it to function even if participants can see through the ideological veils that enshroud them, for even a cynical or indifferent conformity can produce desired systemic effects. So we should perhaps say that though there cannot be administrative production of *ultimate* meaning, it does not seem to follow that no systems-enhancing patterns of meaning can be imposed.

55. N. Luhmann, *Macht* (Stuttgart, 1975), p. 71; cited in Habermas, *The Theory of Communicative Action*, vol. 2, p. 263.

56. Habermas, *The Theory of Communicative Action*, vol. 2, p. 281.

57. *Ibid.*, p. 325.

58. *Ibid.*

59. *Ibid.*, p. 351.

60. *Ibid.*

61. The meals most compatible with the former mode of preparation tend to be self-contained and individually packaged. Further, it is often recommended that only one such meal be prepared at a time. All of these features of the "microwave meal"

encourage the "privatization" of both the preparation and, given the practice of preparing one meal at a time, even the consumption of the meal.

62. Habermas, *The Philosophical Discourse of Modernity*, p. 373.

63. Luhmann, *The Differentiation of Society*, pp. xxv, 236.

64. *Ibid.*, p. 118.

65. *Ibid.*, p. 119.

66. *Ibid.*

67. *Ibid.*, p. 120.

68. Habermas, *Philosophical Discourse of Modernity*, p. 354. The link between systems theory and postmodernism here is a shared suspicion of the project of the rational critique and grounding of social practices. In the case of systems theory, such practices can be *functionally* rationally grounded or criticized, but not *communicatively* rationally grounded. From Habermas's perspective, the missing premise, the burden, for Luhmann would be to demonstrate argumentatively or communicatively that the interests of social agents are implicated in the system's ability to master complexity in such a way that such mastery serves generalizable and not merely particular interests. Habermas sees Luhmann as being uninterested in this.

69. Luhmann, *The Differentiation of Society*, p. 293; and see Note 13 above.

70. *Ibid.*, p. 316.

71. Habermas, *Philosophical Discourse of Modernity*, p. 354.

72. *Ibid.*, p. 375.

73. Habermas, *The Theory of Communicative Action*, vol. 2, p. 186.

74. See Habermas, *Philosophical Discourse of Modernity*, p. 371.

75. *Ibid.*, pp. 420–421.

76. See Nehamas, *Nietzsche*, p. 105.

77. See Habermas, *Knowledge and Human Interests*, trans. Jeremy J. Shapiro (Boston: Beacon Press, 1971), p. 305.

78. Habermas, *The Theory of Communicative Action*, vol. 2, pp. 183, 281, 390.

79. Luhmann, *The Differentiation of Society*, p. 292.

80. *Ibid.*, p. 230.

81. *Ibid.*, p. 322.

82. *Ibid.*

83. Habermas, *Philosophical Discourse of Modernity*, p. 382.

84. Strictly speaking, an important aspect of his critique of systems analysis is that questions concerning the justification of practical norms are not submitted to an unfettered discussion involving those affected by those norms. What systems analysis and poststructuralism share is a suspicion of or cynicism towards the *project* of rational justification, whether it be by those affected or not.

85. Habermas, *The Theory of Communicative Action*, vol. 1, pp. 2, 186.

86. *Cf.* also Benhabib, p. 260.

87. Habermas, *The Theory of Communicative Action*, vol. 1, p. 184.

88. See, for example, Thomas McCarthy, "Rationality and Relativism: Habermas's 'Overcoming of Hermeneutics'," in *Habermas: Critical Debates*; and Mary Hesse's "Science and Objectivity" in the same volume.

89. Habermas, "A Reply to My Critics," pp. 258–259.

90. An example of the latter, disconfirming instance would be provided by Carol Gilligan's pointing to subjects who do *not* prefer moral reasoning in terms of rights. See Carol Gilligan, *In a Different Voice* (Cambridge, MA: Harvard University Press, 1982); and my suggestion of a possible Habermasian response to her position in "On Habermas and Particularity: Is There Room for Race and Gender on the Glassy Plains of Ideal Discourse?", p. 333.

91. See McCarthy, "Rationality and Relativism," pp. 74–75.

92. Habermas understands this collusion in the following way: rational critique is taken to be meaningless as far as orientation in the life-world is concerned; politics is exempt from the requirement of moral-practical justification; and traditions are to be spared demands for justification. (See his "Modernity: An Unfinished Project," in David Ingram and Julia Simon-Ingram, eds. *Critical Theory: The Essential Readings* (New York: Paragon House, 1991), pp. 354–355.)

Chapter 7

1. Sabina Lovibond, *Realism and Imagination in Ethics* (Minneapolis: University of Minnesota Press, 1983), pp. 154–155. This claim must, of course, be qualified by a discussion of the limiting cases, some of which will be taken up below, of what I shall call ironic, dramatic and expeditious discourse.

2. *Cf.* David Wiggins, "Truth, Invention and the Meaning of Life," *Proceedings of the British Academy* (1976), p. 340; and Jürgen Habermas, "Questions and Counterquestions," in *Habermas and Modernity*, ed. Richard J. Bernstein (Cambridge, MA: MIT Press, 1985), pp. 194–195.

3. Habermas, *Ibid.*, pp. 194–195.

4. *Cf.* Wiggins, p. 342.

5. Habermas, *The Theory of Communicative Action*, vol. 2, trans. Thomas McCarthy (Boston: Beacon Press, 1987), pp. 150–152.

6. Habermas, "Questions and Counterquestions," pp. 195–196.

7. *Ibid.*

8. In his recent book, *Contingency, Irony and Solidarity* (Cambridge: Cambridge University Press, 1989), Rorty privatizes the ironic moment, suggesting that the public domain, where his liberal hopes for solidarity find their home, should be protected from the bite of the ironist. He thus makes a strategic distinction between the public and the private that allows one to both be an ironist and be socially committed. He insists, however, that there can be no general account that will allow us in a principled way to adjudicate the claims of the public and private. I suspect that, unless it is suitably relativized, the public/private distinction that Rorty borrows

from the final vocabulary of the liberal tradition, like its cousins the fact/value distinction and the participant/observer distinction, will strain under the weight of systematic scrutiny. On this matter, see also Nancy Fraser, "Solidarity or Singularity? Richard Rorty between Romanticism and Technocracy," in *Reading Rorty*, ed. Alan Malachowski (Oxford: Basil Blackwell, 1990), pp. 312–313. See also Patricia J. Williams, *The Alchemy of Race and Rights* (Cambridge: Harvard University Press, 1991), on the social and economic preconditions of privacy.

9. See, for example, Charles Taylor, "Interpretation and the Sciences of Man," *Review of Metaphysics* 25 (1971); and Peter Winch, "The Idea of a Social Science," in *The Idea of a Social Science and its Relation to Philosophy* (London: Routledge and Kegan Paul, 1958).

10. Peter Winch, a champion of the *verstehenden* approach, does maintain that it is crucial to determine the *point* that following a set of rules has in a society, and, further, that that point must be intelligible to us (see his "Understanding a Primitive Society," *American Philosophical Quarterly* 1 [1964], pp. 307–324). I would thus find his position in keeping with what I am urging.

11. Mary Hesse, *Models and Analogies in Science* (Notre Dame: University of Notre Dame Press, 1966), pp. 1–56.

12. Donald Davidson, "On the Very Idea of a Conceptual Scheme," in *Inquiries into Truth and Interpretation* (Oxford: Clarendon Press, 1984), pp. 183–198.

13. Habermas, "Questions and Counterquestions," p. 194.

14. Habermas, *The Theory of Communicative Action*, vol. 1, trans. Thomas McCarthy (Boston: Beacon Press, 1984), pp. 113–115.

15. *Ibid.*, p. 115.

16. *Ibid.*, p. 116.

17. Benhabib, *Critique, Norm and Utopia: A Study of the Foundations of Critical Theory* (New York: Columbia University Press, 1986), p. 241.

18. Thomas McCarthy, "Contra Relativism: A Thought-Experiment," in *Relativism: Interpretation and Confrontation*, ed. M. Krausz (Notre Dame: University of Notre Dame Press, 1989), p. 257.

19. For another argument to this effect, see McCarthy, "Reflections on Rationalization," in *Habermas and Modernity*, pp. 184–185.

20. Habermas, "Questions and Counterquestions," p. 205. See also *Theory of Communicative Action*, 1, p. 67; and McCarthy, "Contra Relativism: A Thought-Experiment," pp. 267–268.

21. It has been argued, for example, that the Greeks did not take their mythical discourse to be making truth claims, at least not in any ordinary sense. As *muthos*, or likely stories, mythical stories were among those narratives that were understood to be neither true nor false. For a general discussion of this matter, see Paul Veyne, *Did the Greeks Believe in Their Myths?*, trans. Paula Wissing (Chicago: University of Chicago Press, 1988). See also MacIntyre on the role of mythology as a dramatic resource for the construction of social identity (*After Virtue*, p. 201). Further, as Sabina Lovibond reminded me, one might also see Wittgenstein's *Remarks on*

Frazer's 'The Golden Bough' for comments on the scientistic misunderstanding of mythical narrative.

22. McCarthy, "Rationality and Relativism: Habermas's 'Overcoming' of Hermeneutics," in *Habermas: Critical Debates*, eds. J. B. Thompson and David Held (Cambridge, MA: MIT Press, 1982) p. 70.

23. Habermas, *Theory of Communicative Action*, 1, p. 66.

24. Habermas, "Toward a Reconstruction of Historical Materialism," in *Communication and the Evolution of Society*, trans. T. McCarthy (Boston: Beacon Press, 1979), p. 163.

25. *Cf.*, for example, McCarthy, "Rationality and Relativism"; Carol Gilligan, *In a Different Voice* (Cambridge: Harvard University Press, 1982); and Richard Miller, "Ways of Moral Learning," *The Philosophical Review*, vol. XCIV, No. 4 (October 1985), pp. 507–556.

26. David Wiggins too (in "Truth, Invention and the Meaning of Life," pp. 352–355) holds that an observer, in rendering an account of a practice, is herself implicated in participative experiences. Departing from general considerations drawn from the theory of meaning, he invites us to consider the metaethical project of rendering an account of ethical language by constructing for it a recursive theory of meaning. It will entail theorems of the form: "*s* is assertible iff *p*," where *s* stands for the designation of a sentence in the object-language, here the language of morals, and *p* stands for the metalinguistic expression which is the translation or interpretation of that sentence. He goes on to say that:

> [i]f the theorist believes his own theory, then he is committed to be ready to put his mind where his mouth is at least once for each sentence *s* of the object-language, in a statement of assertion conditions for *s* in which he himself *uses* either *s* or a faithful translation of *s*. (emphasis mine)

As Lovibond puts it, the theorist must be able to participate ingenuously in the practice of using moral language, for such language is unavoidably part and parcel of the metalanguage in which she carries out the interpretive task (Lovibond, pp. 88–89). So the theorist cannot stand off from the language of morals or from the point of view which gives it its sense. That language cannot, for the theorist, make its appearance only within inverted commas.

27. Lovibond, pp. 105–107.

28. So Donald Davidson, for example, is not addressing the question: Are there *really* incommensurable conceptual schemes? The question is, rather: What evidence could there be *for us* that there are? See also Hilary Putnam's influential notion of "internal realism" in his *Reason, Truth and History* (Cambridge: Cambridge University Press, 1981); and Rorty's commendation of this notion as being, in important respects, similar to the latter's understanding of pragmatism in "Solidarity or Objectivity," in *Relativism: Interpretation and Confrontation*, p. 39.

29. I owe this example to my colleague, Neale Mucklow. In *Habermas: Autonomy and Solidarity*, ed. Peter Dews (London: Verso, 1986), pp. 208–210, Habermas discusses the American Confederacy of the 1850s as a form of life which was a nested zone within the American capitalist system.

30. Here we might say that the inside or what is encompassed by an existing language game or symbolic system is elastic or expandable. As Lovibond suggests, this can occur through the extension of an existing symbolic system to encompass novel or alien phenomena, or through seeing an alien practice as a new way of acting in accordance with the rules (p. 184).

31. See also Albrecht Wellmer, "Reason, Utopia, and the *Dialectic of Enlightenment*," in *Habermas and Modernity*, p. 61.

32. In his *Beyond Objectivism and Relativism: Science, Hermeneutics and Praxis* (Philadelphia: University of Pennsylvania Press, 1983), pp. 157–158, Richard Bernstein explores the implications of the lack of consensus that marks our situation for the possibility of the exercise of practical judgment or *phronesis*.

33. Among the criterial properties of a "good life" might be such a life's being reflective of norms in which I can recognize myself, and which represent a general, as opposed to particular, interest. The *encouragement* to inquire into the satisfaction of these conditions is lacking from within the "why not my game?" attitude. As Rorty has said, "We would have no reason to question our purposes unless we encountered other purposes that are at right angles to ours." One problem with this response is that our society may not contain the sorts of institutionalized channels that would enable genuinely different voices to be heard.

34. Thomas McCarthy, in a recent publication, pursues a line of thought that leads to a conclusion similar to this in claiming that "truth" functions as an "idea of reason" that allows us to think the inadequacy of, and thus to criticize, the standards of truth that we have inherited ("Private Irony and Public Decency: Richard Rorty's New Pragmatism," *Critical Inquiry* 16 [1990], pp. 369–370.) But McCarthy's argument seems to rest upon disputable internalist presuppositions, such as those of a "developmental logic," "learning process" and a convergence of linguistic-conceptual frameworks.

35. *Cf.* Nancy Fraser, "Foucault on Modern Power: Empirical Insights and Normative Confusions," *Praxis International* 1 (1981), pp. 272–287.

36. Habermas, "Taking Aim at the Heart of the Present," in *Foucault: A Critical Reader*, ed. David Couzens Hoy (London: Basil Blackwell, 1986), p. 108.

37. Lovibond, pp. 118–119.

38. Lovibond, p. 123.

39. McCarthy, *Critical Inquiry*, p. 361, and "Contra Relativism: A Thought-Experiment," p. 260.

40. McCarthy, "Contra Relativism," p. 260.

41. I have phrased the point in this way in order to deflect the Winchean criticism of "pressing Zande thought where it would not naturally go" (see Peter Winch, "Understanding a Primitive Society," p. 315). Of course, it may well require some reconstructive work to determine just what the claims whose justification is in question are, and this is subject to all the uncertainties to which interpretations are heir.

42. Even if we were Humeans, and agnostic regarding intelligible connections, evidence

to the effect that the outcome of a test was an unreliable guide to what we should expect in our practical activity predicated upon such an outcome would give us cause for concern. Suppose it could be shown that a given test would have a positive outcome (with respect to a particular hypothetical claim) no matter what. The apparatus could not then be relied upon to be capable of rendering a falsifying verdict. As a consequence, its "confirming" verdict would be taken to be meaningless.

43. Rorty, *Contingency, Irony and Solidarity*, p. 60.

44. Rorty, "Pragmatism, Relativism, and Irrationalism," in *Consequences of Pragmatism: Essays, 1972–1980* (Minneapolis: University of Minnesota Press, 1982), p. 174.

45. Of course, the distinction between language and purposes is somewhat artificial, or needs to be relativized, for what matters most to us is always linguistically mediated. One might say that there are "master" language games that are expressive of our core purposes and other, more specialized languages that serve those purposes.

46. Rorty, *Contingency, Irony and Solidarity*, pp. 47, 59.

47. *Ibid.*, p. 59.

48. On the idea of forging such a perspective or language, see Charles Taylor, "Understanding and Ethnocentricity," in *Philosophy and the Human Sciences* (Cambridge: Cambridge University Press, 1985), p. 125.

49. For another discussion of humanity as an unfinished project, see my "Community and Difference: Reflections in the Wake of Rodney King," in *Artifacts, Representations and Social Practice: Essays for Marx Wartofsky*, eds. Robert Cohen and Carol Gould (Dordrecht: Kluwer Academic Publishers, 1993).

50. Rorty, *Contingency, Irony and Solidarity*, p. 198.

51. *Ibid.*, p. 60.

52. *Ibid.*, p. 191.

53. *Ibid.*, p. 198.

54. Perhaps these two senses of the "we," referring to those who share our core values and to those who fall under descriptions that also fit us, be they defining core descriptions or not, can be mediated by what Charles Alteri has in conversation called a proleptic sense of the "we." The proleptic "we" is a recommendation or invitation on the part of the we of shared core practices to others that they try on its practices and core values to see if they can flourish by so doing.

55. Rorty, *Contingency, Irony and Solidarity*, p. 192.

56. See Rorty, *Contingency, Irony and Solidarity*, p. 196.

57. *Ibid.*

58. For a few recent examples of critiques of the liberal tradition that are fashioned as specific responses to Rorty, see Allan C. Hutchinson, "Reading/Rorty/Radically," *Harvard Law Review*, vol. 103, No. 2, 1989, pp. 555–585; Cornel West's *The American Evasion of Philosophy: A Genealogy of Pragmatism* (Madison: University of Wisconsin Press, 1989), pp. 205–206, 207, and his "Afterword" in *Post-Analytic*

Philosophy, eds. John Rajchman and Cornel West (New York: Columbia University Press, 1985); and Nancy Fraser, "Solidarity or Singularity?", pp. 303–321.

59. Rorty, *Contingency*, p.61.

60. *Ibid.*, p. 59.

61. Elsewhere, Rorty seems more sensitive to the force of this. In responding to the work of Roberto Unger, Rorty acknowledges that reason, in the sense of being a familiar language game, is "frozen politics," serving to legitimate and make seem inevitable institutions of which one wants to be free. But this is just what ideology consists in, *pace* Rorty. See Rorty, "Unger, Castoriadis, and the Romance of a National Future," *Northwestern University Law Review*, vol. 82, No. 2, 1988, p. 347.

   Moreover, more recently Rorty has spoken of the need for the oppressed to replace the language of the oppressors with a language designed to serve the purposes of the oppressed (see "The Professor and the Prophet," *Transition* 52 (1991), p. 73, and "Feminism and Pragmatism," *Michigan Quarterly Review* 30: 2 (Spring 1991), pp. 231–258). And I think that this is certainly right. But I do not think that Rorty is sufficiently sensitive to the institutionalized structures of power that work to silence the genuinely "other." Though he speaks of present practices being made anachronistic by the common culture's incorporation of the imaginative, transgressive vocabularies and practices of outcasts, he gives scant attention to just how such revolutionary practices and vocabularies are to achieve semantic authority over the common culture. His sometimes implicit appeal to the way things work in the scientific community is unconvincing. Scientists whose work proved revolutionary were in most cases *already sanctioned* (as scientists) by the community whose views they were to revolutionize. By hypothesis the bearers of the voices from the margins are not. I find it difficult to be as sanguine as he that the institutional means are in place for enabling those voices to be heard and potentially persuasive. It is not just a matter of imagining new vocabularies or of having them accepted within particular, marginalized social groups; it is also a matter of having the power, in the sense of actual social recognition, to have those vocabularies taken seriously so that they might make a difference in the common culture. If that recognition is not already institutionally secured, as, almost by definition, it is not for members of marginalized groups, it must be struggled for. Liberal good will is seldom, if ever, sufficient. And often the struggle will be against powerful interests and entrenched vocabularies that are themselves fully compatible with a liberal democracy. This will make thinking about social, political and economic power unavoidable (see my "Evading Theory and Tragedy?: Reading Cornel West," *Praxis International* 13 (1993), pp. 38–39).

62. Rorty replies that to ask him under what conditions he would recognize liberalism to have been falsified is "like asking a physicist under what conditions she would give up the idea that microstructural arrangements can explain macrostructural behavior" (private correspondence with author). Like such a physicist, Rorty avers that he would have no idea. Giving up liberalism, he says, would be as unimaginable for him as would be giving up finding such explanations for her.

   This is a revealing response. It is convincing only insofar as liberalism, a *particular* political paradigm, is likened not to a particular scientific paradigm, but to an assumption underlying *all* modern scientific paradigms. But this seems a false analogy. Further, likening liberalism to an informing presupposition of modern science confirms Rorty's tendency to accord to liberalism the *de facto* status of a project secured at the third level of the scheme proposed in Chapter Three of this work. That is, it betrays a tendency to remove liberalism from the level of contestable paradigms. Just as to deny the thesis that microstructural arrangements can explain macrostructural ones is to give up being a scientist in an important sense, Rorty in effect is suggesting that to challenge bourgeois liberal discourse is to give up public political relevance. What he secures, as if at the third level of my scheme, is what I would want to keep problematizable. And this does not imply that we "jump out of our skins" and assume other identities. For narrative accounts of change in our standards can be given that stress the aspect of continuity under change that is requisite to a sense of identity. It is rather a matter of not immunizing our prevailing purposes to transformative pressure.

63. Rorty, *Contingency*, p. 63.

64. So Rorty's liberalism is (illegitimately, it seems to me) shielded from criticism, because either his account is too vague or it is situated at the third level of my scheme in such a way as to immunize it from critique.

65. Rorty, *Contingency*, pp. 87, 91.

66. *Ibid.*

67. For example, think of a society structured purely along classically liberal lines, in particular, a society where grievances can be discussed only in terms of the violation of individual rights. The advocacy of group-based needs and remedies, remedies such as affirmative action programs, is notoriously difficult to square with such a framework. See also Hutchinson, pp. 564–565.

68. See Rorty, "Unger and the Romance of a National Future," p. 337; and Hutchinson, p. 570.

69. See West's "Afterword," p. 267; and, again, Rorty's admission that tragic liberals like himself affirm Hegel's observation that their narratives attempt to grasp their time (and place) in thought rather than try to change it ("Unger and the Romance of a National Future," pp. 342–343).

70. I say "with some qualification" because, in some of his more recent work, Rorty has quite explicitly acknowledged and highlighted the desirability of *some* of the conditions that I discuss under the rubric of "humanity as an unfinished project." See especially his "Feminism and Pragmatism," pp. 239, 242, 247–249. In some of the passages therein I find much to admire (with the notable exception of his invocation of Hegel's idea of the "cunning of reason" in such a way that, perhaps inadvertently, allows even oppression to be redeemed by the contribution it makes to "the evolution of the species"). Nevertheless, and in a way that is consistent with the foregoing discussion, there are still issues that separate us.

For example, the liberal "we" remains immunized from justificatory pressure. Not being able to imagine attractive alternatives to our institutions and projects, Rorty simply doubts that the basic framework of our society could be unjust ("Feminism and Pragmatism," Note 15). Perhaps he could accommodate some of my concerns with his prescriptive or persuasive (as opposed to reportive) definition of liberal culture as that *ethnos* that makes openness to encounters with other actual and possible cultures central to its self-image (*Objectivity, Relativism and Truth* (Cambridge: Cambridge University Press, 1991), pp. 2, 13 and 14), but I am not sure. For the boundary condition on such encounters remains the spirit of Western liberal democracy (*Objectivity*, p. 212). What about vocabularies that, *in the name of human flourishing*, would challenge liberalism itself? Should they all be kept private and not be permitted in the arena of public political discourse? While Rorty, no doubt, would be happy for a *person* committed to such a vocabulary to speak, it is not clear that Rorty's liberal utopia would have the logical spaces that would permit such a *vocabulary* to get a respectful hearing. It is as if Rorty can only think of a challenge to liberal institutions as being *ipso facto* a challenge to thinking that cruelty is the worst thing we can do, a challenge to democratic values, a challenge to antielitism, in short, a challenge to solidarity. And I deeply respect the concern that motivates his wariness. But why be closed to the possibility that this assumption is false? In other words, how open is Rorty willing for the human conversation to be? As Alisdair MacIntyre has written (though not from a perspective that I necessarily endorse):

> Liberalism . . . is often succesful in preempting . . . debate[s] by reformulating quarrels and conflicts with liberalism . . . so that they appear to have become debates within liberalism, putting in question this or that particular set of attitudes or policies, but not the fundamental tenets of liberalism. . . . There is little place in such political systems for the criticism of the system itself, that is, for putting liberalism in question. (*Whose Justice? Which Rationality?* (Notre Dame: University of Notre Dame Press, 1988), p. 392)

71. Sandra Harding, in her *The Science Question in Feminism* (Ithaca: Cornell University Press, 1986), p. 165, refers to the curious coincidence, with regard to ethics, between African worldviews and what in feminist literature is labeled a distinctively feminine worldview. Assuming there is something to what she says here, and I believe there is, this example would also serve as a scheme for a cultural fusion of horizons.

72. Ronald Dworkin, *Taking Rights Seriously* (Cambridge: Harvard University Press, 1978), pp. 226–227. See also his more recent attempt to mediate the abortion controversy in *Life's Dominion* (New York: Knopf, 1993).

73. Much of what the present discussion implies about the renegotiation of identity was prefigured in the references early in Chapter Five to the reconfiguration and revision of our prereflective meanings.

74. Lovibond, pp. 122–123.

75. Lovibond, p. 123.

76. This formulation was suggested, in conversation, by Karsten Harries.

77. Lovibond, p. 222.

78. Lovibond, pp. 217–218.

79. Habermas, "Labor and Interaction: Remarks on Hegel's Jena *Philosophy of Mind*," in *Theory and Practice*, trans. John Viertel (Boston: Beacon Press, 1973), pp. 150–151. In "On Habermas and Particularity: Is There Room for Race and Sex on the

Glassy Plains of Ideal Discourse?" *Praxis International* 6 (1986), pp. 328–340, I argue that Habermas fails to heed his own good advice in his elaboration of the conception of ideology critique. I refer to that failure as his methodological *a priorism*.

80. Lovibond, pp. 199–200.

81. Alasdair MacIntyre, *Whose Justice? Which Rationality?* p. 352. For this discussion, see more generally the chapter entitled "The Rationality of Traditions."

82. MacIntyre, pp. 364–365.

83. *Ibid.*, p. 367.

84. *Ibid.*, pp. 367–368.

85. Bernstein, *Beyond Objectivism and Relativism*, p. 230.

86. I argue in "Community and Difference" that such communal forms need not exclude matters of difference, be they cultural, gendered or ethnic.

87. See, for example, John Caputo, *Radical Hermeneutics: Repetition, Deconstruction, and the Hermeneutic Project* (Bloomington: Indiana University Press, 1987), pp. 234–267. Caputo suggests that without foundations all that is left is to enforce the fairness of the agonistics between competing interests (p. 234). But this is essentially only to ring a change on the old theme of liberalism, which refuses to press seriously the issue, Can "fairness" be explicated in a way that is neutral with respect to the competing interests?

88. Poststructuralism's celebration of the "decentered subject" can be understood to have unambiguously emancipative potential *only* if the autonomous rational subject is *in itself* the villain. But this is clearly open to question, and not only from the perspective of Habermas's notion of "modernity as an unfinished project." There is often presupposed by those who advocate the emancipative potential of such a fragmented subject a false dichotomy, to wit, *either* one has to do with a self who, under the cloak of a claim to pure rationality, is ethnocentric, patriarchial and so on; *or* one has to do with a decentered, tolerant and pluralistic self. The "impossible" project of a genuinely respectful commensurability is rejected in favor of a thematization of difference. But my notion of "humanity as an unfinished project" is intended to suggest that the project of respectful communities of coherent, though not homogeneous, selves, of nonabsolute, yet not endlessly proliferating, selves is not an idle dream.

Chapter 8

1. I do not wish to engage in the debate over whether the characteristics and styles that I highlight here are those of a stage of modernity, i.e., late modernity, or are those of modernity's successor stage, i.e., postmodernity. What interests me is that those characteristics and styles figure prominently in accounts of our times, however those times are denominated. On the debate, see Margaret A. Rose, *The postmodern and the post-industrial* (Cambridge: Cambridge University Press, 1991). I also do not wish, except perhaps implicitly, to evaluate the existing and proliferating theoretical accounts of the postmodern. I wish instead to think technology in terms

of the postmodern. And indeed, it will not be without interest to us that so-called postmodern society is acknowledged to be highly celebrative of the products, power and potential of high technology. It is also important to remember that 'postmodernity' does not designate a natural kind, but rather a mode of gathering together strands of a particular slice of history, a way of *construing* that highlights or foregrounds certain features and marginalizes others. Lastly, I use the term 'postmodern' to refer both to a characteristic set of social and cultural conditions (sometimes referred to as postmodernity) and to a characteristic sensibility as analyzed by theorists of the postmodern (sometimes referred to as postmodernism), theorists who embrace or reject those conditions and that sensibility in varying degrees. Through the media, advertising, new technologies (in particular "Virtual Reality" entertainment and new communications technology), and, in general, products of the consumer society, the postmodern phenomenon mediates everyday life. In this sense, the intended audience of this chapter, as of this book, includes the postmodern theorist, the self-avowed postmodernist, and the everyday social actor in social and cultural postmodernity.

2. See, among others, Margaret Rose, *op. cit.*, pp. 26, 27; Mark Poster, *The Mode of Information: Poststructuralism and Social Context* (Chicago: University of Chicago Press and Cambridge: Polity Press, 1990); Fredric Jameson, *Postmodernism, or the Cultural Logic of Late Capitalism* (Durham: Duke University Press, 1991), pp. 76, 95; and Jean Baudrillard, "The Ecstasy of Communication," in Hal Foster, ed., *The Anti-Aesthetic: Essays on Postmodern Culture* (Port Townsend: Bay Press, 1983), pp. 126–134.

3. See also Christopher Lasch, *The True and Only Heaven: Progress and its Critics* (New York: W.W. Norton, 1991), p. 527.

4. Fredric Jameson, "Postmodernism, or the Cultural Logic of Late Capitalism," *New Left Review* 146 (1984), pp. 54–55. The "postmodern" is a phenomenon sufficiently overdetermined in meaning that one ought to be wary of any single attempt to capture it whole. Accordingly, I draw upon several theorists of the postmodern, acknowledging that each offers *a* "reading," an interpretive account, and therefore that each analysis will depend upon where in the "system" the theorist begins, i.e., upon what she takes to be the key or "master" element(s).

5. Jameson, *Postmodernism*, p. 284; Jean-François Lyotard, *The Postmodern Condition: A Report on Knowledge*, trans. Geoff Bennington and Brian Massumi (Minneapolis: University of Minnesota Press, 1984), p. xxiv.

6. Jameson, "Postmodernism," pp. 61–62.

7. *Ibid.*, p. 62.

8. Jameson, *Postmodernism*, pp. 95–96.

9. Jameson, "Postmodernism," p. 66.

10. Rose, pp. 83, 103ff.

11. Jean Baudrillard, *Simulations*, trans. Philip Beitchman (New York: Semiotext(e), 1983), p. 100.

12. *Ibid.*, p. 101.

13. See Poster, pp. 43–68, for a Baudrillardian analysis of television ads.

14. Poster, p. 58.

15. Baudrillard, *Simulations*, pp. 150, 151, 152.

16. *Ibid.*, p. 146. There is an interesting parallel between this conception of the real and the conception of nature held by Descartes, the "father of modern philosophy." In maintaining the laws of nature and those of mechanics to be coextensive, Descartes conceived of the natural as the mechanical, as (in principle) the makeable, that is, the reproducible (see René Descartes, *Discourse on the Method of Rightly Conducting Reason and Seeking for Truth in the Sciences, The Philosophical Works of Descartes*, vol. 1, trans. Haldane and Ross (Cambridge: Cambridge University Press, 1972), p. 115). On this point concerning the mechanical conception of nature, within the context of early modern philosophy, see also Marx Wartofsky, "Philosophy of Technology," in *Current Research in Philosophy of Science*, eds. P.D. Asquith and H. Kyburg (East Lansing: Philosophy of Science Association, 1979), pp. 173–174. Early modern thought's rejection of teleological causation in favor of mechanical causality for natural explanation was an important step in achieving what Peter Berger, *et al.*, in *The Homeless Mind: Modernization and Consciousness* (New York: Random House, 1973), refer to as the technological requirements of reproducibility and makeability—the requirements that all elements of the process of technological production be reproducible and that reality be apprehended as makeable (pp. 26, 112). This in-principle identification of human subjectivity with a Platonic demiurge, implied at the dawn of modernity, would inform a case for claiming that postmodernity, rather than constituting a radical break from modernity, is in part a fulfillment of the modern project. I return to this idea below. This notwithstanding, Descartes, of course, remained convinced of the independent existence of the real. Furthermore, for him there was but a single "code" that provided the key to natural reality, and, through our mathematical understanding, we could gain access to it; whereas, for postmodernism, there are endlessly proliferating codes, all of which are fabrications.

17. See Robert Elliot, "Faking Nature," *Inquiry* 25 (1982), pp. 81–93.

18. Jameson, *Postmodernism*, p. 311. On this, with special reference to Colonial Williamsburg, see also Ada Louise Huxtable, "Inventing American Reality," *The New York Review of Books*, December 3, 1992, pp. 24–29.

19. Baudrillard, *Simulations*, p. 4.

20. *Ibid.*, p. 111.

21. *Ibid.*, pp. 88–92.

22. *Ibid.*, pp. 88, 89.

23. *Ibid.*, pp. 130–131.

24. Karsten Harries makes a similar point, suggesting that, ironically, technology increases rather than diminishes the terror of time ("Building and the Terror of Time," *Perspecta: The Yale Architectural Journal* 19 (1982), p. 60). For as we embrace the ideal of perfect security obsessively (colluding obsessively with what, in Chapter Five, I called technology's "will to surpass"), our technical attempts to achieve

such security leave us only more alarmed, as we are conscious of the degree to which that achievement yet eludes us.

25. Jameson, *Postmodernism*, p. 275.

26. David Harvey, *The Condition of Postmodernity* (Oxford: Basil Blackwell, 1989), p. 288.

27. Jameson, *Postmodernism*, p. 202.

28. Jameson, "Postmodernism," p. 56.

29. Harvey, p. 285.

30. *Ibid.*, p. 286.

31. Clive James, in his Public Broadcasting System series, "Fame in the 20th Century," speaks astutely of Madonna's originality lying in borrowing the originality of others. (As I write this (late 1993), such an "original" displacement of origins seems to have devolved into a nostalgic copy of herself.) In his series, James speaks more generally of fame as the product of the global information society.

32. See Gregory Smith, "Heidegger, Technology and Postmodernity," *The Social Science Journal* 28 (1991), p. 371.

33. Paul de Man, *Blindness and Insight: Essays in the Rhetoric of Contemporary Criticism* (New York: Oxford University Press, 1971), p. 197.

34. *Ibid.*, p. 199.

35. *Ibid.*, p. 201. See similar themes sounded in Kierkegaard's *The Concept of Irony: With Constant Reference to Socrates*, trans. Lee M. Capel (New York: Harper and Row, 1965), pp. 233, 240, 278, and elsewhere, where irony is defined as the infinite freedom or the infinite absolute negativity of an abstract subject, hovering over life.

    Another Kierkegaardian text comes to mind in this connection, *Either/Or*, where we see depicted the aesthetic project to transform the real world into one of imaginative possibility. In this text, Johannes the seducer transforms Cordelia the beloved into the idea, the image, of Cordelia, a simulacrum that he can aesthetically *control*.

36. De Man, p. 202.

37. Jameson refers to irony as a modernist concept (*Postmodernism*, p. 122). He further speaks of "fiction," "irony" and "literary language" as being operative in de Man's thought *despite* their modern provenance—as opposed to Derrida's, where they are absent (p. 226). One can speak of irony as a modernist concept, no doubt, because the ironic/nonironic contrast is a modernist opposition. One needs nonironic linguistic practices in order to highlight ironic practices. My contention, however, is that postmodernism, in its attempt to place everything in quotes, wants to universalize irony. If one takes Baudrillard's claims about the ubiquity of the hyperreal seriously, then there is no space cleared for the fictional as such, for there is no longer a real that would contrastively define it.

    De Man's own understanding of irony, as the systematic undoing of understanding or intelligibility, allows us to see irony as a *constitutive* feature of his (poststructuralist) conception of reading (*Allegories of Reading: Figural Language in Rousseau,*

Nietzsche, Rilke, and Proust (New Haven: Yale University Press, 1979), pp. 300–301).

38. As Derrida puts it: "The meaning of meaning is infinite implication, the indefinite referral of signifier to signified . . . a certain pure and infinite equivocality which gives signified meaning no respite, no rest . . . it always signifies again and differs" (Jacques Derrida, *Speech and Phenomena, and Other Essays on Husserl's Theory of Signs* (Evanston: Northwestern University Press, 1973), p. 58).

39. As a more or less self-conscious example of this phenomenon, one might look to Jameson's discussion of experimental video tapes as privileged exemplars of postmodernist texts (*Postmodernism*, p. 91). In the "total flow" of experimental video, each narrative element or sign gets renarrativized or reinterpreted in a *ceaseless* fashion with no closure and an indefinite trumping (p. 88). Hence we have a self-consciously postmodern text constituted by a sign flow which resists meaning, whose inner logic excludes the emergence of a "theme as such" and which systematically sets out to short-circuit traditional interpretation (p. 92).

40. For hermeneutics, what is real is the thing *for us*, the thing as expressed in our language, as it gets parcelled out in our logical space. For deconstruction, it is as if the recognition that our access to things is, to say the least, linguistically mediated (*"il n'y a pas d'hors texte"*) straightaway makes of things a fiction, an artifact, a simulacrum. To avoid this conclusion one would have to say that the simulacrum is tied to a *particular way* in which communication takes place, to the way in which it takes place in postmodernity, for instance. Baudrillard does this, but Derrida, as far as I can tell, does not make the effort to historicize or de-essentialize this phenomenon. This all or nothing logic, characteristic of deconstruction, is contested by hermeneutics. If for deconstruction language fictionalizes (though Derrida may not use the term), then for hermeneutics language realizes. It is as if deconstruction at some level presupposed a truth/illusion contrast, but denied our access to truth since language has always already mediated. (This is consistent with my earlier claims in this study that poststructuralism presupposes some of the distinctions that it wishes to deconstruct.) In this way it would be haunted by the aperspectival that it presupposes. In hermeneutics, on the other hand, the truth/illusion contrast gets made *within* language: rigid prejudices prevent our seeing the truth, which is always revealed, insofar as it can be revealed, in language. We approach the truth through being open to what the other has to say to us. These contrasting approaches to meaning ("the glass is half empty; the glass is half full") highlight the way in which deconstruction is informed by an infinitely remote standard of objectivity in terms of which anything achievable must be found infinitely wanting, and, in being found infinitely wanting, is a *mere* illusion, a simulacrum.

41. In having previously argued for this claim, I find myself in agreement with Habermas's assessment that, in so-called postmodernity, "what is expressed in the . . . value accorded the transitory and the ephemeral and in the celebration of dynamism is the longing for an immaculate and unchanging present . . . [a] 'nostalgia for true presence'" (Habermas, "Modernity: An Unfinished Project," in David Ingram and Julia Simon-Ingram, eds. *Critical Theory: the Essential Readings* (New York: Paragon House, 1991), p. 344).

42. Paul Bové, *Destructive Poetics: Heidegger and Modern Poetry* (New York: Columbia University Press, 1980), p. 113.

43. This brings the temporal dimension of the last chapter's critique of philosophical nihilism to the fore: the standpoint of the atemporal is the aperspectival measure that informs the observer's ironic stance; from that point of view, the participant is taken to be enmeshed in external history, and engaged in essentially meaningless practices.

   I encountered, in a recent interview with Derrida that appeared after the completion of the basic work on this book, rather striking support for my suggestions that at least some strands of poststructuralism are informed by an anxiety towards death. In the piece, Derrida clearly gives credibility to the hypothesis that his precocious awareness of, and continuing obsession with, mortality is not unrelated for him to the genesis and practice of deconstruction (Mitchell Stephens, "Jacques Derrida," *The New York Times Magazine* (January 23, 1994), pp. 22–25).

44. De Man, *Blindness and Insight*, p. 207.

45. Harvey speaks of postmodernism as being accompanied by "space-time compression" in the organization of capitalism, whose history is characterized by speedup in the pace of life (Harvey, p. 240).

   In this book I have not claimed that technology is unique in giving rise to a particular experience of time; my interest has been in characterizing and in assessing the implications of the experience of time of which technology is a sufficient if not necessary condition. In fact, as Kierkegaard's discussion of the aesthetic style of life in *Either/Or* (written in the mid-nineteenth century) attests, the possibility for the experience of temporal fragmentation is by no means unique to the postmodern, or even the technological, era. It is just that technology is central among the conditions that today contribute to making such a temporal experience so pervasive.

46. Jameson, "Postmodernism," p. 64.

47. *Ibid.*, p. 72.

48. Christopher Lasch, p. 521.

49. Baudrillard, "The Ecstasy of Communication," p. 128; and Poster, p. 136. See also Lyotard, who suggests that "a person is always located at 'nodal points' of specific communication circuits" (*The Postmodern Condition*), p. 15. It is as if a latent Cartesianism informed this postmodern view of the subject. Just as the subject's very being, for Descartes, was hostage to thought, for the postmoderns it is hostage to information exchange—I transmit and receive, therefore I am.

50. Jameson, "Postmodernism," p. 73; and Harvey, p. 350.

51. Lasch, p. 82.

52. *Ibid.*, p. 82, 83, 88. If we understand memory as an interpretive grid for understanding the present, then Lasch's notion of memory is reminiscent of Herbert Marcuse's (see my "Marcuse, Time and Technique: Concerning the Rational Foundations of Critical Theory," *The Philosophical Forum* 17 (1986), pp. 245–270). As I pointed out in Chapter Seven, a *sittliche* account need not be a conservative communitarian

account, because for Marcuse, unlike Lasch, memory condemns the present; this is the source of its critical potential.

53. Lasch, p. 83.

54. *Ibid.*, p. 83.

55. *Ibid.*, pp. 88–89. Lasch also mentions Wordsworth's commitment to the "fructifying," "vivifying," and "renovating virtue" of memory, which elicits in us *gratitude* in response to our indebtedness to the past, as opposed to *regret* over the loss of the past (*ibid.*, pp. 89–90).

56. See *ibid.*, p. 81.

57. *Ibid.*, p. 118. Related to this is the presumption that authentic culture is timeless, that it is not subject to historical development. Accordingly, notions of authenticity with respect to cultural production, say, in the case of so-called "primitive" art, are quite likely informed by this sort of nostalgia.

58. See Jameson, "Postmodernism," pp. 66–67; and Baudrillard, *Simulations*, p. 72.

59. See Jameson, *Postmodernism*, p. 156. Though even this, my argument suggests, *ultimately* betrays a longing for something "deeper" than the image can provide.

60. Harvey, p. 286.

61. *Ibid.*, p. 288.

62. Jameson, "Postmodernism," p. 71 and *Postmodernism*, pp. xvi, 154, 156.

63. *Postmodernism*, p. 154.

64. Jameson, "Postmodernism," p. 65.

65. *Cf.* Gadamer on the alienation of aesthetic and historical understanding, in "The Universality of the Hermeneutical Problem," in *Philosophical Hermeneutics*, trans. David E. Linge (Berkeley: University of California Press, 1976).

66. Jameson, *Postmodernism*, pp. 109–129.

67. *Ibid.*, p. 118.

68. *Ibid.*, p. 285. Jameson's distinction between historicity and historicism, essentially mirroring the distinction between the "ontological" hermeneutics of Gadamer and Heidegger, on the one hand, and the "romantic" hermeneutics of Dilthey and Schleiermacher, on the other, reproduces one of the informing distinctions of this book, namely, that between temporalities of repetition and those of the autonomous, aesthetic values-perspective. Postmodernism, like technology, rejects the "weight" of the past *cum* repetition.

69. See Gregory Bruce Smith, "Heidegger, Technology and Postmodernity," p. 376.

70. I acknowledge that there are readings of postmodernism that emphasize its *rejection* of gestures of mastery and that emphasize its Romantic and creative, as opposed to its technological, intentions (see, for example, Jane Flax, *Psychoanalysis, Feminism and Postmodernism in the Contemporary West* (Berkeley: University of California Press, 1990), the work of George Bataille, and my discussion of Lyotard below). But the version of mastery that Bataille, for example, rejects is one where it takes the form of an instrumental reason that is in thrall to the values and codes of conventional, bourgeois, productivist society. One could say that a genuinely post-

modern society would liberate this form of mastery by freeing it of such constraints. So one might argue that it is not *mastery* that is rejected, so much as it is certain kinds of *constraint* on a mastery that could otherwise realize itself as "sovereignty" or as the "will to power." This would, accordingly, leave standing two problems: what I have called postmodernism's relativism, and its lack of constraints on the transformation of world (*Welt*) into resource (*Bestand*). Central to my understanding of postmodernism are technological attempts to produce or simulate reality (discussed below) and ironic gestures to aestheticize or derealize (historical) reality—projects either to realize fictions or to fictionalize the real. Both projects are manifestations of the will to control. One aspect of the connection between the strands of postmodernist thought that I wish to highlight is aptly characterized by Richard Rorty: "[L]ight-minded aestheticism . . . [like] the insouciant pluralism of contemporary culture, . . . helps make the world's inhabitants . . . more receptive to the appeal of instrumental rationality" ("The Priority of Democracy to Philosophy," in *Reading Rorty*, ed. Alan Malachowski (Oxford: Basil Blackwell, 1990), p. 293).

71. See Jameson, "Postmodernism," p. 87.

72. Lyotard, pp. 46, 62 and 65.

73. *Ibid.*, pp. 46, 47. See also Habermas, *The Philosophical Discourse of Modernity: Twelve Lectures*, trans. Frederick Lawrence (Cambridge: MIT, 1987), p. 385.

74. In Chapter Seven, I suggested that, in addition to meaningfulness, among examples of criterial properties of the right game, though they cannot be given a foundationalist justification, are what I have gathered under the rubric of "humanity as an unfinished project," namely, the ideas of universal self-recognition and of generalizable interests. Given the reinscription of the values-perspective in our postmodern context, the notion of humanity as an unfinished project was elaborated as a response to the problem of community by suggesting an "outside" measure that might guide our conversation. By invoking such a dimension of experience, I do not, of course, intend a rehabilitation of metaphysics, a contingent framework blind to its own contingency, but rather to keep the ethical dimension open.

75. Moreover, I find congenial some of Lyotard's recent critical statements, couched in the metaphorics of economic exchange, about the contemporary drive to save or gain time. They occur in *The Differend: Phrases in Dispute*, trans. Georges Van Den Abbeele (Minneapolis: University of Minnesota Press, 1988), and in *The Inhuman: Reflections on Time*, trans. Geoffrey Bennington and Rachel Bowlby (Stanford: Stanford University Press, 1991). Except for seemingly asserting capitalism to be the exclusive culprit in the obsession to control time, Lyotard's analysis of temporality seems quite close to Luhmann's.

76. Lyotard is critical of the status of performativity as a criterion of legitimation because it implies a deep commensurability at odds with the postmodern condition (*The Postmodern Condition*, p. 60). (We should recall, however, Baudrillard on the relation between simulation, commensurability and control.) Lyotard is critical of the hegemony of the system's point of view (*ibid.*, p.xxiv). However, he seems to criticize it on largely theoretical grounds, e.g., because of the impossibility of stable systems, of perfect control, etc. This leads him to speak of legitimation by paralogy (science as "heuristics," privileging what the positivists called the "context of genera-

tion"). But one might ask of Lyotard: Is not paralogy enlightened performativity; cannot the creative move be the one that leads to the increased efficiency of the system? Lyotard might respond by conceding that it could be, but that it might be an inefficient way to increase efficiency (see Lyotard, *The Postmodern Condition*, p. 66). But one would think that performativity would not work in technology, either. Hence this line of thought suggests that Lyotard is not so much offering a critique of technology as he is perhaps a critique of an unenlightened way of pursuing it.

77. This discussion brings us to the threshold of considering whether there can be a postmodern critical social theory. This is a matter which I cannot pursue here, though I have made some comments relevant to it in Chapter Seven, where I suggest that discourses of rational critique are rejected too sweepingly and uncritically by many with postmodernist sympathies (see especially Note 88). On this, see also my "Evading Theory and Tragedy?: Reading Cornel West," *Praxis International* 13 (1993), pp. 32–45.

78. Borgmann, *Technology and the Character of Contemporary Life: A Philosophical Inquiry* (Chicago: University of Chicago Press, 1984), pp. 59–62, 97.

79. Baudrillard, "The Ecstasy of Communication," p. 129. With regard to the issue of social interaction, psychologists are finding that "computer-compulsive" people tend to find it increasingly difficult to engage in smoothly functioning, face-to-face contact. Craig Brod, in *Technostress* (Reading: Addison-Wesley, 1984), p. 45, indicates that traditional ways of temporally organizing social interaction are violated by people who "relate to others entirely in terms of information exchange." Geoff Simons, in *Silicon Shock: The Menace of the Computer* (Oxford: Basil Blackwell, 1985), p. 113, reports, albeit rather hyperbolically, that as our affairs are more and more conducted by computer and less and less by face-to-face interaction, "we are seeing the gradual destruction of human-to-human contact, the elimination of traditional social intercourse, the projection of a new model for human life in which individuals work and play in contact with computer terminals rather than people." And sociologist Sherry Turkle, in *The Second Self: Computers and the Human Spirit* (New York: Simon and Schuster, 1984), p. 216, writes that "[t]he hacker culture appears to be made up of people who need to avoid complicated social situations, who for one reason or another got frightened off or hurt too badly by the *risks* and complexities of relationships" (emphasis mine).

80. Baudrillard, "The Ecstasy of Communication," p. 129.

81. Smith, pp. 371, 376.

82. Lasch, p. 528.

83. See Dennis Hayes's *Behind the Silicon Curtain: The Seductions of Work in a Lonely Era* (Boston: South End, 1989). He suggests that technological innovation is no longer "linked to the public good," that computer products are increasingly "ephemeral," and that "computer work has become more and more detached from social contexts" (cited on p. 522 of Lasch). Of course, admittedly, the question remains concerning the extent to which the phenomenon reported by Hayes is driven by technology as opposed to capitalism.

84. To such strong claims asserting postmodernity to be the "unleashing" of technology's "will to power," one might well object that ecological consciousness and a sense of limits are very much with us today, and that there are affinities between such sensibilities and both poststructuralism and postmodernism. To this there are several responses. To the extent that ecological concerns are anthropocentric, it can be argued that they do not escape the ambit of the "will to power." To the extent that they are not, as is the case in some versions of "deep ecology," such concerns might be more properly understood as anti- or premodern, as opposed to postmodern (see Habermas, "Modernity: An Unfinished Project," pp. 354–355). Another response, apparently with considerable currency in Japan, is that *technology itself* can allay our ecological concerns. As for the affinities, it is true that the poststructuralist deconstruction of binary oppositions, such as that of reason vs. nature, would seem congenial to ecological concerns. It does remove the *metaphysical* underpinnings from projects of domination. But surely, to remove such a justification, along with metaphysical justifications for a host of other practices, does not entail a special concern for nature, nor necessarily even a critique of projects of domination which make no such metaphysical appeal. Indeed, by the poststructuralist's own lights, in the name of what could such a critique of nonmetaphysically grounded projects of domination be made? It is also true that many postmodern theorists have been drawn to the so-called "new social movements," a collection in which the ecological movement is typically included. But the affinity of postmodernist *theory*, as opposed to individual postmodernists, with such movements would seem to have more to do with revalorizing marginalized *identities* (of members of dispossessed social groups) than with a concern with the fate of nature *per se*.

85. Jameson, *Postmodernism*, p. ix.

86. Lasch, p. 520; and Harvey, pp. 284–285.

87. See, for example, Karl Lowith, *Meaning in History* (Chicago: University of Chicago Press, 1949).

88. Hans Blumenberg, *The Legitimacy of the Modern Age*, trans. Robert M. Wallace (Cambridge: MIT Press, 1983).

89. See Lasch, p. 528.

90. The often dizzying pace of technological progress in certain sectors threatens to undermine technology's promise to hold the future in thrall to the present, to make of present futures "future presents." This would seem to call for a metatechnology, a means of planning for and managing the tempo of change.

91. See, for example, Baudrillard, *Simulations*, pp. 119, 123, 126. And Jameson has suggested that the deepest subject of postmodernism is reproductive technology itself (*Postmodernism*, p. 95).

92. Harvey, p. 300.

93. Gadamer, *Truth and Method* (New York: Seabury Press, 1975), pp. 78f.

94. Of course, this is also true of the material reproductions that populate theme parks such as Disney World and Euro Disney (see Ada Louise Huxtable, "Inventing American Reality" and Baudrillard, *Simulations*). Ringing a rather different change on the nostalgia theme, as well as attempting to cash in on the commodification of

a simulation of socialism, there are plans afoot to turn part of the former German Democratic Republic into a theme park, with itself as the theme. A replica of the GDR is planned with the "utmost in historical accuracy in mind," down to being surrounded by barbed wire, being walled in, having guards patrol the border, having badly stocked stores, snooping state secret police officers, static-ridden transmissions of West German TV, black marketeers, an underground opposition, and scratchy toilet paper (*The Week in Germany*, November 5, 1993).

95. Allucquere Rosanne Stone, "Will the Real Body Please Stand Up?: Boundary Stories about Virtual Cultures," in *Cyberspace: First Steps,* ed. Michael Benedikt (Cambridge: MIT Press, 1991), p. 94.

96. Gary Stix, "Reach Out: Touch is Added to Virtual Reality Simulations," *Scientific American*, February 1991, p. 134.

97. For this account of Virtual Reality technology, I have relied upon Benedikt, "Introduction," in *Cyberspace*, pp. 11–12.

98. Howard Rheingold, "Travels in Virtual Reality," *Whole Earth Review*, No. 67 (Summer 1990), pp. 80–83.

99. John Holusha, "Carving Out Real-Life Uses for Virtual Reality," *The New York Times*, October 31, 1993, Section 3, p. 11.

100. Andrew Pollack, "Where Electronics and Art Converge," *The New York Times*, September 15, 1991, Section 3, pp. 1, 6.

101. Rheingold, "Travels in Virtual Reality," p. 87.

102. William Gibson, *Neuromancer* (New York: Ace Books, 1984).

103. Kevin Kelly, Adam Heilbrun and Barbara Stacks, "Virtual Reality: An Interview with Jaron Lanier," *Whole Earth Review* 64 (Fall 1989), p. 115.

104. Meredith Bricken, "Virtual Worlds: No Interface to Design," in *Cyberspace*, p. 372.

105. Michael Heim, "The Erotic Ontology of Cyberspace," in *Cyberspace*, p. 69.

106. Baudrillard, "The Ecstasy of Communication," p. 128.

107. Howard Rheingold, *Virtual Reality* (New York: Summit Books, 1991), p. 388.

108. Jameson refers to cyberpunk—a form of science fiction, most notably the work of William Gibson, predicated upon the fantastic possibilities of Virtual Reality technology—as perhaps the supreme literary expression of postmodernism (*Postmodernism*, Note 1, p. 419; *cf.* also pp. 37–38). See also Peter Fitting, "The Lessons of Cyberpunk," in *Technoculture*, ed. Constance Penley and Andrew Ross (Minneapolis: University of Minnesota Press, 1991), pp. 295–315.

109. Stone, "Will the Real Body Please Stand Up?" p. 85.

110. Meredith Bricken, "Virtual Worlds: No Interface to Design," in *Cyberspace*, p. 373. This is already possible on the Internet through MUDs (Multi-User Dungeons or Multi-User Dimensions), which are a multiparticipant, user-extensible, exclusively word- or text-based Virtual Reality (Pavel Curtis, "Mudding: Social Phenomena in Text-Based Virtual Realities," *Intertek* 3.3 (Winter, 1992), pp. 26–34). As Jacques Leslie points out, the allure of MUDs is that they are "laboratories for

exploring identity" ("MUDroom," *The Atlantic*, vol. 272, No. 3 (September, 1993), p. 28).

111. See Allucquere Rosanne Stone, "Will the Real Body Please Stand Up?" pp. 83–85.

112. Kelly *et al.*, "An Interview with Jaron Lanier," p. 112.

113. *Ibid.*, p. 113.

114. *Ibid.*, p. 112.

115. One might object that the "mineness" of an experience cannot be so reified; nor can the associations and interpretations that we think of as constituting experience. Only its purely sensory content can be. And that is true. Neither what Kant called the transcendental unity of apperception nor Heidegger's *Jemeinigkeit* can be stored in a computer file. And it is also true, of course, that a repeated experience, even if identical in sensory content to an earlier one, is nonetheless different in that the earlier experience forms part of its temporal context.

116. Bricken, "Virtual Worlds," p. 372.

117. Heim, "The Erotic Ontology of Cyberspace," pp. 73–74.

118. Gibson, *Neuromancer*, p. 6, cited in Heim, p. 75.

119. Leslie, in the original manuscript for the article cited in Note 110, reports on a MUD user, turned cynical by the experience, who described interaction in MUD as "talking to a lie" and who claimed that, as a result of his experience, he no longer trusted his ability to distinguish truth from deception. His is, no doubt, an extreme case, but it serves to illustrate my point.

120. Heim, p. 71.

121. See, for example, Robert Elliot, "Faking Nature."

122. In this regard, the utopian talk of a global village, of community and even, astonishingly, of a new sense of the sacred that is supposed to be ushered in by cyberspace betrays a nostalgia for what has been lost. But how can we regard a realm as sacred that is produced completely by human powers, that is purely a product of our freedom and a projection of our desires, a realm whose secrets we can know exhaustively?

123. Jameson, *Postmodernism*, p. 96.

124. On computer technology's implication in the deaths of the author and of the novel, see Robert Coover, "The End of Books," *The New York Times Book Review*, June 21, 1992, pp. 1, 23–25.

125. I discuss these responses in more detail in my "Evading Theory and Tragedy?: Reading Cornel West."

126. Lasch, pp. 71–72, 79.

127. Borgmann's discussion of focal practices is not free of this *aporia* (*Technology and the Character of Contemporary Life*, pp. 196–210). Borgmann tends to focus almost exclusively upon healing the disconnection between means and ends, between effort and enjoyment. As important as this project is, and indeed I am myself also engaged in it, an exclusive focus on it runs the risk of being subvertible by

a kind of aestheticism or voluntarism that is all too easily assimilable to the technological paradigm. We could make anything we wanted a meaningful practice if the only stipulation were that we do it for its own sake. Hence my concern to focus also upon the *worldlessness* of the means-ends schema and to reconnect both ends (values) and means to structures of meaning. This would block the potential for the reaesthetization or instrumentalization of *praxis* to which Borgmann's analysis would leave us vulnerable. For it is possible for practices to reconnect ends and means yet still be *disconnected* from structures of meaning.

128. See also Benhabib's reconstruction of Weber's diagnosis of modernity (*Critique, Norm, and Utopia: A Study of the Foundations of Critical Theory* (New York: Columbia University Press, 1986), pp. 258–260).

129. In his discussion of the prerequisites of an ideal dialogical community, Richard Bernstein points to an analogous circle, where incipient forms of such a community must be presupposed by any projects to establish one (*Beyond Objectivism and Relativism: Science, Hermeneutics and Praxis* (Philadelphia: University of Pennsylvania Press, 1983), p. 226).

130. But see Note 54 of Chapter Six of this work.

131. Jameson refers to postmodernism as a "cultural dominant," suggesting that despite pervasive postmodern tendencies, there yet remains a residue of something other, for example, our continued preoccupation with history, though it gets expressed in a "distorted" form as historicism (*Postmodernism*, pp. 286–287).

132. David Wiggins, "Truth, Invention and the Meaning of Life," *Proceedings of the British Academy* (1976), p. 363.

133. Wiggins, p. 378.

134. See Kierkegaard's *Either/Or*, vol. I, trans. David F. Swenson and Lillian Marvin Swenson (Princeton: Princeton University Press, 1959), p. 356. On the idea of rooting an ethics in experience, see Werner Marx's attempt to ground a nonmetaphysical ethics in our experience of being-towards-death (*Is There a Measure on Earth?: Foundations for a Nonmetaphysical Ethics* (Chicago: University of Chicago Press, 1987), esp. pp. 55–56).

135. See Note 79 above.

136. Plato's discussion of the integrity of a craft in the *Republic*, where he criticizes the shoemaker for subordinating the good of the shoes to an interest in the money the shoes would procure, though based upon the model of *techne*, provides a model for what I have in mind here.

137. The ennobling experience of beholding such integrity, such steadfastness and loyalty to what matters, amidst ever-present demands for convenience, time-savings and shortcuts, helps to keep the very idea of morality alive. Such an integrity sets up the very sort of contrast that structures the space of morality (on this, see Neale H. Mucklow, "A Case for Teaching Students to Think Critically in the Disciplines," *Proceedings of the South Atlantic Philosophy of Education Society* (1986), pp. 47–48).

138. Patricia Benner and Judith Wrubel, *The Primacy of Caring: Stress and Coping in Health and Illness* (Menlo Park: Addison Wesley, 1989), pp. 86–87.

139. *Ibid.*, p. xii.

140. *Ibid.*, pp. 152–153.

141. *Ibid.*, p. xi.

142. *Cf. ibid.*, pp. xiii, 58.

143. *Ibid.*, p. 212.

144. I am aware that the use of diagnostic technology is also driven by concern about malpractice suits. And my friend is a lawyer. But this does not alter the fact that his concerns took second place to, and were bracketed because of, the imperatives of technology.

145. The human practices stand to the humanities or the explicitly interpretive disciplines roughly as material technology stands to the natural sciences. I have in mind practices such as psychotherapy, teaching, parenting, friendship, nursing and management. Of course, application in the case of such practices is more adequately understood on the model of *phronesis* or practical judgment than on the model of applied science.

146. Benner and Wrubel illuminate how one gets implicated in the practice of nursing. They suggest that in expert caring, the agent of caring is enriched in the process. One discovers a self of "membership related to a common humanity and given over or defined by specific concrete concerns and human relationships" (*The Primacy of Caring*, p. 398).

147. Lasch, p. 488.

148. *Ibid.*, p. 491.

149. *Cf. ibid.*, pp. 527–529.

150. *Ibid.*, p. 530.

151. See, for example, "Mining Deep Underground for Energy," *The New York Times*, November 3, 1991, on the potential for generating energy from hot rock deep in the earth's core; and Michael D. Lemonick, "Blinded by the Light," *Time*, December 20, 1993, p. 54, on progress in the area of nuclear fusion, which may yield virtually limitless clean energy.

152. One can also generate an immanent critique of Lasch by raising the question: Does his discussion invoke a nostalgic idealization of America's agrarian past that violates his own critique of nostalgia?

153. See also *Technoculture*, p. 130. On "technology as ideology" and the self-legitimating status of technological progress, see Chapter Six of this study.

Index

action, 4, 5, 9, 10, 14, 15, 17, 22, 27,
    31, 44, 45, 47, 49–50, 51, 54, 55,
    56–58, 60, 63, 65–69, 71, 79, 85,
    86, 87, 90, 99–100, 101, 105, 107,
    151, 162, 164, 181n18, 184n7,
    189n14, 191n33, 193n10, 194–
    195n25. *See also praxis*
  communicative, 81–83, 90, 99, 100
  and meaning, 66–68
  and time, 56–60, 67–68
Adorno, T., 54, 80
aesthete, 29, 71, 72, 142, 145
aesthetic distance, 29, 66, 70–72, 74, 77,
    97, 98, 100, 109, 115, 136, 148,
    149, 158, 211n35. *See also* observer
aesthetic retrieval of meaning, 72, 164–
    165, 219–220n127
Agassi, J., 179–180n15
allegory, 144, 193n13
Apel, K. O., 77, 185n12
architecture, 139, 156, 160. *See also*
    Gehry
Arendt, H., 44, 57, 65, 188n2, 189n14,
    191n33
Aristarchus, 118, 119
Aristotle, 49, 74
art, 65, 73, 74, 138, 146, 156, 160–161,
    162, 178n5, 192n3, 214n57
authenticity, 59, 137, 214n57

bad infinite, 57, 140
Bataille, G., 214–215n70
Baudrillard, J., 137–140, 144, 151, 152,
    157–159, 209nn2 and 11, 210n13,
    211n37, 212n40, 215n76
Bell, D., 164, 173
Benhabib, S., 196n19, 198n54, 220n128
Benner, P., 169, 170, 220n138, 221n146
Berger, P., 210n16
Bernstein, R., 132, 203n32, 220n129
Blumenberg, H., 154, 191n28
Borgmann, A., 152, 164, 171, 177n1,
    192–193n8, 219–220n127
Bové, P., 213n42
Brumbaugh, R., 189n24
Bunge, M., 17, 178n10, 180n15, 191n26

Camus, A., 47, 59, 69
capitalism, 19, 20, 137, 140, 141, 144,
    150, 153, 154, 182n26, 183–
    184n41, 196n10, 213n45, 215n75,
    216n83
Caputo, J., 189n20, 208n87
care, 127, 128, 167, 170, 171, 174
Carr, D., 73, 192n6, 193n10, 194–
    195nn14,16 and 25
causality, 53, 190–191n26, 210n16
chance, 55, 91. *See also* contingency;
    risk
clock, 22–24, 54, 55, 68, 69, 74, 152,
    162
code, 102, 137, 138, 140, 147, 210n16
coherence, 10, 71–74, 96, 97, 151, 164
Coleridge, S. T., 145
communicative action. *See* action, com-
    municative

223

communicative rationality. *See* rationality, communicative
Communism, 20. *See also* Marx, K.; Marxism
communitarianism, 121, 175
community, 113, 114, 120–124, 127, 129, 132, 208n86, 215n74, 219n122, 220n129
computer, 12, 17, 21, 54, 79, 135, 138, 155–160, 168, 216nn79 and 83, 219nn115 and 124
computer aided design (CAD), 156, 160
conceptual scheme, 103
concern, 57, 169, 170, 171,
contingency, 51, 66, 74, 79, 91, 140, 152, 172. *See also* chance; risk
of language games, 100, 101, 115, 128, 131, 151, 215n74
control, 3, 4, 7, 16, 24, 29, 46, 53–57, 60, 73, 74, 76–77, 78–79, 90, 139, 140, 153, 158, 159, 172, 178n8, 179n15, 185n12, 196n13, 211n35, 215n70
conversation, 3, 168, 174–175, 187n20, 215n74
copy, 11, 137, 161, 211n31. *See also* counterfeit; fake
counterfeit, 139, 140, 161. *See also* copy; fake
Critical Theory, 5, 6, 10, 11, 75, 77, 92, 114, 177n1, 179n15. *See also* Habermas
cybernetics, 150
cyberpunk, 156, 218n108
cyberspace, 152, 157, 159, 219n122
cynicism, 88, 90, 136, 146, 159, 163, 199n84

Davidson, D., 103, 202n28
De Man, P., 142–144, 162, 193n13, 211–212n37
death, 59, 60, 143, 147, 148, 162–163, 194n25, 213n43, 220n134. *See also* mortality
death of the subject, 161
deconstruction, 77, 109, 132, 212n40, 213n43, 217n84. *See also* Derrida

demiurge, 140, 210n16
Derrida, J., 77, 142, 143, 211n37, 212nn38 and 40, 213n43
Descartes, R., 43, 140, 149, 155, 210n16, 213n49
desire, 3, 11, 12, 13, 63, 135, 139–141, 143, 146, 152–154
diachrony, 147
Dialectic of Enlightenment (Adorno and Horkheimer), 54
dialogue, 82, 83, 92, 93, 130. *See also* conversation; ideal speech situation
Dictatorship Over Needs (Feher, Heller and Markus), 20
différance, 142
difference:
   community and, 197n44, 208nn86 and 88
   meaningful, 10, 63, 66–69, 75, 96, 164, 167, 188n4
   postmodernism and, 154–155, 162, 208n88
Dilthey, W., 194n14, 214n68
discourse, 89, 150. *See also* language
   argumentative, 105, 173
   ideal, 28
   practical, 82–84, 128, 129
   theoretical, 83
Discourse on the Method (Descartes), 149
discourses of modernity, 5–7, 77, 80, 116
disease, 15, 169, 170
disenchantment, 140, 165
disengagement, 152
domestication of time. *See* time, domestication of
Don Giovanni, 63
Dworkin, R., 128, 207n72

E-mail, 69, 159
ecology, 217n84
economy, 8, 81, 86, 135
effective-historical consciousness (*wirkungsgeschichtliches Bewusstsein*), 57, 89, 100, 189n22
efficiency, 4, 7, 15, 18–23, 36, 48, 53,

56, 76–78, 151, 164, 181n18,
182n26, 216n76
Either/Or (Kierkegaard), 29, 51, 112,
211n35, 213n45
Eliade, M., 191n27
Elliot, R., 210n17
Ellul, J., 19–21, 23, 54, 55, 181–
182nn17 and 26
embodiment, 9, 49, 99, 159–160, 170
emotivism, 97
engineering, 13, 17, 18, 179n15
epistemology, 112
equality, 88, 111, 121, 127, 128
ethics, 5, 10, 12, 50, 112, 127, 135,
163, 168, 169, 170, 172, 207n71,
220n134. *See also* morality; resolve
ethics of satisfaction, 50, 189n17
ethnocentrism, 7, 92, 126, 155
existentialism, 97, 124
experience, 3, 6, 9, 27–38, 40, 47, 48,
56, 58, 77, 79, 86, 89, 112, 113,
167, 183n41, 184nn4,6,8 and 9,
185n10, 186–187n20, 194n25,
219n115
  and ethics, 12, 168–169, 171, 173,
  220n134
  and time, 8, 43, 51–53, 67, 68, 70,
  144, 147, 152, 213n45
  and Virtual Reality technology, 155–
  162
  reduction of, by science, 34–38, 48
  reduction of, by technology, 43, 48,
  77, 79, 86
explanation, 54, 106, 187n20, 210n16

fake, 160–161, 162. *See also* copy; counterfeit
fame, 211n31
Feenberg, A., 177n6, 181–182n26
Feher, F., 20, 181n22
feminism, 207n71
fiction, 70, 90, 110, 138, 211n37,
212n40, 215n70
finitude, 9, 14, 66, 72, 108, 112, 143,
166, 184n41
Finlay, M., 178n8
Flax, J., 214n70

forgery. *See* fake
Foucault, M., 35, 72, 77, 89, 115, 116,
125, 137, 140
Fraser, N., 201n8, 203n35
freedom, 4, 28–29, 30, 32, 34, 40, 45, 47,
53, 55, 66, 71, 83, 84, 121, 122,
125, 128, 142, 151, 153, 157, 159,
161, 163, 173, 211n35, 219n122
friendship, 5, 168–169, 171, 221n145
functional rationality. *See* rationality,
functional
fusion of horizons, 65, 111, 121, 122,
127, 128, 207n71
future, 24, 53, 54, 57, 91, 148–149. *See
also* time
Future Shock (Toffler), 148

Gadamer, H. G., 6, 10, 32, 33, 57, 59,
65, 89, 93, 94, 100, 108, 111, 114,
154, 173, 184–185n9, 186n20,
214nn65 and 68
Geertz, C., 193–194n13
Gehry, F., 148
generalizable interest, 84, 127, 129
Gestell, 144
Gibson, W., 156, 159, 218nn102 and
108
Giddens, A., 183–184n41
Gilligan, C., 127, 200n90
good life, the, 28, 40, 115, 122, 164
Goodman, N., 138
Gorgias (Plato), 33
Gramsci, A., 129

Habermas, J., 3, 5, 6, 10, 11, 17, 28,
29, 48, 55–57, 65, 75–94 *passim*,
95, 96–97, 99, 100, 103–108, 111–
116, 125, 126, 128–130, 149, 152,
164, 169, 173, 174, 180n15, 184n3,
185n12, 189n14, 195n7, 196nn19
and 20, 197n44, 199n68, 200nn90
and 92, 202n29, 207–208n79,
208n88, 212n41. *See also* action,
communicative; rationality, communicative
  critique of functional rationality, 81–
  82, 84–86, 87, 89–90, 91, 92

Hanson, N., 9, 33
Harding, S., 207n71
Harries, K., 189n17, 194n24, 210n24
Harvey, D., 141, 144, 147, 211n26,
    213n45
health care practices, 12, 15, 21, 169–
    171, 182–183n30
Hegel, G. W. F., 57, 112, 130, 136,
    159, 184nn3,4 and 8, 188n3,
    206nn69 and 70
Heidegger, M., 4, 22–24, 32, 34, 35,
    37, 43–45, 58–60, 68, 72, 75–77,
    79, 96, 140, 144, 149, 163, 173,
    177n1, 179n15, 188–189nn4 and 13,
    194n25, 195nn1 and 5, 214n68,
    219n115
Heim, M., 159, 218n105
Heller, A., 20, 181n22
hermeneutics, 5, 6, 10, 75, 85, 108, 143,
    185n10, 212n40, 214n68. See also
    Gadamer
    and Critical Theory, 6–7, 93–94, 173
    and deconstruction, 142–143, 212n40
Hesse, M., 9, 27, 28, 33, 102, 184–
    185nn1 and 9, 187n20, 201n11
historicality (Geschichtlichkeit), 58, 72
historicism, 7, 93, 148, 214n68,
    220n131. See also relativism
historicity, 89, 110, 114, 116, 137, 147,
    149, 160, 161, 169, 214
history, 53–58, 60, 63, 73, 89, 91, 100,
    129, 136, 154, 161–163, 186n20,
    196n13, 209n1, 220n131
    end of, 7
    external, 50–51, 54, 55, 56, 57, 58,
    63, 91, 136, 143, 146, 170, 213n43.
    See also time, linear
    internal, 50–51, 58, 69, 146, 163. See
    also repetition
    postmodernism and, 143–149
hope, 5, 112, 120, 132, 146, 163, 170
Horkheimer, M., 54, 80
Hughes, T., 56, 178–179nn12 and 14
The Human Condition (Arendt), 44,
    188n2
humanism, 126, 137. See also humanity
    as unfinished project

humanity, 3, 6, 7, 9, 120, 122, 124,
    126–129, 132, 174, 221n146
humanity as unfinished project, 7–8,
    122–127, 128, 129, 132, 174,
    187n21, 189n20, 204n49, 206n70,
    208n88, 215n74
hyperreal, 138–139, 157, 211n37
hypertext, 162

ideal speech situation, 82–83, 92, 130,
    152
identity, 51, 57, 59, 71, 72, 109–110,
    121–123, 127–129, 159, 189n20,
    201n21, 206n62, 207n73, 219n110
    moral, 127–128
    personal, 59, 72, 85
ideology, 22, 31, 79–81, 88, 125, 137,
    174, 205n61, 221n153
ideology critique, 208n79
image, 11, 135, 137, 138, 141, 146–148,
    155, 158, 211n35, 214n59. See also
    simulacrum
incommensurability, 102, 103, 145
instrumental rationality. See rationality,
    purposive
integrity, 12, 57, 67, 72, 85, 86, 100,
    163, 189n20
integrity of a practice. See practice, integ-
    rity of
Internet, 218n110
interpretive sociology, 102
irony, 7, 115, 124, 141–144, 148, 162,
    193n13, 200n8, 211nn35 and 37

James, C., 211n31
Jameson, F., 137, 139, 141, 144–149,
    153, 162, 209nn2 and 4, 211n37,
    212n39, 214n68, 217n91, 218n108,
    220n131
judgment, 93, 203n32. See also Ga-
    damer; hermeneutics
justice, 86, 88, 150

Kant, I., 100, 112, 130, 190n26,
    219n115
Kern, S., 183n37, 192n2
Kierkegaard, S., 29, 50, 51, 58, 59, 72,

112, 142, 145, 168, 189nn15 and
  19, 211n35, 213n45
Kuhn, T., 9, 33, 34, 36–39, 151,
  180n15, 184–185nn9 and 14,
  186n16, 194n25

Lacan, J., 145
language, 30–34, 37–39, 46, 76, 77, 82,
  83, 85, 87, 96, 98, 99, 102, 103,
  107, 109–112, 114–116, 118, 120–
  121, 122, 125, 126, 129, 137, 138,
  140, 142, 150, 165, 166, 168,
  184n9, 187nn20 and 23, 202n26,
  203n30, 204nn45 and 48, 205n61,
  211n37, 212n40. *See also* discourse
language games. *See* language
Lanier, J., 158, 218n103
Lasch, C., 12, 145–147, 153, 154, 172,
  173, 209n3, 213–214nn52 and 55,
  221n152
Lenin, V., 20
liberalism, 120, 121, 123–126, 204–
  205n58, 205–206nn61,62 and 64,
  207n70, 208n87
life:
  tragic sense of, 145, 146
life as a work of art, 73, 74
life-world, 14, 27, 81, 82, 84–87, 90,
  91, 100, 160
  colonization of, 73, 85, 90, 169
  rationalization of, 84
limits, 15, 145, 149, 152–153, 169,
  172–173, 217n84
love, 5, 168
Lovibond, S., 11, 80, 96, 107, 114, 116,
  126, 128–131, 196n17, 200n1,
  202n26, 203n30
Luhmann, N., 10, 78, 79, 86, 88–91,
  100, 140, 148, 150, 196n13,
  199n68, 215n75
  systems theory of, 88–91, 196n13,
  199n68
Lukács, G., 35, 196n10
Lyotard, J., 77, 137, 140, 143, 150–152,
  191n34, 213n49, 214n70, 215–
  216nn75 and 76

MacIntyre, A., 11, 59, 60, 63, 114, 126,
  130, 131, 192nn45 and 5, 195n3,
  201n21, 207n70, 208n81
Madonna, 141, 211n31
Marcuse, H., 35, 50, 129, 184n3,
  191n30, 213–214n52
Markus, G., 20, 181n22
Marx, K., 19, 78, 144, 147, 181nn19
  and 20, 191n30. *See also* Communism; Marxism
Marx, W., 220n134
Marxism, 121, 124. *See also* Communism; Marx, K.
McCarthy, T., 105, 106, 117, 119,
  200n88, 201n19, 203n34
meaning, 4–6, 8–12, 14, 22, 27–33, 43–
  50, 57, 58, 63, 67, 68, 75–77, 78,
  79, 80, 81–82, 95–98, 99, 100–101,
  102, 108, 110, 125, 132, 163–171,
  173, 184nn5 and 7, 188n6, 193n12,
  194n13, 198n54, 202n26, 220n127
  and postmodernism, 136, 137, 138,
  139, 142–144, 147, 149, 151, 152,
  154, 162, 212nn38,39 and 40
  and science, 34, 35, 38–40, 186nn14
  and 20
  and systems theory, 86–92, 196n13
  distinguished from value, 43–50
  of life, 69–74, 167
  prereflective, 27, 32, 33, 38, 39–40,
  70, 168, 171, 186n20
meaningful difference. *See* difference,
  meaningful
meaningful effects, 4, 43, 58, 171
means and ends, 9, 16, 44, 45, 48, 64,
  76, 77, 153, 219n127
  worldlessness of, 45, 48, 76, 220n127
medicine. *See* health care practices
memory, 59, 63, 67, 137, 145, 155, 157,
  158, 213–214nn52 and 55
metanarrative, 7, 136, 145, 154
metaphysics, 5, 7, 51, 52, 56, 76, 100,
  142, 149–151, 172, 215n74
metaphysics of presence, 7, 100, 142
military, 20, 135, 156
Models and Analogies in Science
  (Hesse), 102

modernity, 5, 6, 53, 77, 80, 85, 112,
113, 116, 135, 136, 139, 140, 149,
153, 164, 172, 173, 208nn88 and 1,
210n16, 217n84, 220n128
moral complicity, 116
moral theory, 92–93. *See also* ethics
morality, 5, 93, 112, 130, 220n137. *See
also* ethics
mortality, 23, 124, 163, 171, 213n43.
See also death
MTV, 141
multiculturalism, 7
Mumford, L., 22, 183n33
mythos, 70, 201n21

narrative, 10, 59, 60, 63, 69, 70, 72, 73,
77, 106, 144, 159–161, 193nn9, 10
and 13, 194–195n25, 206nn62 and
69, 212n39. *See also* story
mythical, 106, 201–202n21
Nehamas, A., 193n9, 195n25
networks, 9, 27, 65, 144, 152, 159
information, 150
Neuromancer (Gibson), 156, 159,
218n102
New Age, 72, 164
Nietzsche, F., 4, 75–77, 79, 80, 87, 90,
140, 149, 163, 195nn3 and 5,
196n14
nihilism, 4, 6, 10, 11, 28, 66, 75–77,
79, 80, 87, 91, 92, 96, 112, 113,
126, 131, 132, 135, 143, 149, 158,
164, 165, 166, 188n4, 213n43. *See
also* perspectivism; relativism; values-perspective
critique of, 11, 97–110, 112–113
nonconvergence thesis, 119, 186n20
nostalgia, 143–147, 212n41, 214n57,
217n94, 219n122, 221n152
nursing, 169, 170, 221n145

objectivism, 93, 94, 114, 132
observer, 29, 71, 81, 97–101, 103–105,
107–110, 112, 115, 132, 142, 149,
155, 158, 165, 166, 200n8, 202n26,
213n43. *See also* aesthetic distance

optimism, 146, 163, 164, 173
Other, 10, 11, 43, 123, 127, 130, 136,
152–153, 159, 161, 168, 203n33,
205n61, 207n70, 212n40, 220n131.
See also resistance
otherness, 31, 152, 153. *See also* resistance

paradigm, 36, 39, 48, 65, 125, 126,
205n62, 220n127
paralogy, 151, 215–216n76
participant, 31, 97–101, 103–105, 107–
110, 112, 128, 158, 165, 200n8,
213n43
participant/observer distinction, 99–101,
109, 200n8
critique of, 97–110, 112
past, 9, 57, 91, 144, 146–148, 196n13,
214n55. *See also* time
performativity, 86, 150–152, 215–
216n76
perspectivism, 6, 7, 10, 79–81, 87–89,
91, 97, 101, 108, 140, 196n14. *See
also* nihilism; relativism; values-perspective
*The Philosophical Discourse of Moder-
nity* (Habermas), 80, 116, 195n7
planning, 15, 20, 52, 53, 78, 172,
181n26, 217n90
temporality of, 52–53
Plato, 33, 50, 99, 188n12, 189n22,
220n136
play, 69, 71, 136, 137, 143, 148, 153,
158, 174, 216n79
plot, 63, 70
Polanyi, M., 185n14
politics, 8, 20, 125, 172, 182n26,
188n12, 200n92, 205n61. *See also*
liberalism
Popper, K., 33, 179–180n15
Poster, M., 177n2, 210n13
postindustrial society, 150
postmodernism, 5, 7, 10–12, 89, 95,
122, 135–137, 139–141, 143–145,
147, 148, 150, 151–155, 157, 161–
163, 172, 199n68, 208–209nn1,2

and 4, 210n16, 212nn39 and 41,
213n45, 214–215nn68 and 70,
217nn84 and 91, 218n108, 220n131.
See also poststructuralism
postmodernity. *See* postmodernism
poststructuralism, 10, 11, 87, 91, 93, 94,
113, 132, 141–143, 145, 151,
199n84, 208n88, 212n40, 213n43,
217n84. *See also* postmodernism
power, 4, 11, 14, 18, 20, 21, 39, 43, 46,
48, 49, 76–79, 83, 85, 87, 89, 90,
93, 110, 113, 115, 116, 125, 139,
140, 145, 149–151, 153, 156, 158,
163, 173, 205n61
practice, 5, 12, 14–17, 27, 30, 39, 46,
68, 69, 79, 87, 101–105, 107, 116,
117, 119, 132, 138, 139, 155, 164,
168–171, 179n13, 180n15, 192–
193nn5 and 8, 199n68, 202n26,
203n30, 204n54, 205n61, 211n37,
213n43, 219–220n127
    focal, 164, 171, 192–193n8, 219–
    220n127
    goods internal to, 87
    human, 18, 167, 171
    integrity of, 12, 85–86, 164, 169–170,
    220nn136 and 137
    technological, characterized, 14–17
    understanding of, 101–104
pragmatism, 5, 113–115, 120, 122,
179n15, 202n28. *See also* Rorty, R.
praxis, 5, 9, 49–51, 56–58, 60, 63, 68,
69, 87, 144, 174, 178n5, 189n14,
220n127. *See also* action
prereflective meaning. *See* meaning, prereflective
present, 57, 70, 148, 158, 212n41. *See
also* time
progress, 7, 8, 12, 15, 18–20, 23, 45,
52, 53, 55, 58, 66, 68, 75, 79, 123,
130, 144, 145, 146, 154, 172, 174,
182n26, 191n28, 217n90, 221n151
Proust, M., 60, 74
psychology, industrial, 22
psychotherapy, 168, 221n145
Putnam, H., 202n28

quotation, 98, 142, 148

rational critique, 87, 90, 95–97, 114,
129, 130, 166, 199n68,84, 200n92,
216n77
rationality, 3–11, 13, 14, 16, 19, 27, 43,
53, 56, 75–82, 85, 87, 90, 91–93,
95–100, 102, 107–114, 118, 120,
126, 130–132, 135, 136, 149–151,
163–167, 172, 173, 182n26,
183n30, 188n4, 196n10, 199n68,
208n88, 215n70
    communicative, 11, 80–82, 87, 91–93,
    100
    critique of, 92–94, 200n90
    functional, 10, 75–79, 81, 82, 84, 87,
    90–92, 97, 139, 150, 151
    purposive, 14, 53, 80, 81, 85, 87, 96,
    112, 215n70
    technological, 3–8, 10, 11, 13, 14, 16,
    19, 63, 66, 75, 76, 97, 113, 149,
    151, 153, 163, 164, 167, 173
rationalization, 12, 16, 82, 84, 85, 151,
159, 164–166, 174
    of life-world, 84
    of systems, 84
recollective experience, 58. *See also* repetition
reference, 68, 80, 82, 137–138, 147,
161. *See also* sign
relativism, 6, 88, 93, 94, 105, 108, 109,
110, 114, 131, 132, 135, 139, 148,
215n70. *See also* historicism; perspectivism; values-perspective
religion, 136, 140, 154, 163
Remembrance of Things Past (Proust), 60
repetition, 9, 10, 12, 51, 56–60, 63, 66,
68–69, 71–75, 89, 145–148, 162,
168, 172, 173, 174, 193n13,
214n68. *See also* history, internal
representation, 23, 35, 44, 46–48, 51,
137, 138, 151, 159, 162
reproduction, 12, 77, 82, 85, 86, 137,
138, 141, 150, 154, 161, 217n91
resistance, 60, 92, 152, 159–160. *See
also* Other; otherness

resoluteness (*Entschlossenheit*), 59, 163.
  See also resolve
resolve, 38, 51, 58, 163, 164, 169, 172.
  See also ethics
resource, 15, 22, 136, 144, 149, 153,
  173, 215n70. *See also* standing reserve
Rheingold, H., 218n107
Ricoeur, P., 70, 73, 193n11
risk, 11, 31, 32, 35, 36, 40, 85, 90–91,
  106, 107, 128, 143, 163, 164, 172,
  216n79. *See also* chance; contingency
  and postmodernism, 163
Rorty, R., 5, 7, 11, 27, 40, 72, 77, 100,
  114, 115, 119–127, 129–131, 170,
  184n2, 187nn20 and 23, 200–201n8,
  202n28, 203n33, 204–
  207nn58,61,62,64,69 and 70,
  215n70
  critique of, 120–126, 205nn61 and 62,
  206nn64 and 70
Rose, M., 208n1
Royce, J., 163
rules, 20, 54, 99, 101, 102, 105, 107,
  109, 114, 151, 185n14, 190n26,
  201n10, 203n30

St. Augustine, 74
Sartre, J. P., 29, 47, 59, 98, 124, 168,
  194n25
Saussure, F., 142
Schiller, F., 144
schizophrenia, 71, 128, 157, 158
Schlegel, F., 142
Schopenhauer, A., 50, 163
Schrag, C., 192n37
science, 6, 8, 9, 16–18, 21, 23, 27–29,
  33–40, 43, 46, 48, 52–53, 54, 59,
  60, 70, 80, 81, 102, 125, 126, 178–
  181nn5,12,13,14,15 and 18, 184–
  187nn3,6,9,12,13,14,15,16,20,22,23
  and 24, 190–191n26, 206n62,
  210n16, 215n76, 221n145
  distinguished from technology, 16–18
  three-tiered analysis of, 36–38

worldlessness of, 33, 48
scientism, 28
  critique of, 33–40
secularization, 140
self, 10, 29, 32, 40, 57, 58, 59, 68, 70–
  73, 127, 142, 152, 153, 159, 169,
  170, 171, 208n88, 221n146. *See
  also* identity; subject
self-reflection, 32, 34, 36, 38, 39
sex, 67, 156
sign, 68, 137, 138, 147, 157, 193n13,
  212n39. *See also* reference
signified, 48, 137, 138, 212n38. *See also*
  sign
signifier, 48, 137, 138, 212n38. *See also*
  sign
simulacrum, 11, 40, 137–141, 146–148,
  154, 155, 157, 158, 161, 162,
  211n35, 212n40
skeptic, 98, 99
Smith, B. H., 73, 194n21
social theory, 82, 91, 152, 216n77
solidarity, 68, 81, 114, 123, 124, 168,
  188n6, 200n8, 207n70
space, 3, 9, 47, 141, 144, 147, 148,
  154, 157, 158, 159, 186n15, 213n45
spatialization, 51, 147–148
Stalin, J., 20
standing reserve (*Bestand*), 22, 76, 149,
  152. *See also* resource
story, 59, 60, 65, 69–71, 73, 74, 148,
  164, 194n25. *See also* narrative
structure of meaning. *See* meaning
The Structure of Scientific Revolutions
  (Kuhn), 39
subject, 3, 34–35, 68, 70, 76, 78, 79,
  98, 141, 142, 144, 146, 147, 151,
  158, 159, 161, 166, 167, 170,
  196nn10 and 19, 208n88, 211n35,
  213n49. *See also* self
  disengaged, 97, 211n35
subject-centered reason, 77, 80, 196n19
synchrony, 147–148
system, 23, 32, 44, 47, 56, 78, 79, 81,
  82, 85, 86, 88, 90, 91, 106, 129,
  141, 142, 156, 193n13, 198n54,
  199nn68 and 84, 215–216n76

systems theory, 10, 23, 55, 75, 77–79, 85, 89–91, 139, 140, 152, 196n13, 199nn68 and 84
Szondi, P., 142

Taylor, C., 46, 101, 145, 187n23, 188n8, 204n48
Taylor, F.W., 22–23
techne, 5, 22, 49, 51, 57, 58, 63, 69, 140, 152, 174, 188n12, 189nn14 and 22, 220n136
technological rationality. *See* rationality, technological
technology, 3–24, 36, 40, 43–45, 48, 49, 51–56, 58, 60, 63, 64, 66–71, 75–81, 89, 91, 95–97, 111, 113, 132, 135, 136, 138–140, 147–175, 177n2, 178–184nn5,8,12,13,14,15, 17,18,19,26,39 and 41, 189nn13 and 14, 196n13, 208–209n1, 210–211nn16 and 24, 213n45, 214n68, 216nn76 and 83, 217nn84,90 and 91, 218n108, 219–220nn124 and 127, 221nn144 and 145
  autonomy of, 14–15, 19–21
  as infrastructure of postmodern society, 135–136, 153–155
  relationship to human values, 13–14
  relationship to science, 16–18
  relationship to time, 22–24, 51–56
  social constructivist theory of, 22, 178n8, 179n13
  totalitarian character of, 21–22
  worldlessness of, 14, 22, 48, 49
temporality, 4, 9, 10, 43, 50, 52–54, 56–58, 63, 66, 67, 69, 71, 75, 89–91, 143, 144, 146, 147, 193–194n13, 213n43, 215n75. *See also* time
text, 30–31, 32, 73, 74, 146, 161, 162, 186–187n20, 212nn39 and 40
  life as a, 69
  life unlike, 73–74
  literary, 73
theme park, 157, 217–218n94
theoria, 29, 34, 38, 39, 98

The Theory of Communicative Action (Habermas), 99, 100, 197n20
Thompson, E. P., 183n38
time, 3–6, 8–12, 14, 16–18, 20, 22–24, 27, 29, 31, 37, 43, 45, 50–60, 63, 64, 66, 67–71, 73–75, 77, 79, 81, 90, 91, 96, 99, 104, 111, 116, 117, 135, 136, 138, 139, 141–148, 150, 152, 154, 155, 157, 158, 160–163, 165, 166, 169, 171–173, 182n26, 183nn38,39 and 41, 189nn22 and 24, 190–191n26, 191n30, 193nn10 and 13, 196n13, 210n24, 213n45, 215n75. *See also* past; present; future
  domestication of, 4, 5, 51, 53, 54, 56–57, 75, 79, 91, 182n26
  linear, 52, 53, 54, 55, 145 *See also* history, external
time-compression, 144
time-contraction, 3, 69, 144
tradition, 6, 11, 33, 45, 49, 57–59, 72, 85, 96, 103, 113, 114, 115, 130, 131, 136, 147, 173, 200n92
tragic sense of life, 145, 146
The True and Only Heaven: Progress and its Critics (Lasch), 172, 209n3
truth, 39, 77, 83, 84, 87, 88, 90, 92, 104, 111, 116–119, 131, 195n25, 198n54, 201n21, 203n34, 212n40
  and postmodernism, 137, 138–140, 149, 150
  and science, 179–180n15
  consensus theory of, 83
TV advertisements, 138, 141

underdetermination thesis, 59, 119
understanding, 100, 101–107, 114, 201n10
  and evaluation, 104–107

value, 3–5, 9, 10, 12, 13, 19, 34, 35, 39, 40, 43–51, 56, 59, 63, 70, 71, 76, 78, 80, 83, 87, 88, 90, 100–102, 105, 109, 112, 114, 121–123, 129, 137, 138, 139, 144, 147, 149, 153, 154, 162, 167, 170, 171,

180n15, 184n5, 188nn4 and 6,
189n13, 193n12, 196n14, 220n127
internal relationship to meaning, 12,
46–47, 76, 147, 169, 171, 193n12
values-perspective, 4, 5, 7, 10–12, 71,
72, 76, 80, 96, 97, 101, 107, 113,
126, 132, 139, 143, 147, 149, 151,
157, 173, 193n12, 214n68, 215n74.
See also nihilism; perspectivism; relativism
critique of, 4, 11, 12, 97–110
van Fraassen, B., 190–191n26
verstehenden social inquiry, 101. *See
also* understanding
Veyne, P., 201n21
video art, 162
video game, 71
Virtual Reality, 12, 136–138, 153, 155–
162, 209n1, 218nn108 and 110

Wartofsky, M., 210n16
Weber, M., 4, 14, 34, 77, 80, 112, 173,
190n26, 192n3, 220n128
West, C., 204–205n58, 205n61, 206n69
Wiggins, D., 97, 103, 167, 188n4,
202n26
Wilde, O., 72

The Will to Power (Nietzsche), 76
will to power, 4, 11, 14, 43, 76, 78, 79,
87, 90, 113, 149, 151, 153, 163,
215n70, 217n84
will to surpass, 66, 78, 154, 210n24
Winch, P., 188n10, 201n10, 203n41
Winner, L., 33, 63, 64, 94, 181n25,
189n13
Wittgenstein, L., 5, 36, 96, 107, 201–
202n21
word processor, 3, 66, 158, 162
world (*Welt*), 4, 5, 9, 11, 14, 15, 22, 23,
27, 30, 34, 35, 37, 38, 40, 44, 45,
48–50, 51, 66, 67, 68, 76, 77, 81,
82, 84–87, 90, 91, 100, 110–111,
136, 149, 152–153, 154, 160, 165–
166, 167–168, 169–170, 200n92,
215n70
world-as-picture, 23, 35, 44–46, 49, 149
worldlessness, 14, 22, 27, 33, 45, 48,
49, 76, 97, 220n127
of means-ends scheme, 45, 48, 76,
220n127
of science, 33, 48
of technology, 14, 22, 48, 49
of value, 45
Wrubel, J., 169, 170, 220n138, 221n146